INVESTMENT CROWDFUNDING

Investment Crowdfunding

ANDREW A. SCHWARTZ

OXFORD
UNIVERSITY PRESS

Oxford University Press is a department of the University of Oxford.
It furthers the University's objective of excellence in research, scholarship,
and education by publishing worldwide. Oxford is a registered trade mark of
Oxford University Press in the UK and certain other countries.

Published in the United States of America by Oxford University Press
198 Madison Avenue, New York, NY 10016, United States of America.

© Andrew A. Schwartz 2023

All rights reserved. No part of this publication may be reproduced, stored in
a retrieval system, or transmitted, in any form or by any means, without the
prior permission in writing of Oxford University Press, or as expressly permitted
by law, by license, or under terms agreed with the appropriate reproduction
rights organization. Inquiries concerning reproduction outside the scope of the
above should be sent to the Rights Department, Oxford University Press, at the
address above.

You must not circulate this work in any other form
and you must impose this same condition on any acquirer.

Library of Congress Cataloging-in-Publication Data
Names: Schwartz, Andrew A., author.
Title: Investment crowdfunding / Andrew A. Schwartz.
Description: New York : Oxford University Press, [2023] |
Includes bibliographical references and index.
Identifiers: LCCN 2023003792 (print) | LCCN 2023003793 (ebook) |
ISBN 9780197688526 (hardback) | ISBN 9780197688540 (epub) |
ISBN 9780197688533 (updf)| ISBN 9780197688557 (digital-online)
Subjects: LCSH: Crowd funding—Law and legislation—United States. |
Crowd funding—Law and legislation—English-speaking countries. |
Crowd funding—Law and legislation—European Union countries. | Investments—Law
and legislation—United States. | Investments—Law and legislation—English-speaking
countries. | Investments—Law and legislation—European Union countries.
Classification: LCC K1330.S39 2023 (print) | LCC K1330 (ebook) |
DDC 346.0666—dc23/eng/20230403
LC record available at https://lccn.loc.gov/2023003792
LC ebook record available at https://lccn.loc.gov/2023003793

DOI: 10.1093/oso/9780197688526.001.0001

Printed by Integrated Books International, United States of America

Note to Readers
This publication is designed to provide accurate and authoritative information in regard to the subject
matter covered. It is based upon sources believed to be accurate and reliable and is intended to be
current as of the time it was written. It is sold with the understanding that the publisher is not engaged
in rendering legal, accounting, or other professional services. If legal advice or other expert assistance is
required, the services of a competent professional person should be sought. Also, to confirm that the
information has not been affected or changed by recent developments, traditional legal research
techniques should be used, including checking primary sources where appropriate.

*(Based on the Declaration of Principles jointly adopted by a Committee of the
American Bar Association and a Committee of Publishers and Associations.)*

You may order this or any other Oxford University Press publication
by visiting the Oxford University Press website at www.oup.com.

For my parents, Leslie and Ken.

Contents

Acknowledgments		ix
Table of Abbreviations		xi
Introduction		1
Chapter One:	Investment Crowdfunding	11
Chapter Two:	Purpose	27
Chapter Three:	Challenges	45
Chapter Four:	Private Ordering	57
Chapter Five:	American Law and Practice	99
Chapter Six:	Comparative Law and Practice	143
Chapter Seven:	Lessons Learned	175
Conclusion		183
Index		187

Acknowledgments

This book is the culmination of ten years of research and writing on investment crowdfunding, making it difficult to acknowledge everyone who made it possible for me to reach this moment.

With that said, I appreciate the support of my home institution, the University of Colorado Law School, which provided me with a Gilbert Goldstein Faculty Research Fellowship as well as a sabbatical to work on this project. I also thank the University of Auckland Law School for graciously hosting me (twice) as I researched New Zealand law and practice, one time as a Fulbright Scholar. On that point, I must acknowledge the United States Department of State, the J. William Fulbright Foreign Scholarship Board, and Fulbright New Zealand for their financial support.

Thank you very much to those who read and commented on earlier drafts of the manuscript: Joan Heminway, Christine Hurt, Darian Ibrahim, Akshaya Kamalnath, Trish Keeper, Mark Loewenstein, Eugenia Macchiavello, Seth Oranburg, Jim Park, Allison Schwartz, Jeremy Schwartz, and Kenneth Schwartz. I also thank the Institute for Humane Studies for sponsoring a manuscript workshop for several of these readers.

I especially want to thank Ming Lee Newcomb, my primary research assistant on this project, for her superlative work as a Research Assistant and editor. Many other RAs from the University of Colorado Law School also deserve credit, including Meredith Ashlock, Elizabeth Field, Nate Goergen, Savanna Griffis, Cori Hach, Carter Hilty, Morgan Pullam, Emily Wasserman, and Lisa Willcox, as does my industrious faculty coordinator, Kelly Ilseng.

Finally, my deepest gratitude goes to my wife, Allison, for her love, support, and chalance in all things.

Table of Abbreviations

ASIC	Australian Securities and Investments Commission
ASX	Australian Stock Exchange
CMA	Competition and Markets Authority
CROWDFUND Act	Capital Raising Online While Deterring Fraud and Unethical Non-Disclosure Act
CSA	Canadian Securities Administrators
CSF	crowd-sourced funding
FCA	Financial Conduct Authority
FMA	Financial Markets Authority
FMCA	Financial Markets Conduct Act
GAAP	generally accepted accounting principles
ICO	initial coin offering
IPO	initial public offering
JOBS Act	Jumpstart Our Business Startups Act
KIIS	key investment information sheet
LLC	limited liability company
NFT	non-fungible token
NZVIF	New Zealand Venture Investment Fund
NZX	New Zealand Stock Exchange
OMB	Office of Management and Budget
SAFE	Simple Agreement for Future Equity
SEC	Securities and Exchange Commission
SME	small and medium-size enterprise
SPAC	special purpose acquisition company
SPV	special purpose vehicle
VC	venture capital, venture capitalist

Introduction

It's a wonder that anybody invests in startup companies. Sure, a successful startup company creates jobs, grows the economy, and generates a healthy return for its early investors—but the *typical* startup company achieves none of these things. For every venture that makes it big, there are thousands of others that simply burn through all their investors' money with nothing to show for it.

This makes it tough for entrepreneurs to raise capital in the first place. Potential investors are rightfully wary that any given startup company is much more likely to go out of business than to grow tenfold. But if a startup can't raise seed money at the outset, it will never have the chance to grow and succeed—to the detriment of us all. Where would we be without Uber rides, Facebook posts, or Amazon Prime?

For the past half-century, startup companies have mainly been funded by courageous (and wealthy) angel investors and venture capitalists (VCs). These are not legal or technical terms, but they have a well-understood meaning: VCs are professional startup investors, usually found in Silicon Valley and certain other hotspots, while angel investors are wealthy amateurs based in many major cities. VCs and angels invest in a diversified portfolio of startup companies, hoping that a couple of huge successes will more than make up for the many that will fail. They also invest locally, allowing them to advise, and keep an eye on, the companies they own.

With the advent of the internet, however, geography is no longer a constraint, and a radically inclusive new form of startup finance has become suddenly possible. In a break from the analog past, entrepreneurs now have the ability to solicit investments directly from the broad public—the "crowd"—simply by posting an idea to a website and asking each person to pitch in a small amount. If 1,000 people each contribute $1,000, you've got $1 million in capital right there—and you don't have to trek out to Palo Alto and convince a bunch of guys in fleece vests.

Sounds great, there's only one problem: this sort of "investment crowdfunding" was previously illegal—and remained so prior to the recent legal changes that are the subject of this book.

Century-old laws, designed to protect the public from losing our shirts in speculative ventures, make it illegal to offer "securities"—meaning shares of stock, bonds, or any other financial investment—the same way you would a

Investment Crowdfunding. Andrew A. Schwartz, Oxford University Press. © Andrew A. Schwartz 2023.
DOI: 10.1093/oso/9780197688526.003.0001

2 INTRODUCTION

bicycle or a piece of land. You can't offer shares of stock in a company on a website like Craigslist or via Twitter.

Rather, a suite of federal laws enacted in response to the great stock market crash of 1929 require that all securities first be "registered" with the government before they can legally be offered to the public. This registration process—sometimes called an IPO or "initial public offering"—is run by the Securities and Exchange Commission (SEC), and other jurisdictions have similar laws operated by analogous regulators, such as the Australian Securities and Investments Commission (ASIC) or the United Kingdom's Financial Conduct Authority (FCA).

The registration process is covered by hundreds, if not thousands, of rules and regulations. To register securities, you must provide the SEC with extensive mandatory disclosures about the business and its finances. It is complex and technical and requires the assistance of specialized (and highly paid) attorneys and accountants. It is like filing a tax return—times ten thousand.

The regulations are as thick as an old-fashioned phonebook, and the costs of compliance can run to millions of dollars, which is way too expensive for most startup companies to afford. It doesn't make sense to spend $3 million in compliance costs when you only want to raise $1 million in the first place. It would be like paying for a building permit to construct a Lego skyscraper in your attic.

This legal framework explains why startup companies have traditionally been funded by VCs, angels, and the friends and family of the founders—but never the broad public. If an entrepreneur privately offers the chance to invest to a limited number of close friends and family, this does not count as a public offer, and so it is specifically exempted from the registration requirement. There is also a legal exemption for offers made to so-called "accredited" investors, sometimes called "wholesale" investors. This group includes professional investors (like VCs) as well as wealthy investors (angels), as they have the expertise to identify promising companies, or at least the deep pockets to withstand significant losses.

The practical effect of these rules is that, as long as entrepreneurs studiously exclude the public and limit investment to accredited investors and their personal contacts, they can raise startup capital without going through the registration process. No surprise, that is just what they have done—and who can blame them?

The unfortunate result, however, is that our market for startup finance became more like a private club than a public market, for both investors and for entrepreneurs. On the investor side, ordinary people—those who don't know an entrepreneur personally and who aren't wealthy enough to qualify as accredited—have been completely left out of the market for startup finance.

On the entrepreneur side, women and many marginalized groups have found it especially tough to raise seed money for their startups. This would include

INTRODUCTION 3

many racial minorities, rural populations, and those raised in poverty. Fewer of them have wealthy friends and family, and few of them know any VCs or angels, making it less likely that they will raise the money they need. This is not just a problem for these frustrated entrepreneurs, it is a social problem, as we will never see the companies they might have developed if given the chance.

In response to these concerns, as well as a general desire to foster startup activity, countries around the world, led by the United States, amended their securities laws over the past decade to expressly authorize and regulate a new type of online stock market that I call "investment crowdfunding."[1] The goal is to give everyone—regardless of wealth or whom they know—the chance to invest in startup companies and to likewise give all entrepreneurs the chance to pitch their ideas to the broad public. It is not formally limited to startup companies—a local café could surely participate—but the emphasis is on new ventures in their early stages.

Investment crowdfunding is modeled on the earlier, and highly successful, concept of "reward crowdfunding," as practiced on Kickstarter, Indiegogo, and other websites. In reward crowdfunding, entrepreneurs use the internet to obtain financing from strangers to produce a creative or consumer product, such as a documentary or a wristwatch. The funders are later compensated with the product itself or some other reward, like having their names listed in the film credits.

Investment crowdfunding works much the same way, except instead of getting a physical product or some other reward, investors receive a financial interest in the company. On a specialized website, entrepreneurs post information about their companies and the targeted level of funding that they need. Potential investors peruse the various opportunities and decide which to invest in, as well as how much to contribute.

If investors collectively pledge enough to meet the funding target, the deal goes through: the startup company[2] gets the money, and the investors receive shares of stock, or some other security, in return. If the target is not met by the specified deadline, the pledges are voided and there is no deal. The whole endeavor is on a small scale, as each company is only allowed to raise a limited amount of capital, such as $5 million per year.

---

[1] I and others have also used other names for the same concept, including "equity crowdfunding" and "securities crowdfunding."

[2] When I use the term "startup company," I mean to include all types of entrepreneurship, including small businesses and SMEs (small and medium enterprises). Some people reserve the term "startup company" exclusively to refer to a company that plans to "scale up" and grow into a significant player in the business world, like Netflix or Uber. They would call other companies, those that have more modest ambitions, small businesses. In this book, however, I am just using the term as a shorthand, not to make a point. I use the term "startup company" to refer to all types of small and early-stage companies, as they are all invited to participate in investment crowdfunding.

4   INTRODUCTION

Consider a hypothetical rock band that needs $50,000 to record and promote its first album. The band has talent, and the album might generate a huge number of sales—perhaps $500,000 or more—although this is obviously speculative, as there are countless highly talented bands that never make it big.

The band has been playing live concerts in small, local venues for the past two years and has a hundred loyal fans who attend regularly, as well as a thousand "followers" on social media websites like Facebook. The album could do well—the loyal fans are almost certain to buy it—but the band lacks the seed money it needs to rent a recording studio, hire a sound engineer, and advertise the album.

Investment crowdfunding enables the band to raise the $50,000 it needs and provides an avenue for its fans and followers to invest in a band they love and want to see succeed. The band simply posts information to an investment crowd-funding website, including a video of a recent concert, and invites the public to invest.

Likely, the loyal fans and followers will be the first to buy in, and the campaign will have some momentum. Other people, who had never heard of the band before, will see that it has caught the attention of the crowd, and some of them will invest as well. (This is called the "snowball effect" or, more negatively, "herding," and will be addressed in Chapter Four.)

If the $50,000 target is reached, the band gets the money, and the investors each receive a share of the band's profits. Hopefully, it will be a success, and the investors will all make money, along with the band. This outcome is far from certain, of course, and the very nature of releasing a new rock album—like all startup ventures—is inherently uncertain. Most albums don't sell a million copies, and most startups aren't worth a billion dollars.

Importantly, however, the very fact that the album was crowdfunded increases its chances of success. The fans are now investors, making them highly motivated, for both aesthetic and economic reasons, to buy the album, post about it on social media, and otherwise support the band. These efforts, in turn, make the album more likely to succeed. This idea that crowdfunding investors are also consumers and advocates—I call them "brand ambassadors"—represents an important advantage of crowdfunding over traditional forms of startup finance, a point to which we will return in Chapter Four.

In short, investment crowdfunding makes good sense, and the only thing standing in the way has been the law. But the law can be changed at any time—and so it was. In 2012, a strongly bipartisan Congress passed the Jumpstart Our Business Startups (JOBS) Act, which introduced a new legal regime to authorize and regulate this new form of stock market in the United States. In signing the JOBS Act into law in 2012, President Barack Obama offered these cogent remarks on investment crowdfunding:

INTRODUCTION 5

And for start-ups and small businesses, this bill is a potential game changer. Right now, you can only turn to a limited group of investors—including banks and wealthy individuals—to get funding. Laws that are nearly eight decades old make it impossible for others to invest. But a lot has changed in eighty years, and it's time our laws did as well. Because of this bill, startups and small business will now have access to a big, new pool of potential investors—namely, the American people. For the first time, ordinary Americans will be able to go online and invest in entrepreneurs that they believe in.[3]

This is a compelling vision, and it was ultimately put into effect in 2016, when the SEC issued the final regulations, known as Regulation Crowdfunding.

Investment crowdfunding, though born in America, quickly spread around the world, with dozens of other countries following suit and amending their securities laws to allow this new form of stock market. The JOBS Act and Regulation Crowdfunding provided what I will call the "standard model" for investment crowdfunding regulations, and countries around the world used it as their template. To date, most countries with a legal regime for investment crowdfunding have hewed closely to the American original, in places as disparate as Australia, Brazil, Canada, France, Israel, Korea, Malaysia, Nigeria, and many more.

Two jurisdictions—namely, the United Kingdom and New Zealand—took a different path and adopted a more lightly regulated version of investment crowdfunding, which I will refer to as the "liberal model." In contrast with the standard model, which emphasizes law and regulation, the liberal model relies primarily on private ordering, where market participants, incentivized by market forces, make their own rules and structures.

For example, the standard model requires that companies provide certain mandatory disclosures on official government forms. The liberal model, by contrast, allows each platform and company to decide, based on investor demand, what type of information to disclose, and in what format.

A primary purpose of this book is to compare the standard model with the liberal model, with an eye toward finding the best, and worst, aspects of each one. I focus on a set of six jurisdictions. Four of them follow the standard model: America, Australia, Canada, and the European Union. Two of them follow the liberal model: New Zealand and the United Kingdom.

In Chapters Five and Six, I will describe and analyze the investment crowdfunding regulations in these countries using legal and economic theory, as well as in light of the real-world experience to date (as limited as it may be). I spent the past decade researching investment crowdfunding on four continents. I have spoken with legislators, regulators, platform operators, entrepreneurs, and

---

[3] Press Release, White House, Remarks by the President at JOBS Act Bill Signing (Apr. 5, 2012).

6 INTRODUCTION

others. I've collected statistics myself and reviewed those collected by others. I've read dozens of journal articles, as well as innumerable news stories and blog posts on the subject. In the end, I have a lot of anecdotes, and a fair bit of data to boot—my empirical report could fill the entire book.

Even so, I will try not to cram a full statistical analysis and global history of investment crowdfunding into the following pages. A comprehensive review would be overwhelming, repetitive, and quickly outdated—several jurisdictions completely overhauled their investment crowdfunding laws while I was drafting this book, forcing me to go back and make revisions. (I'm looking in your direction, Canada.) Nevertheless, I have learned a lot in my empirical research, and I will insinuate relevant data, anecdotes, and my observations throughout the book.

Most basically, what I've learned is that investment crowdfunding has a sound footing and significant promise—but that it has not yet reached its full potential. Moreover, the legal regime in place makes a big difference, and the liberal approach followed in New Zealand and the United Kingdom is, with a few tweaks, what I would recommend for any country designing or reforming a regulatory scheme for investment crowdfunding.

That's my conclusion—but to get there will take the entire book. I proceed as follows.

In Chapter One, I introduce the concept of "investment crowdfunding," describe its background and origins, and situate it within its broader context. "Crowdfunding" is a broad concept, and so I must delineate the parameters of what exactly we are talking about. To that end, I define investment crowdfunding as the *public offering of unregistered securities through an independent online platform*. Each word is pregnant with meaning, but I will hold off on a full explanation until Chapter One—which is only a few pages away.

For now, permit me to highlight that this definition excludes a number of related areas of "fintech," such as initial coin offerings (ICOs) and non-fungible tokens (NFTs). Those types of transactions, although they take place online, are not conducted through independent online platforms. The definition also excludes certain types of online platforms that call themselves "crowdfunding" but are only open to accredited investors rather than the public. I don't begrudge them the use of the word, I am just trying to clearly define the subject matter at hand.

In Chapter Two, I elucidate the three policy goals investment crowdfunding is meant to achieve: (1) to provide a simple and inexpensive method for startup companies and other small businesses to raise business capital from the public; (2) to create an inclusive market where all entrepreneurs—regardless of location, gender, race, or anything else—have an equal opportunity to access investors; and (3) to democratize the market for startup investment by allowing ordinary people to make investments that have traditionally been limited to the wealthy and connected. At times, these goals are in tension—in particular with respect to "gatekeeping," a major subject of Chapter Four. For the most part, however, they all live in harmony.

Chapter Two also reports that investment crowdfunding is making significant progress toward these goals—in the United States and around the world. As for the first goal, the dollar value of crowdfunding investments is relatively small, but growing quickly. In the year 2021, for instance, more than 1,000 American companies raised money through investment crowdfunding; each company raised about $400,000, on average, for a total of more than $400 million. The numbers are even larger in other countries, especially the United Kingdom.

Investment crowdfunding is also succeeding in creating an inclusive and democratic market for startup finance. Female and minority entrepreneurs have found a receptive audience that is not only open to investing in their companies but affirmatively seeking out such opportunities. And from the investor side, their numbers are small but growing. Looking again at 2021 in the United States, over 500,000 investors participated that year, from every corner of the land, with each of them investing an average of roughly $800.

Chapter Three interrupts this happy story by focusing on the challenges facing investment crowdfunding. Recall how it works: retail investors convey their hard-earned money to someone they've never met, to buy in to a startup company with little or no track record, entirely on the internet, all without the benefit of the usual disclosures or professional advice. What could go wrong?! A lot. For one thing, the entrepreneur might perpetrate a fraud, meaning that she fibs to the investors to get them to buy in. Even an honest entrepreneur might nonetheless fail in her business; indeed, that happens all the time. Either way, the crowd loses its entire investment.

In Chapter Three, I employ a widely used theoretical framework, developed by economists and legal academics over the past fifty years and crystallized by Ronald Gilson. The core of the idea is that investment crowdfunding—like all forms of entrepreneurial finance—must respond to three fundamental challenges: (1) uncertainty: nobody can predict the future, including how a startup company will perform; (2) information asymmetry: entrepreneurs know much more about their business than do potential investors; (3) agency costs: entrepreneurs are human and will be tempted to shirk and enrich themselves at the investors' expense. If it cannot surmount this "trio of problems," nobody will participate, and the market will collapse.

There was widespread fear in the early days of investment crowdfunding that, by exempting the market from the usual disclosure and registration rules of a public offering, the market would devolve into a snake pit full of fraudsters and thieves. *The Wall Street Journal*, for instance, published an article in 2017 titled

8 INTRODUCTION

"Investors, Beware of [Investment] Crowdfunding," in which it reported on an academic article itself called "Crowdfrauding."[4] The *Journal* author painted a dire picture:

> In a paper published in the journal Business Horizons, [the authors] say it's easy for swindlers to circumvent safeguards in the Jumpstart Our Business Startups Act. . . . [T]he researchers say that because many small investors simply aren't sophisticated enough to evaluate a startup, they could be sucked into investing in a fraudulent company. . . . The required level of disclosure is lower than that for a company planning an initial public offering, the researchers say, and swindlers can fabricate documents that appear legitimate.[5]

In practice, things haven't been nearly so bad! We have seen very few allegations of fraud or other illegal behavior, across all jurisdictions. Consider that the SEC has only ever brought one single, solitary case alleging fraud (or anything else) in the context of investment crowdfunding, in a case involving roughly $2 million.[6] By way of comparison, the SEC has brought more than eighty cases alleging misbehavior among ICOs, NFTs, and the like, leading the SEC to establish a special Crypto Assets and Cyber Unit that has recovered more than $2 billion in fines and damages.[7]

How has investment crowdfunding achieved such a clean record, despite the fears of malfeasance? Looking again to theory, there are two basic ways for a market to respond to Gilson's three fundamental challenges. One is to rely on market forces, incentives, and other aspects of "private ordering." The other is to use formal law and government regulation. Investment crowdfunding, wisely, uses both methods, as I describe in Chapters Four, Five, and Six—which is the heart of the book.

I begin with private ordering. In Chapter Four, I describe the most important methods that private parties use to govern the investment crowdfunding market, the most important of which is probably "gatekeeping." This is the idea that entrepreneurs cannot solicit investors directly and are required to act through an online platform. The platform—like a medieval gatekeeper—stands at the

---

[4] Louise Lee, *Investors, Beware of Crowdfunding*, WALL ST. J., Nov. 27, 2017, at R2 (reporting on Melissa S. Baucus & Cheryl R. Mitteness, *Crowdfrauding: Avoiding Ponzi Entrepreneurs when Investing in New Ventures*, 59 BUS. HORIZONS 37 (2016)).

[5] Louise Lee, *Investors, Beware of Crowdfunding*, WALL ST. J., Nov. 27, 2017, at R2; Melissa S. Baucus & Cheryl R. Mitteness, *Crowdfrauding: Avoiding Ponzi Entrepreneurs when Investing in New Ventures*, 59 BUS. HORIZONS 37, 41 (2016) (asserting that the "JOBS Act unlocks the door to crowdfrauding"); *id.* at 48 (claiming to "demonstrate the ease with which scheming individuals can engage in crowdfrauding").

[6] Complaint, Sec. and Exch. Comm'n v. Shumake, No. 21-cv-12193 (E.D. Mich. Sept. 20, 2021).

[7] Sec. and Exch. Comm'n, *SEC Nearly Doubles Size of Enforcement's Crypto Assets and Cyber Unit*, May 3, 2022.

metaphorical "gate" between entrepreneurs and investors and is expected to only allow legitimate and promising companies to list on the platform. We can count on the gatekeepers because they want investors to come back again tomorrow (and because they can lose their license), so it is in their self-interest to be a diligent gatekeeper.

Another key method of private ordering is the fear that "brand ambassadors"—like the fans and followers of our hypothetical rock band—might become "brand assassins." If a crowdfunded company were to mislead its investors or misuse the money it raised, it would not only be abusing its investors, it would be ticking off its biggest fans—who might respond by trashing the company on social media and in real life. So it probably won't.

Gatekeeping and brand ambassadors are just two of the numerous methods of private ordering described in Chapter Four. The key takeaway is that, collectively, these private methods have considerable force, meaning that law and regulation should focus on enhancing and complementing them, rather than piling on additional regulatory burdens.

Chapters Five and Six then turn to the law. Chapter Five describes and critiques the American legal regime for investment crowdfunding, namely, the JOBS Act and Regulation Crowdfunding. Chapter Six, in turn, does the same for the investment crowdfunding laws of Australia, Canada, the European Union, New Zealand, and the United Kingdom.

I sort the legal regimes adopted in these different jurisdictions into two types, which I call the "standard" model and the "liberal" model, and distinguish as follows: the standard model depends primarily on legal regulation to address the three challenges of uncertainty, information asymmetry, and agency costs. By contrast, the liberal model depends primarily on private ordering, supplemented by a light-handed set of regulations, to address the trio of problems. This is not a binary distinction, but more like a range of possibilities, with shades between them.

The United States created the standard model when it passed the JOBS Act and Regulation Crowdfunding, and many countries around the world followed its lead. In Chapter Six, we will see that Australia, Canada, and the European Union all adhere to the standard model. The United Kingdom and New Zealand, in contrast, went their own way and adopted a much lighter set of regulations that are specifically designed to harness the power of private ordering, which I call the liberal model.

Notably, the countries that adopted the liberal model, that is, the United Kingdom and New Zealand, have larger and more impactful investment crowdfunding markets than the United States and the others that followed the standard model—and without higher levels of fraud or failure. In the United Kingdom today, there are more investment crowdfunding deals each year than there are

10 INTRODUCTION

angel rounds, and numerous British crowdfunding companies have gone on to an IPO or have been acquired. Tellingly, the UK antitrust regulator blocked a merger between that country's two leading platforms in 2021 on the ground that investment crowdfunding had "become an important part of the overall financial ecosystem."[8] This is consistent with my general support for the liberal approach.

Finally, in Chapter Seven, I summarize the thesis of the book: because investment crowdfunding only allows companies to raise a limited amount of money, the only workable legal regime is a simple one that imposes very low costs. Rather than depending on legal regulation to police the market, we should rely primarily on the powerful methods of private ordering described in Chapter Four and shape our laws to enhance them. We should, in short, follow the liberal approach, not the standard model.

That said, I do not favor a laissez-faire approach to the regulation of investment crowdfunding. There are certain aspects of the form that do call for legal regulation, where private incentives will not lead to the optimal outcome. In fact, I recommend beefing up Regulation Crowdfunding in certain ways, such as by mandating annual reports after a company has raised money on an investment crowdfunding platform, and putting some legal limits on the company's choice of funding target—both points to which we shall return in Chapter Five.

With that introduction, let us proceed to define investment crowdfunding and take a look at its origins and how it works today.

---

[8] UK COMPETITION & MARKETS AUTHORITY, ANTICIPATED ACQUISITION BY CROWDCUBE LIMITED OF SEEDRS LIMITED PROVISIONAL FINDINGS REPORT 5 (2021) (observing that investment crowdfunding platforms "have grown from accounting for a negligible number of equity raises at the start of the last decade to accounting for almost 500 equity raises in 2020").

Chapter One
Investment Crowdfunding

Investment crowdfunding is one species of the broader genus known as "crowdfunding," which is "the practice of obtaining needed funding (as for a new business) by soliciting contributions from a large number of people especially from the online community."[1] Multiple varieties of crowdfunding have developed since the turn of the millennium, including "reward" crowdfunding (as on Kickstarter) and "donation" crowdfunding (as on GoFundMe). But those are not the subject of this book.

Rather, this book is about "investment" crowdfunding. Before going any further, then, allow me to clarify just what I mean by this term. This chapter accordingly defines the concept, explains is origins, and begins to describe how it works in law and practice—a topic that we will cover throughout the rest of the book.

A. HISTORICAL ORIGINS

The word "crowdfunding" was only added to the dictionary in 2014.[2] The concept, however, is far older. Crowdfunding is seen whenever a group of people—a crowd—gathers their funds together in a common pool and for a common purpose. The internet has energized crowdfunding into a powerful global phenomenon, but the basic notion of crowdfunding is ancient.

A church collection plate is one of the oldest and simplest examples of crowdfunding. A plate (or bowl or basket) is passed around the congregation, from hand to hand, and each person drops a couple of coins on it. After completing a lap around the church, the plate is full of money to pay the pastor, provide charity, purchase Bibles, and otherwise fund the expenses of the church. Slightly more sophisticated techniques, such as tithing or membership dues, are really just variations on the theme. All of them accomplish the same goal: gather funds from all (or nearly all) members of the congregation to finance the church and keep it running.

---

[1] Merriam-Webster's Collegiate Dictionary (11th ed. 2019).
[2] Press Release: Merriam-Webster, Merriam-Webster's Collegiate Dictionary Updated for 2014 (May 19, 2014).

Investment Crowdfunding. Andrew A. Schwartz, Oxford University Press. © Andrew A. Schwartz 2023.
DOI: 10.1093/oso/9780197688526.003.0002

12   INVESTMENT CROWDFUNDING

Crowdfunding is not the only way to fund a church, of course. It is certainly possible for a single person or family to build a church and cover its expenses. But there is something special about a community of people coming together and collectively contributing their money to the church. The funders feel invested in the project, because they are. It is not just a church; it is *their* church. They are more likely to attend services or Mass, serve as ushers, and bring in new members.

Beyond churches, many types of charities have long raised money through crowdfunding, rather than soliciting large donors. The March of Dimes is a notable example. This organization was founded by President Franklin D. Roosevelt in 1938 as the National Foundation for Infantile Paralysis (NFIP) to conquer polio, an infectious disease that can paralyze its victims. At the time, the United States was in the midst of a polio epidemic, with tens of thousands of diagnoses each year, many of them children who suffered greatly. President Roosevelt himself had been diagnosed with polio as a young man and was forced to use a wheelchair in his later years.

The NFIP needed to raise money to fund research, education, and assistance. Instead of targeting a few wealthy donors, as with prior anti-polio organizations, the NFIP sought a huge number of small donations. Upon its establishment in 1938, a radio celebrity of the time went on the air and urged every American to contribute just ten cents apiece to the NFIP; his goal was to generate a "march of dimes to reach all the way to the White House." The call was answered, and within weeks, the White House was deluged with tens of thousands of letters, each containing just one dime. That first campaign raised nearly $100,000 (roughly $2 million today) and started a long tradition of dime-based donations. Over time, the organization collected more than 7 billion dimes ($700 million), demonstrating the power of crowdfunding for charity.[3]

Crowdfunding is not only for charities, however. In colonial America, canals, bridges, and even universities were commonly financed via crowdfunding. Projects like these required tremendous sums, with money often raised through the sale of lottery tickets. Hundreds or thousands of people would each pay a small sum to buy a lottery ticket, and a few lucky winners would win the prize money. The rest of the collected funds would go toward building the canal or bridge—or Harvard.[4]

The chance of winning the lottery was one reason people bought tickets, but that was not the only motivation. Most of them surely realized that their chances of winning were slim and that the prize money was not enough to make it a

---

[3] DAVID W. ROSE, THE MARCH OF DIMES 9, 43 (2003).

[4] *Records Reveal Harvard Lottery to Bolster Early Building Funds—Stoughton and Holworthy Owe Existence to Tickets*, HARV. CRIMSON, Mar. 15, 1927.

HISTORICAL ORIGINS 13

sensible bet. Rather, they were contributing their money toward the project because, once completed, it would benefit the whole community, including themselves. A new canal or bridge is a "public good" (meaning something that benefits the whole community) that could be expected to expand trade, bring new settlers to the town, and lower the cost of doing business for everyone.

One of the most famous examples of crowdfunding in American history is the pedestal for the Statue of Liberty, situated in the harbor of New York City. The colossal monument was a gift from France to honor the United States' centennial of independence and the friendship between the two countries. It was designed by a French sculptor and constructed in Paris in the late 1870s and early 1880s, at which point it was shipped to the United States. While the gift was welcome, the monumental sculpture needed a massive pedestal to support its tremendous weight, and it fell to the Americans to construct that pedestal.

After it was shipped from France, the Statue of Liberty's pedestal was not yet complete. Wealthy donors in Boston and New York could not raise the $300,000—roughly $8 million in today's dollars—it would cost, and neither New York nor the federal government agreed to pay for it. Joseph Pulitzer, publisher of the *New York World*, a leading newspaper at the time, called upon the American people to contribute what they could toward the cost of the pedestal. "Let us not wait for the millionaires to give us this money," he wrote, and he set a goal of raising $100,000—nearly $3 million today—in small donations from the public to pay for the pedestal.

In a brilliant marketing maneuver, Pulitzer promised to print the name of every person who contributed to the "Pedestal Fund," regardless of how little they gave, and the campaign caught on like wildfire. Beyond publicity, donors who gave at least $1 received a small replica of the Statue of Liberty as a token of appreciation, with the size of the replica increasing with the size of the donation. This foreshadowed the modern practice of "reward" crowdfunding, to be discussed shortly.

Within six months, 125,000 people had donated to the cause, with most of them giving less than $1 (roughly $25 today), and more than $100,000 was raised, enough to complete the pedestal. The following year, 1886, the pedestal was finished and the Statue of Liberty was placed upon it, where it still stands as a symbol of liberty, brotherhood—and crowdfunding.[5]

Crowdfunding continued into the twentieth century, most famously with the Green Bay Packers, an NFL football team based in an obscure city in northern Wisconsin of just 100,000 souls. Most NFL teams, of course, are based in giant

---

[5] Yasmin Sabina Khan, Enlightening the World: The Creation of the Statue of Liberty 168–73 (2011).

metropolises, like Los Angeles, New York, or Miami. So how did Green Bay end up with an NFL team? Crowdfunding, of course.

The team was organized in 1923 as a nonprofit corporation, and the local people of Green Bay purchased enough shares to get the team off the ground; additional stock offerings were held in 1935 and 1950. The shares do not pay a dividend, and cannot be sold or traded—but people have bought them up whenever the team has put them on sale. In 1997, more than 100,000 people each paid $200 per share, yielding $24 million to renovate Lambeau Field, and more than 250,000 investors participated in another sale in 2011 at $250 per share, giving the team another $67 million to improve the facility. Most recently, the Packers sold roughly 200,000 shares in 2022 at $300 per share, raising another $60 million.[6] Crowdfunding and the Green Bay Packers go hand in hand. The NFL's internal rules prohibit public ownership of franchises—but it includes a grandfather clause just for the Packers.

Overwhelmingly, the purchasers come from the team's rabid fan base, the same people who are willing to endure subzero temperatures to cheer on the Packers on the "frozen tundra" of their iconic stadium, Lambeau Field. They love the team so much that they just want to support it, in any way they can. Indeed, the only real benefit of holding Packers shares is the ability to purchase special Packers merchandise that is exclusively available to shareholders. (These supporters are precisely the sort of "brand ambassadors" to whom we will return in Chapter Four.)

B. REWARD AND DONATION CROWDFUNDING

While examples of crowdfunding exist across history, the technological advances at the turn of the twenty-first century revolutionized the practice. Widespread access to the internet allowed groups of people to connect—and to crowdfund—in ways previously impossible. A new form of crowdfunding emerged at this time, sometimes called "reward" crowdfunding.

Reward crowdfunding is where large groups of people use internet-based platforms to fund a project with the promise of something tangible in return, usually the fruits of the project itself. Reward crowdfunding came on the scene around 2010 and exploded in popularity, quickly growing into a multibillion-dollar industry. It bears close attention here because it was the inspiration for investment crowdfunding, and also created the basic format for it.

---

[6] Talal Ansari, *NFL's Packers Sell Symbolic Shares of Stock to Fans*, Wall St. J., Nov. 17, 2021, at B7; *Packers Shareholders*, Green Bay Packers, https://www.packers.com/community/shareholders (last visited Oct. 28, 2022).

The leading pioneers in reward crowdfunding are two American websites: Kickstarter and Indiegogo. Both established in 2008–2009, the primary mission of these two websites—as well as similar ones around the world—is to connect artists and creators with people who want to finance their projects. Unlike in past centuries when the arts were primarily financed by wealthy individual patrons, these sites allow a modern-day Mozart to broadcast his project to the masses and to raise funds from a multitude of people, each willing to pitch in a little bit to meet his needs. Rather than one wealthy person writing a check for $50,000, the composer might get the same funding from 10,000 people who each pitch in $5.

Why would these individuals contribute $5? They may just like the idea or the artist and want to show support. Furthermore, $5 is a very small amount, less than many of them would spend on a cup of coffee, which makes contributions easier for the common man. Beyond that, funders of projects on Kickstarter and Indiegogo typically receive a reward in return for their investment, following the path blazed by the colonial lotteries and Pulitzer's campaign for the Statue of Liberty's pedestal. Most commonly, the reward is the fruit of the project, though this is not necessarily the case. For example, a rock band might crowdfund the money it needs to record its next album, and, as a reward, the funders are promised the album itself once it is completed. This type of crowdfunding is accordingly known as "reward" crowdfunding.

Kickstarter's self-described mission is to "help bring creative projects to life."[7] The site originally focused on artistic endeavors, but over time, the concept of "creative projects" proved rather expansive, reaching greatly beyond traditional artistic endeavors. In contrast, Indiegogo, for its part, has always had a broad view of what can be crowdfunded, describing its purpose as helping "ideas come to life."[8]

Across both sites, art, books, and music are all well represented, but so are gadgets, clothing, and other consumer products, such as drones, 3-D printers, headphones, computers, and lots of other "stuff." For example, Kickstarter's most successful projects of all time include a jacket designed for travelers, a food cooler, and several smart watches. In fact, it seems that you can crowdfund just about anything. In one notable—and satirical—case, an Ohio man crowdfunded the creation of a potato salad and received more than $50,000 from nearly 7,000 backers![9]

---

[7] *About*, KICKSTARTER, https://www.kickstarter.com/about (last visited Oct. 28, 2022).
[8] *Learn about Indiegogo*, INDIEGOGO, https://www.indiegogo.com/about/our-story (last visited Oct. 28, 2022).
[9] Zack Danger Brown, *Potato Salad*, KICKSTARTER, https://www.kickstarter.com/projects/zack dangerbrown/potato-salad (last visited June 5, 2021).

16   INVESTMENT CROWDFUNDING

In a typical reward-crowdfunding campaign, the creator posts to Kickstarter or a similar website a description of the project she wants to pursue, the minimum amount of money she needs to fund it, and usually a promise of some sort of reward or benefit to those who provide funding. Members of the public—the "crowd"—peruse the various projects available on the website, decide which one they want to support, and then pledge their money to the cause. Each campaign runs for a certain period of time, announced at the outset.

If a given project reaches its target amount—or more—within the given timespan, the money is collected and transmitted to the creator. On Kickstarter, which follows an "all-or-nothing" model, if a project fails to meet its target, then the deal is off and no money changes hands. On Indiegogo, which does not follow the "all-or-nothing" rule, any and all money funders pledge by the deadline is shunted over to the creator.

Frequently, there are different levels of rewards depending on the amount invested. An author planning to write a book might promise a bookmark for contributions of $5, a paperback copy of the book itself for those who provide $20, a hardcover version of the book for those who pledge $50, and a signed copy of the hardcover version for those who contribute $100. Sometimes the reward is related to the project but not the fruit of the project itself. For instance, an artist raising money to paint a mural obviously cannot send funders the mural itself. In such a case, the artist might offer a thank-you email to smaller donors and send prints of mural's art to larger donors, with the size of the prints increasing in tandem with the size of the donation.

The rewards are often not a physical object but rather some measure of publicity, akin to Pulitzer's publication of the names of donors to his Statue of Liberty campaign. Donors to the mural project, for instance, may have their names recorded on a sign or plaque placed next to the mural. Similarly, contributors to a film may get their name in the credits, with the largest backers receiving top billing. At times, the rewards are distinctive experiences, especially for the largest funders. Major backers of a film production, for instance, may be offered a chance to attend the premiere of the film. Large funders of a rock band may get front-row concert tickets or backstage passes when the band next comes to town.

Sometimes the reward is nothing at all, as supporters may contribute to a project purely as a matter of philanthropy. Especially for small amounts, like $10, the contributor typically receives nothing more than an automatically generated thank-you note. Even larger amounts may be donated, as well, if backer simply wants to support the project. Indeed, this type of "no-reward" crowdfunding has itself grown into another form of internet-based crowdfunding, commonly known as "donation" crowdfunding.

In donation crowdfunding, funders receive nothing in return—apart from the satisfaction of helping someone or supporting a cause. One leading donation crowdfunding is GoFundMe, which specializes in campaigns to raise money for charitable causes and people in need. On the site, organizations or individuals can solicit funds, and campaigns run the gamut from financing an individual's expensive surgery or cross-country bike tour to generating donations established charities like UNICEF or the American Cancer Society.

Since its founding in 2010, GoFundMe has generated more than $9 billion in contributions from more than 120 million donors. In fact, despite the lack of incentive to funders, GoFundMe holds the title for the largest crowdfunding platform in the world, generating more money than the combined sum of Kickstarter's near $6 billion and Indiegogo's over $1 billion total funds raised. While GoFundMe may be the most successful example, it is not alone in its donation-crowdfunding model, with other sites including JustGiving and Fundly.

With the internet's widespread reach, reward (and donation) crowdfunding has exploded in popularity over the past decade or so. On Kickstarter alone, 18 million people contributed nearly $5 billion to support nearly 200,000 projects in the decade following its founding in 2009.[10] During that stretch, roughly 500 different Kickstarter campaigns raised $1 million or more, while 7,000 projects topped the $100,000 mark. To offer some perspective, the $5 billion crowdfunded on Kickstarter during its first decade is roughly comparable to the total of all the grants ever awarded by the National Endowment for the Arts, which was established by Congress in 1965—and Kickstarter's numbers are growing fast.

Thanks in large part to Kickstarter and Indiegogo, reward crowdfunding has become a cultural phenomenon. Now, similar reward-crowdfunding sites exist in countries around the globe, focusing on reward crowdfunding for their domestic audience. Examples include Wadiz in Korea, Catarse in Brazil, and Verkami in Spain. It is the popularity of reward crowdfunding that led the term "crowdfunding" to be added to the dictionary in 2014.

To conclude, internet-based reward and donation crowdfunding became firmly established in our market and culture in the early 2010s. In the decade since, backers have financed a huge number of campaigns, sometimes receiving some incentive and sometimes for the benefit of the common good. With the rise in popularity of these crowdfunding platforms, the next logical step was "investment" crowdfunding—where companies use the internet to raise capital from the crowd by promising backers some financial stake in their business.

---

[10] *Kickstarter Stats*, KICKSTARTER, https://www.kickstarter.com/help/stats (last visited June 5, 2021).

C. THE LEGAL CONTEXT FOR INVESTMENT CROWDFUNDING

Investment crowdfunding builds directly on reward crowdfunding, as funders receive some sort of financial interest in return for their contributions. Recall the hypothetical rock band discussed in the introduction that offered people a portion of the profits from their album sales in exchange for the seed money needed to record the album in the first place.

In an earlier age, investment crowdfunding would not have been feasible. Modern technology, however, especially inexpensive computing power and effective telecommunications systems, have allowed startups and small businesses to solicit, collect, and keep track of a large number of investments, and investors spread across the country. Further, small businesses traditionally could not realistically afford to send promoters door to door or to run advertisements that could reach the entire populace to obtain their necessary capital. Yet the internet makes it easy for any business to solicit funds from anyone and everyone, nationwide, at minimal cost. In economic terms, the "transaction costs" are now low enough to pursue investment crowdfunding.

Investment crowdfunding is a norm-shattering and inclusive proposition. Historically and in modern times, the vast majority of businesses have been funded by a small handful of people, not a large crowd. Nearly all new businesses get their initial capital from the founders themselves, as well as the founders' friends and family (e.g., a "rich uncle"). Sometimes, an "angel investor" will provide a substantial amount of seed money to a fledgling startup, or a venture capital (VC) fund may offer to invest in a promising company.

But what about founders of modest means, who lack a rich uncle and don't know any angel investors or VCs? No matter how great their business idea, without capital, their business is unlikely to ever get off the ground. Investment crowdfunding, however, offers these entrepreneurs the chance to pitch their business to the crowd to obtain the funding they need. When looking at the benefits in aggregate, investment crowdfunding can lead to inclusive economic growth and expanded employment, in addition to the new and useful products and services these otherwise likely defunct companies may provide.

Given the great promise it holds, attempts at creating investment crowdfunding platforms in the United States were made as early as 2005. At that time, however, doing so was clearly illegal. Federal securities laws in the United States and other similar enactments around the world strictly regulate the offer of "securities," meaning stocks, bonds, or any other financial investment. These laws, passed as part of the New Deal in the early 1930s, required that those engaged in investment crowdfunding, just like anybody else, follow these rules and regulations.

THE LEGAL CONTEXT FOR INVESTMENT CROWDFUNDING   19

The basic rule of securities regulation is that, prior to selling any securities, you must first "register" the security with the appropriate regulatory body; in the United States, this is the Securities and Exchange Commission (SEC). Offering *un*registered securities to the public is a civil and even criminal offense, and people who purchase the securities can likewise bring suit against the offender.

Indeed, this happened to one pioneering online platform. Prosper Marketplace was founded in 2005 as an internet-based "peer-to-peer" lending service. On the Prosper website, individuals would post anonymous requests to borrow up to $25,000, explain why they sought the money, and state the maximum interest rate they were willing to pay. Interested people could review the various requests, which also included basic credit information, and bid on funding all or a portion of the loan for a specified interest rate. Once the loan was fully funded, often by a consortium of dozens of lenders, additional lenders would have to offer a lower rate than the bids already made. The effect was to drive down the interest rate until no one would offer a lower bid. After a preset time, the loan would be granted at the lowest interest rate acceptable to enough bidders.

Prosper was an early leader in crowdfunding personal loans, generating nearly $200 million in loans in its first two years—and catching the attention of the SEC, state securities agencies, and private attorneys. Prosper never registered its loans as securities with the SEC or state regulators, leading to lawsuits by both, as well as a private class action brought in the name of all Prosper lenders who purchased the unregistered loans. Prosper settled all of these lawsuits, agreeing to pay a $1 million fine to the states and a $10 million settlement in the class action. It also promised to register its loans as securities, a process that took the site offline for the better part of a year.[11]

This lengthy outage was no surprise, as the process of registering securities— sometimes known as an IPO (initial public offering)—is a complex and expensive endeavor that calls for mandatory disclosure of important information about the security and the business venture. Specialized attorneys and accountants are needed, and the total price tag can run to several million dollars. For large companies, that is the cost of doing business; spending $3 million to raise $100 million is just 3 percent of the total.

Startup companies and small businesses, however, are simply unable to afford costs of that magnitude. These sorts of companies need to raise hundreds of thousands of dollars, or perhaps a couple of million, and it obviously does not make financial sense to spend $3 million to raise $1 million. For this reason, it has always been imperative for startup companies to figure out a way to sell

---

[11] NASAA, *Prosper Marketplace Inc. Enters Settlement with State Securities Regulators over Sales of Unregistered Securities*, Dec. 1, 2008; Prosper Marketplace, Inc., Form 8-K, July 17, 2013. (Disclosure: The author has invested modest amounts in Prosper from 2006 to the present, with currently roughly $3,000 invested there.).

20 INVESTMENT CROWDFUNDING

securities and thereby raise capital, yet avoid the requirement to register with the SEC.

Fortunately, the Securities Act of 1933 and analogous foreign laws include a series of exceptions to the general rule that all securities must be registered before sale. These are officially known as "exempt" offerings, and they are exactly what they sound like: offerings of securities without prior registration.

For startup companies, the two most important exemptions are the private placement exemption, where one offers securities to an exclusive group of family and friends, and the accredited investor exemption, where one sells securities solely to wealthy people (known as "accredited" investors in America, or "wholesale" in other countries). Although these two exemptions may come across as elitist, they are well intentioned and make good sense, as these two groups are particularly well suited to invest in a startup company or small business.

First, friends and family of an entrepreneur are in a good position to judge the prospects of his company, given their relationship and familiarity with his past successes and failures. If your old college buddy was a straight-A student and was constantly being promoted at work, it may be sensible to invest in her startup. If your sister has been unsuccessfully bouncing from job to job for the past decade, you know that contributing to her startup company is probably not a good idea.

Total strangers, without a preexisting relationship with your college buddy or sister, lack the background knowledge of the type of person they are and their likelihood of success. For this reason, traditional securities law only allowed people to invest in private startup companies or small businesses when they personally knew the entrepreneur.

Accredited investors are also well placed to make investments in startup companies—but not for the reason often given. Under current law, you qualify as accredited if you have investible assets exceeding $1 million or an annual income of over $200,000. Professional investors, like VCs, also qualify as accredited investors. One reason to exempt offerings made solely to these sorts of investors is that they are sophisticated and knowledgeable, and therefore do not need the paternalistic protection of securities registration. But not every millionaire is a sophisticated financier; to take an easy example, consider a regular Joe who wins $1 million in the lottery. He doesn't become a shrewd investor overnight.

The better reason for the accredited investor exemption is simply that members of this group have a lot of money, making it less harmful if they lose some of it on an ill-fated investment. Even if an accredited investor loses his entire investment in some risky startup company, he has a large pool of assets to fall back on. He will not go hungry. In addition, accredited investors have enough money to spread their bets around, rather than placing all their eggs in one basket. Angels and VCs both understand that most of their portfolio companies will never make it big—or even survive. So instead of picking their favorite company and going all in, they diversify their investments and hope that a few "home runs" will more than make up for their losses on the others.

Nonaccredited investors (known as "retail" investors) face different circumstances. They may be as smart as any millionaire and have an eye for promising companies, but they face different consequences if they are wrong—which will surely happen, at least sometimes. Unlike an accredited investor, who has a million-dollar cushion, retail investors can easily invest more than they can afford to lose. If retail investors lose a substantial amount of money in a startup company, this could put them in real financial trouble.

Furthermore, many, if not most, startup companies will end up failing and shutting down, for one reason or another. They are totally different from the public companies listed on the New York Stock Exchange, which are all well-established concerns that may suffer a bad quarter or year, but almost never suddenly go poof, as startup companies are wont to do. This is why, until crowdfunding came along, retail investors were legally excluded from the market for startup capital, while accredited investors (VCs and angels) were given the privilege of investing in these risky, but potentially lucrative, ventures.

These arguments for excluding retail investors only carry you so far, however. In a free economy, people are generally free to spend their money as they see fit. If they want to buy an electric skateboard for $1,000 or attend a concert with VIP seats for $1,000, why not let them invest $1,000 in a speculative startup company? Indeed, given that startup companies are a key engine of job growth and the economy, there is a public interest in at least allowing retail investors to participate in the market for startup capital.

One thoughtful response to my rhetorical question is that shoes and concerts are forms of consumption, not investment. People understand that they are "spending" their money on these things, rather than "investing" their money, and they get use and enjoyment by wearing the shoes and attending the concert (perhaps in conjunction). With investment crowdfunding, however, people do not get any use or enjoyment from their securities. They are just intangible assets that give the holder a financial stake in the company.

Yet the dividing line between consumption and investment may not be as clear as it appears, and crowdfunding investors often have mixed motivations for investing. On the one hand, they hope for a financial return, but on the other, they often have nonfinancial reasons for investing.

For one thing, crowdfunding investors may—and do—invest in companies in order to endorse and advance certain social or political goals. People buy organic vegetables, fair-trade coffee, environmentally friendly power, and so on in part to support those industries and practices. They are more expensive than the regular type, but people are keen to pay the extra amount. This practice translates directly to investment crowdfunding. For example, supporters of solar energy could invest in a new company formed to build a solar array, thereby advancing their political goal of advancing solar power. If the solar array ultimately loses money, and the investors do the same, they may be pleased nonetheless with their choice of investment.

Another social rationale for investing in a crowdfunding company is to support entrepreneurship among a certain demographic group, especially one that is underrepresented among entrepreneurs. Indeed, this is one of the primary purposes of investment crowdfunding, as will be discussed in Chapter Two. In that chapter, we will see that Black founders received less than 1 percent of VC capital in recent years and that less than 3 percent of VC funding went to women-led startup companies. In response to figures like these, many crowdfunding investors specifically want to fund a company founded or managed by a person that fits a certain demographic profile. To be sure, they hope that the company does well—for the sake of the founder and of themselves—but they may well be satisfied just that the founder had the opportunity to give it a try.

A final nonfinancial motivation for crowdfunding investors is to serve as a "patron of the arts." Artists—from glassblowers to ballet dancers—commonly cannot support themselves purely from sales or performances and require the financial backing of one or more "patrons" in order to practice their art. This is true even for august institutions like the New York Philharmonic, which have financial backers who make donations over and above the cost of tickets. These donors, in turn, are inducted into societies like "Golden Circle" and the "Friends of the New York Philharmonic." This type of giving has played a major role in reward crowdfunding, which has funded countless movies, books, CDs, and other products of artistic expression—with no potential for financial return. It plays a similar role in investment crowdfunding, where artistic endeavors might even turn a profit. The names may be different—"Beta Tester" rather than "Golden Circle"—but the idea is more or less the same.

These are just a few of the many types of nonpecuniary benefits that motivate crowdfunding investors, and there are certainly many more. The key point is that crowdfunding investors with negative financial returns cannot be said to simply have "lost" their money. Rather they will have "spent" it—at least in part—to support the people and causes they believe in.

D. DEFINITION

Given this background and context, I will now offer a formal definition of investment crowdfunding. The definition I offer is my own and intended to be universal, by which I mean generally applicable regardless of legal jurisdiction or the specific legal rules in place. My definition is not meant to explain every aspect of investment crowdfunding—that is what the whole book is about—but is rather designed to state the essential features that distinguish it. Read it slowly, for each word plays a role.

Investment crowdfunding is *the public offering of unregistered securities through an independent online platform*. Permit me to elaborate.

Public offering: Everyone is invited to participate in investment crowdfunding, not just those with sufficient wealth to qualify as an accredited investor, and not just those with personal connections to the entrepreneur. This inclusive aspect of investment crowdfunding distinguishes it from VC, angel investing, and other fundraising methods that are limited to accredited investors.

Unregistered: For the past one hundred years, public offerings of securities have needed to be registered with the SEC (or analogous foreign regulator), but this registration process is too expensive for startup companies and small businesses to afford. Investment crowdfunding challenges this paradigm by allowing entrepreneurs to offer securities to the public without first registering them. This eliminates a huge amount of regulatory red tape, slashing the cost of raising capital, but risks stripping investors of the protections disclosure traditionally offered.

Securities: Crowdfunding investors receive a financial interest in the company, like shares of stock, options, warrants, bonds, notes, or any sort of investment contract. This distinguishes investment crowdfunding from its precursors, reward and donation crowdfunding, described earlier. The term "security" is a legal concept that we will return to in Chapter Five.

Online: Investment crowdfunding is conducted entirely online—over the internet, World Wide Web, apps, metaverse, and similar—and never in person. This online nature makes geography irrelevant and allows anyone, from anywhere, to easily pitch her business plan to millions of potential investors. Investment crowdfunding harnesses the power of telecommunications technology to create an inclusive and efficient nationwide market. This represents a break from the traditions of VCs and angel investors, who generally invest only in their home city or region. The online context also means that every utterance of everyone involved is set down in writing and etched forever in binary code. This "digital trail" encourages honorable behavior, or at least makes it easier to detect and punish wrongdoers, a subject we will cover in Chapter Four.

Independent platform: Investment crowdfunding is always conducted through an independent intermediary, often called a "platform," and never directly between entrepreneur and investor. This portion of the definition serves to exclude many types of online offerings that lack an independent

24   INVESTMENT CROWDFUNDING

middleman, including initial coin offerings (ICOs), non-fungible tokens (NFTs), and so on.

E. INVESTMENT CROWDFUNDING IN PRACTICE

The remainder of this book will provide a detailed description of the law and practice of investment crowdfunding in the United States and selected other countries. For now, though, permit me to offer an overview of how investment crowdfunding works, and a summary report on the American market as of the present day (the early 2020s).

At its core, investment crowdfunding operates very much like reward crowdfunding. It takes place entirely on internet-based platforms like Wefunder, StartEngine, or Crowdcube. These sites look very much like Kickstarter or Indiegogo, but there is a key difference: investment crowdfunding sites are dealing in securities and thus must comply with a special set of securities laws and regulations. The laws and regulations that govern investment crowdfunding vary somewhat from country to country, as I will discuss in Chapters Five and Six, but the basic rules and procedures are similar across the world.

Although investment crowdfunding takes place on the internet, which is a global system, the practice is regulated on a country-by-country basis. Thus, American investment crowdfunding platforms are licensed by the SEC, while their Australian counterparts are licensed by the Australian Securities and Investment Commission. Offerings made to UK investors must comply with UK law.

An entrepreneur seeking to raise funds for her business begins by applying to one or more investment crowdfunding platforms, which are websites available on the internet. These platforms need a special license from the government in order to legally conduct this type of business.

Large countries like the United States boast dozens of licensed platforms, with a number of serious competitors; current leaders in the field are Wefunder, StartEngine, Republic, and SeedInvest. Smaller countries, by contrast, may have only a couple of licensed platforms and only one or two significant players. In the United Kingdom, for instance, the two leading platforms (Seedrs and Crowdcube) reportedly control more than 90 percent of the investment crowdfunding market in that country.[12]

---

[12] For this reason, the UK Competition and Markets Authority raised significant antitrust concerns when the two companies proposed merging in 2020, leading to the subsequent scuttling of the merger in 2021. UK Competition and Markets Authority, *CMA Finds Competition Concerns in Crowdcube and Seedrs Merger* (Mar. 24, 2021).

Investment crowdfunding platforms do not endorse or guarantee the investments they host—indeed, that would likely violate the terms of their license—but they do curate their offerings, rather than take all comers, as was the tradition in reward and donation crowdfunding. Some of the platforms, especially the leaders in each jurisdiction, claim to be highly selective and demanding, and only allow a very small percentage of interested entrepreneurs to list on their sites, often less than 5 percent. I refer to this phenomenon as "gatekeeping," and we shall return to it in Chapter Four.

As we will discuss in that chapter, gatekeeping makes good business sense. Investment crowdfunding platforms want to establish and maintain a reputation as a reliable place to invest. That way, investors will come back again and again, generating fees for the platform every time. If the platform hosts low-quality (or, worse, fraudulent) offerings, burned investors are unlikely to return, and the platform may fail entirely. Thus they act as strict gatekeepers.

Still, as we will see in the next chapter, one goal of investment crowdfunding is to give all entrepreneurs a chance to seek funding from the crowd. A highly vetted platform has its merits, but it is clearly more exclusive than inclusive, and one might worry that investment crowdfunding platforms are overly selective. Never fear. Anecdotal evidence suggests that some platforms are more selective than others and that almost any real company can get itself listed on one site or another. Even on many of the leading sites, there appears to be a lot of chaff for each bit of wheat.

Once a platform decides to list a company, the latter posts information on the platform, describing the business and the investment opportunity on offer. The offer is posted for a limited amount of time, such as sixty days. Usually, the offer period can be extended, or cut short, as long as investors are given sufficient notice.

Investors, for their part, deposit funds into an account at the platform and peruse the various companies listed on the site. Unlike traditional venture capital and other vehicles only open to accredited investors, everyone is invited to participate, so long as they are within the jurisdiction.

Investors may choose to buy in to one, two, or dozens of the companies they see there, and they can invest in small increments. The minimum investment is determined by each company, and it is typically in the range of $100 to $500. In the United States as of the early 2020s, the average "check size" is roughly $1,000 per investor.

Even if they are enthusiastic and want to "bet the house," individuals face legal limits in the amount they are allowed to invest in a crowdfunding company. To protect investors from losing more than they can afford in the risky world of startup finance, the law in nearly every jurisdiction (New Zealand is the outlier) places a legal limit on the amount they may invest. In some countries, this is a

26 INVESTMENT CROWDFUNDING

flat limit, such as A$10,000 per company in Australia. In other countries, like the United States, this investor cap is based on a percentage of the individual's net worth or income.

How do investors choose among the companies seeking their money? Investment crowdfunding listings almost always include videos, testimonials, and graphics, as well as business and financial information about the company, all posted to the hosting platform. The listings commonly include a "Q&A" function, where potential investors can ask questions and receive answers directly from the company. These online bulletin boards are lively, and often include sophisticated questions about valuations, business plans, and other key issues.

In most jurisdictions, including the United States, the company must also provide certain mandatory disclosures on an official government form and file it with the SEC or equivalent securities regulator. Two countries—which I will call the "liberal" jurisdictions in Chapter Six—do not require companies to provide any specific information, or submit a specific form. Rather, in New Zealand and the United Kingdom, it is up to each company, with guidance from the platform, to decide what information to disclose and in what format.

Investment crowdfunding follows the "all-or-nothing" model. This means that a company must announce at the outset a target funding amount and a deadline for meeting it. If the crowd of investors does not pledge enough to reach the target before the listing expires, the deal is off and everybody gets their money back. If the target is met (or exceeded) in time, the transaction is completed. The investors receive whatever security they purchased, and the company receives the money raised, minus the fees paid to the platform (which are substantial).

After that, the platform recedes into the background, and the company and its new investors go forth together. In some jurisdictions, however, crowdfunding companies are legally obliged to provide their investors with an annual report every year going forward.

* * *

In this chapter, we introduced and defined investment crowdfunding—but we have yet to examine the reason why we have it in the first place. Thus, in the next chapter, we will turn our attention to the policy goals behind investment crowdfunding.

Chapter Two
Purpose

What is the point of investment crowdfunding? The goal is to promote startup companies and the economic growth they generate in an inclusive way that is open to all.

More precisely, investment crowdfunding has three essential purposes: First, to provide a simple and inexpensive method for startup companies and other small businesses to raise business capital from the public. Second, to create an inclusive market where all entrepreneurs—regardless of location, gender, race, or anything else—have an equal opportunity to access investors. Third, to democratize the startup capital market by inviting everyone to participate, not just the wealthy and connected.

At times, these goals may be in tension, and we may not be able to achieve them all simultaneously. For example, a totally inclusive system (the second goal) would ensure that platforms list any and every company that wants to participate. But platforms need to curate and select the companies they list in order to establish a reputation as a reliable market for investors. This gatekeeping function—a major subject of Chapter Four—enhances efficiency (the first goal), but is exclusive by its nature.

Before getting to these complexities, however, this chapter will lay out the three primary purposes of investment crowdfunding.

A. A NEW SOURCE FOR STARTUP CAPITAL

Entrepreneurship is vital to innovation, economic growth, and employment in a contemporary economy. Startup companies in their first year have been responsible for all net job creation in the United States since at least the 1970s, having added an average of three million jobs per year over many decades.[1] Startup companies are similarly important for innovation and general economic growth. Although many of them crash and burn, those that survive often become the companies whose products or services improve our quality of life and where people want to work.

---

[1] TIM KANE, EWING MARION KAUFFMAN FOUND., THE IMPORTANCE OF STARTUPS IN JOB CREATION AND JOB DESTRUCTION 2 (2010) (analyzing a data set from the federal government).

Investment Crowdfunding. Andrew A. Schwartz, Oxford University Press. © Andrew A. Schwartz 2023.
DOI: 10.1093/oso/9780197688526.003.0003

28 PURPOSE

Amazon is one famous example. This company, founded in a garage in 1994, created a convenient online shopping platform where people can buy almost everything they need. Over time, its services have become a significant part of our society, with a majority of American households subscribing to its free-shipping service known as Amazon Prime. Amazon currently employs 1.3 million people and is one of only a handful of companies in the world valued at more than $1 trillion.

Other examples of recent startups with outsized impact include Facebook, which created a new channel for interpersonal communication and is used regularly by roughly half the global population; Netflix, which fundamentally altered both the movie and television industry; and Uber, which revolutionized the taxi business around the world. Of course, these companies are exceptional, but they illustrate the awesome power of entrepreneurship.

Apart from high-growth startup companies, there is another type of entrepreneurship that is also valuable and important—namely, small businesses. Any individual small business, by definition, will never reach the scale and scope of a startup like Amazon or Netflix, but their collective impact is huge.

There are tens of millions of small businesses in the United States, accounting for roughly half of both employment and economic activity. The multitude of independent small businesses offers a tapestry of different products and services, leading to a rich set of choices for consumers and business partners. Local restaurants, boxing gyms, and bookstores offer a unique and distinctive experience. Beyond consumer-facing outfits, many small businesses work directly with large businesses to provide the goods and services the latter need, from automobile components to legal services. Their small size allows them to try novel ideas and methods, some of which will flourish.

Startup companies and small businesses garner widespread support from all sides of the political spectrum. Presidents Barack Obama and Donald Trump may not see eye to eye on many things, but they did both agree that "entrepreneurialism is the key to our continued global leadership and the success of our people."[2] President Obama proclaimed the first "National Entrepreneurship Month" in 2011, and President Trump gladly continued the tradition.[3]

Congress, for its part, has twice officially declared that "it is the continuing policy and responsibility of the Federal Government to . . . provide an opportunity for entrepreneurship . . . and the creation and growth of small businesses."[4]

---

[2] Barack Obama, *Toward a 21st-Century Regulatory System*, WALL ST. J., Jan. 18, 2011, at A17.

[3] Proclamation No. 9816, 83 Fed. Reg. 55457 (Oct. 31, 2018) (President Trump: "During National Entrepreneurship Month, we celebrate the Americans who forge new frontiers of possibility and prosperity, and we reaffirm our commitment to creating an environment in which they can continue to drive our country's economic success.").

[4] 15 U.S.C. §§ 631a(a), 631(a).

A NEW SOURCE FOR STARTUP CAPITAL   29

And this has not been empty rhetoric: a portion of all federal contract dollars are legally required to go to small businesses, and the federal Small Business Administration has for decades guaranteed loans for small businesses and provided free counseling and training to entrepreneurs. More recently, a new Office of the Advocate for Small Business Capital Formation was established in 2019 within the SEC to advance the interests of small businesses and their investors. State and local governments likewise expend resources attracting entrepreneurs and small businesses to their communities.

To summarize: entrepreneurship is firmly in the public interest, and startup companies are actively encouraged as a matter of public policy.

Unfortunately, however, startup companies and small businesses commonly have great difficulty obtaining the financing they need. This is not because they are unworthy—it is because they are so risky. Some startup companies will find great success, but the vast majority will not, with 90 percent failing outright and most of the remaining 10 percent achieving only modest success at small scale.

In the aggregate, many startup companies do quite well, and the tremendous success of a few startups makes up for the losses of the many, to our collective benefit. In real life, however, it is not possible to invest "in the aggregate." Every investment goes into a single startup or small business, and the odds are firmly against any specific one of them being the rare success story.

What will be the next batch of startup companies to change the world in the future? There are lots of hard working VCs, in Silicon Valley and elsewhere, trying to figure out that question right now. But future tastes and preferences are impossible to predict, and financial success is subject to chance and severe randomness. Who knew that the Pet Rock—or Harry Potter, or trucker hats—would be "the next big thing"? Nobody.

If you can avoid the hindsight bias, it's unlikely you would have invested in a company that sells photos that disappear in ten seconds (Snapchat), or that lets anybody send text messages to the whole world (Twitter), or that makes it easy to rent your couch to strangers (Airbnb). The chances of success would have seemed so remote—and yet!

The point is that there may well be wonderful entrepreneurs and startup companies whose potential is not apparent to VCs, banks, or maybe even their own family. If they can get off the ground, they can make it big, develop great products and services, hire lots of employees, and make the world a better place. By providing a venue where entrepreneurs can put their ideas out to the broad public, investment crowdfunding increases the chances that the next great startup company will get funded, rather than fizzle out for lack of funding. Furthermore, since we have no idea which companies will be the world-changers we seek, the more opportunities we take, the better our chances of finding one.

30   PURPOSE

Vitally, because investment crowdfunding companies are, by my definition, limited to raising only a certain amount of money (currently $5 million per year in the United States), the failure of any one cannot have a significant social impact. This reduces the potential harm that can be caused by "herding," where people pile into an asset (meme stocks, bitcoin, houses) just because others are doing so. Although the investors in the many losers may be worse off (though the law protects them from grievous harm—see Chapter Five), the social benefits from the couple of huge successes outweigh the costs of the many failures. This is just a restatement of the principle that entrepreneurship is socially useful.

Hence the first purpose of investment crowdfunding is to create a new avenue for entrepreneurs to raise a modest amount of capital for startup companies and small businesses. Recognizing the importance of startup companies, as well as the difficulty entrepreneurs face in raising capital, and aware of the success of reward crowdfunding, the United States (soon followed by countries around the world) enacted new legislation that adapted the concept to serve as a new method for raising business capital.

Investment crowdfunding can be used by entrepreneurs with little capital of their own and who lack wealthy friends or family members. They can use the power of the internet to solicit capital from people across the country whom they have never met, but who might be interested in supporting their idea. Rather than applying to a single bank, which may be reticent to offer a loan to a budding startup company, investment crowdfunding gives entrepreneurs the chance to pitch their idea to millions of people simultaneously. Instead of trying to land a large investment from angel investors or VCs, who may not be interested because of the location or type of business, entrepreneurs can call upon a large crowd of dispersed investors to each put in just a small amount of money.

A crowdfunding investor in a microbrewery, for instance, is likely to select her company's beer at a shop or bar and to extol its virtues to her friends and family. She loves the product, believes in the company, and has a financial stake in its success. Similarly, crowdfunding investors in a software or tech company can serve as beta testers, meaning that they try out new products and features before they are rolled out to the public. The beta testers help the company identify bugs and resolve problems and thereby improve the product, which benefits the company and its investors. In this way, a crowdfunded company can sign up 500 or 1,000 investors as free brand ambassadors, which could never happen if it were funded by VCs or angels. This is particularly valuable for consumer companies, which form a significant part of the crowdfunding market.

Finally, investment crowdfunding is not purely about financial success. The history of reward and donation crowdfunding shows that people are willing to contribute money to a project or cause that they believe in and want to support, even in the absence of any financial return. This tradition carries through to investment crowdfunding where many participants seek both to support a project or cause and, at the same time, to obtain a financial return. The upshot is that investment crowdfunding is particularly well suited to companies that seek to achieve nonpecuniary goals as well as an economic return, known broadly as "social enterprises."

Organic farms and solar panel producers, for instance, are likely to find a receptive audience among crowdfunding investors. Such businesses may not be highly profitable but can nonetheless attract investors who want to support the cause of organic farming or solar power. The potential for an economic return is only part of the story; the investors may be satisfied if the company simply gets off the ground and remains in business. Similarly, investors may be keen to support artistic endeavors, female founders, or local favorites, not strictly for their economic potential but for aesthetic, ethical, political, or personal reasons.

In short, the first objective of investment crowdfunding is to promote startup companies and small businesses by creating a new and simple way to solicit financial capital from the public. Like an IPO, investment crowdfunding allows a company to tap the public market for capital. Unlike a full IPO, however, with all its regulations and duty to register, investment crowdfunding is legally exempt from complying with all those rules. This allows startups and small businesses to sell stock, bonds, or other investments to the public in a simple, low-cost manner without having to comply with the heavy legal, regulatory, and practical costs of issuing registered securities.

1. Empirical Report

So, what has happened in the real world? Has investment crowdfunding succeeded in creating a new source of startup capital for aspiring entrepreneurs? The answer is a qualified yes. As of the early 2020s, thousands of American companies raise hundreds of millions of dollars each year through investment crowdfunding. This is a lot of money, although still quite small compared to the amounts invested by VC or angel investors.

The market is expanding quickly, however, and experience in other countries shows that investment crowdfunding might soon approach the volumes invested by traditional angel investors. The United Kingdom, in particular, has the most well-established system for investment crowdfunding in the world. British platforms opened up as early as 2010, giving them a five-year head start on the United States—and in that country, investment crowdfunding overtook angel investing as a source of entrepreneurial finance in the year 2020.[5]

---

[5] British Business Bank, Small Business Finance Markets 2020/21, at 92–93 (2021).

32 PURPOSE

Table 2.1 Investment Crowdfunding in the United States (2016–2021)[a]

Year	No. of Offerings	% Successful	No. of Investors	Avg. Amt. Invested	Total Amt. Raised	Avg. Amt. Raised	Raises over $1 Million
2016	188	49%	20,291	$1,378	$27,958,329	$170,420	6
2017	514	62%	70,431	$1,071	$75,439,310	$149,513	18
2018	756	59%	104,479	$862	$90,020,501	$155,411	17
2019	713	63%	198,263	$733	$145,403,265	$257,344	57
2020	1,156	69%	350,775	$895	$314,013,035	$292,541	106
2021	1,488	72%	529,906	$835	$442,600,595	$397,473	113

[a] The statistics in this table come from CROWDFUND CAPITAL ADVISORS, 2021 ANNUAL REPORT: TIME TO CELEBRATE SUCCESS 47, 54, 57, 62–63, 92 (2022).

Looking at the entire (short) history of investment crowdfunding in the United States, from 2016 through 2021, there was a total of over $1 billion raised by more than 4,000 companies, located in every state from coast to coast. Over 300 of these companies raised at least $1 million. Finally, more than 1.3 million people invested in these crowdfunded companies, on one of the sixty-plus active platforms licensed by the SEC. The average amount each person invests in any given company is about $1,000.[6]

Table 2.1 shows key indicators of the American market since it went live in 2016.

The trend seems clear. Activity, participation, and transaction volumes are rising fast, albeit from a modest base. The American investment crowdfunding market is quite small, at least at present, but it is growing quickly: the number of offerings, the number of investors, and the total amount raised has increased by an order of magnitude in just five years.

The year 2021 marked an inflection point, as several legal changes came into effect that year. The SEC made several key liberalizing (deregulatory) changes to Regulation Crowdfunding in late 2020: it raised the issuer limit to $5 million from $1 million, excused accredited investors from the investor cap, and authorized the use of a special purpose vehicle (SPV). (An SPV is a legal entity that has only one, special purpose, namely, to act as a single shareholder on the company's formal list of shareholders; the investors own an interest in the SPV, rather than directly in the company, thereby simplifying corporate governance matters like shareholder votes.)

[6] CROWDFUND CAPITAL ADVISORS, 2021 ANNUAL REPORT: TIME TO CELEBRATE (2022).

When those reforms went into effect in early 2021, the market leaped in response: that single year saw nearly 1,500 crowdfunding offerings, raising a cumulative total of roughly $440 million, representing a 40 percent growth rate from the prior year. This growth rate may not be sustainable, however, since the reforms of early 2021 were a one-time event. But even if the market grows at a more modest rate in the 2020s, it has already become a material part of the entrepreneurial landscape in the United States. One measure of the increased relevance of investment crowdfunding is that is has begun to attract an ecosystem of consulting firms and other sorts of hangers-on (such as professors who write books on the subject).

A variety of different types of companies pursue investment crowdfunding, although they can be split largely into two halves. About half the companies are in the embryonic stage, having just recently been founded and without any assets, revenue, or employees (apart from the founders). The other half of the companies are actually in operation, hold some assets, generate some revenue, and employ more than just a couple of people. They may not be "mature," but let's call them that anyway.

Over the brief history of investment crowdfunding, the mix has shifted from the embryonic stage to mature companies. Even still, as of the early 2020s, the split remains roughly fifty-fifty, and the average age of a crowdfunding company is just about three years old.

How have these investments performed? We do not really know, as there have been very few "exits" or "liquidity events" by crowdfunded companies, and even fewer whose details have been publicly disclosed. Anecdotally, numerous American companies have progressed from crowdfunding to collectively raise billions in additional "follow-on" investments from VCs.[7] Other crowdfunded companies have merged or been acquired by larger players.[8]

Consider, for example, renewable energy company Heliogen, which raised over $1 million in 2017 through investment crowdfunding platform SeedInvest. In 2021, Heliogen was listed on the New York Stock Exchange by merging with a special purpose acquisition company (SPAC), providing crowdfunding investors with an exit and a ten-times return after four years.

For another example, Meow Wolf, an immersive art company founded in New Mexico, raised over $1 million via investment crowdfunding in 2017, selling shares to more than 600 people at a price of $25 (for the early birds) or $50 (for the rest). The shares included a "redemption" provision that allowed the company to redeem the shares at any time for their fair market value, as determined

---

[7] Wefunder, for instance, reports that companies that initially raised money on its site went on to raise an additional $5 billion from VCs. *Our Public Benefit Impact Report*, WEFUNDER, https://wefun der.com/pbc (last visited Oct. 28, 2022).

[8] CROWDFUND CAPITAL ADVISORS, 2021 ANNUAL REPORT: TIME TO CELEBRATE 73 (2022).

34   PURPOSE

by the board of directors. In 2019, as the company's shows were gaining in popularity, the shares were redeemed for about $84 per share.[9] Some investors were disappointed, largely because they wanted to remain involved. From a financial perspective, doubling or tripling your money after two years represents a successful exit.

Anecdotes aside, a fair number of crowdfunded companies have surely gone out of business, officially or otherwise. But these represent only a small fraction of the thousands of companies that have raised money from the crowd. For the large majority of crowdfunded companies, they are operating, but their fortunes are unknown.

Shares in small, private companies, such as the ones that have participated in investment crowdfunding, are not liquid securities like those listed on the New York Stock Exchange, and which can be sold at the push of a button on E-Trade or Robinhood. As angel investors well know, you commonly have to wait as long as five years to realize any return on these sorts of investments. So we just have to wait a few more years to see how these investments performed.

Even then, it will be hard to say, both for a lack of data and because the types of companies participating is changing over time, from lower quality to higher quality, as investment crowdfunding has gained credibility and prestige.

At least that is the story in the United States. But investment crowdfunding is a global phenomenon. So what has the experience been in other countries? I will say much more about this question in Chapter Six. For now, consider two further tables. Table 2.2 shows the annual amount raised via investment crowdfunding in four comparable countries, the United States, Australia, New Zealand, and the United Kingdom. I exclude Canada and the European Union from this report because they have only just implemented their legal regimes. The data begins in 2016, the year that Regulation Crowdfunding went live in the United States.

Table 2.3 provides this same information but is scaled to the population of each country. New Zealand has five million people; the United States has 300 million. By scaling by the size of their populations, we can clarify the comparison. All figures are rough approximations, as the point is not to report on precise dollar values but to give a sense of the progress over the years and to compare across jurisdictions.

The story from the United States has been largely replicated in another country that follows the standard model, namely, Australia: small market, slow start, but showing recent acceleration. However, in the two jurisdictions, the United Kingdom and New Zealand, the numbers are much larger, and investment

---

[9] Judith Kohler, *Meow Wolf Putting the Bite on Investors Who Anted Up When It Needed Help, Critics Say*, DENVER POST, Aug. 7, 2019.

Table 2.2 Total Amount Raised by Country in Millions of Local Currency (and Millions of US Dollars) (2016–2021)[a]

	United States[b]	Australia[c]	New Zealand[d]	United Kingdom[e]
2016	$28	n/a	NZ$11 ($7)	£401 ($501)
2017	$75	n/a	NZ$12 ($8)	£255 ($319)
2018	$90	A$14 ($11)	NZ$17 ($11)	£342 ($428)
2019	$145	A$31 ($23)	NZ$14 ($9)	£405 ($506)
2020	$314	A$29 ($22)	NZ$16 ($10)	£498 ($623)
2021	$443	A$71 ($53)	NZ$16 ($10)	£991 ($1,239)

[a] I use the following exchange rates for all years: A$1 = $0.75; NZ$1 = $0.65; £1 = $1.25. These are not perfectly accurate, since the rates change from year to year, but they are sufficient for present purposes. Figures are rounded to the nearest million.

[b] CROWDFUND CAPITAL ADVISORS, 2021 ANNUAL REPORT: TIME TO CELEBRATE SUCCESS 47 (2022).

[c] BIRCHAL, CSF YEARBOOK 2021, at 13.

[d] Data for 2017–2021 comes from the annual PEER TO PEER AND CROWDFUNDING SECTOR SNAPSHOT published by the New Zealand Financial Markets Authority, *available at* https://www.fma.govt.nz/library/reports-and-papers/peer-to-peer-and-crowdfunding-sector-snapshot (last visited Oct. 28, 2022). Data for 2016 comes from Calida Smylie, *Equity Crowdfunding Numbers Slump After First Year*, NAT'L BUS. REV., Nov. 7, 2016.

[e] Data comes from combining the amounts reported annually in the annual YEAR END REVIEW published by Seedrs, *available at* https://www.seedrs.com (last visited Oct. 28, 2022), and the annual Q4 UPDATE published by Crowdcube, *available at* https://www.crowdcube.com (last visited Oct. 28, 2022), as these two platforms controlled nearly the entire UK market during these years.

crowdfunding has begun to rival angel investing and VC funding as the key sources of entrepreneurial finance.

New Zealand jumped out to an early start, opening its market in 2014, two years ahead of the United States. Within a couple of years, investment crowdfunding volumes quickly grew to be in the same ballpark as domestic angel and VC funding (which were notoriously anemic). The annual crowdfunding volume has stayed fairly steady since then—although these formal statistics are somewhat understated due to one specific legal restriction in the Kiwi regime.

New Zealand has a very low issuer limit of NZ$2 million (approximately $1.4 million), but if a company wants to raise more than that, the platform can easily shift accredited ("wholesale") investors into a different legal "bucket," leaving room for nonaccredited investors to "fill up" the crowdfunding offer. For instance, imagine a company wants to, and believes it can, crowdfund NZ$5 million. Working with the platform, the company simply runs two simultaneous

36 PURPOSE

Table 2.3 Total Amount Raised by Country per Capita in US Dollars (2016–2021)[a]

	United States	Australia	New Zealand	United Kingdom
2016	$0.09	n/a	$1.40	$7.16
2017	$0.23	n/a	$1.60	$4.56
2018	$0.28	$0.44	$2.20	$6.11
2019	$0.45	$0.92	$1.80	$7.23
2020	$0.97	$0.88	$2.00	$8.90
2021	$1.36	$2.12	$2.00	$17.70

[a] The data for this table comes directly from Table 2.2 and, as there, I use the following exchange rates for all years: A$1 = $0.75; NZ$1 = $0.65; £1 = $1.25. I also use the following rough approximations for the population of each country during these years: United States—325 million; Australia—25 million; New Zealand—5 million; United Kingdom—70 million. None of these figures are precise, but they are sufficient for present purposes.

offers, one under the crowdfunding regulations and one for accredited investors. Some call this a "side-by-side" offer.

If an accredited investor wants to participate, the platform politely directs her to the accredited side of the offer, leaving space under the issuer limit for the nonaccredited investors. The end result is that the company can raise NZ$3 million from accredited investors (often in large chunks) and NZ$2 million from the "crowd." This is all conducted via a single platform, and everyone receives the same shares for the same price.

Had the crowdfunding issuer limit been much higher (as it is in the United States, the European Union, and the United Kingdom), the whole process could have taken place in a single offering. That would be preferable, as actually executing a side-by-side offer often entails calling dozens of investors and asking them to sign some additional paperwork—which is no fun for anybody and a waste of resources. For present purposes, though, the key point is that the low issuer cap makes New Zealand's crowdfunding numbers appear artificially low.[10]

Another confounding issue is that the United Kingdom has special tax benefits (known as EIS and SEIS) for people who invest in startup companies. This is not specific to crowdfunding, but it probably inflates their numbers when compared

---

[10] In 2021, for example, Table 2.2 shows that all New Zealand companies collectively raised a national total of NZ$16 million. But one platform in that country, Snowball Effect, reported that companies raised a total of nearly NZ$40 million that year on its site alone. The bulk of the NZ$40 million presumably came from accredited ("wholesale") investors, and thus was not formally reported to the Financial Markets Authority as investment crowdfunding.

to the United States and other jurisdictions without similar tax rules. It also bears noting that other countries have begun to adopt special tax incentives that are specific to investment crowdfunding. Malaysia, for instance, enacted a limited income tax deduction for money invested in crowdfunding companies.

Despite these caveats, the United Kingdom has clearly outpaced the rest of the world in the field of investment crowdfunding. The amounts raised there are significant by any measure, and the industry has become an important part of the financial marketplace in the United Kingdom. Notably, however, the United States and Australia, both of which are much younger than the United Kingdom, may be on similar growth paths, just a few years behind.

All in all, investment crowdfunding has succeeded in creating a viable new source of startup capital in every country addressed. In the United States, things started slowly, but the market has begun to grow at a rapid clip in recent years.

B. INCLUSIVE ENTREPRENEURSHIP

Beyond advancing startup companies and small businesses generally, investment crowdfunding was specifically conceived as a way to encourage an especially inclusive form of entrepreneurial finance. As discussed previously, many of the most important routes to raising business capital rely on location, wealth, and connections. Financing from personal savings, friends and family, and local angels and VCs may be realistic options for those who have significant wealth themselves or connections to those who do. But what about entrepreneurs of modest means who live far from Silicon Valley and don't know any angel investors? Entrepreneurs who are "out-of-the-loop" for one reason or another have long had exceptional difficulty in attracting investment for their ventures, and investment crowdfunding is especially useful for them.

Entrepreneurial financing has traditionally depended on geography. Local banks are the source for business loans; local angels and VCs tend to focus on startups in their area; and investors are often courted over coffee or a beer at a favorite local place. Initial investments commonly come from friends and neighbors who know the entrepreneur personally, perhaps from PTA meetings or the local Rotary Club. All this is well and good, but it has the effect of putting out-of-town entrepreneurs at a severe disadvantage.

A startup based in San Francisco has a better chance of being funded than one based in Toledo, Ohio, simply because there is a much larger community of potential funders in the former. More generally, entrepreneurs in rural areas are at a distinct disadvantage compared with their urban counterparts. An entrepreneur with big dreams is still given the same advice today that Horace Greely is said to have offered in the late 1800s: "Go West!" Many ambitious entrepreneurs

38   PURPOSE

have physically relocated from one part of the country to another in order to find investors for their fledgling business. Even for rural entrepreneurs who would prefer to remain in, say, Iowa, rather than move to California, the siren song of wealthy and experienced angel investors is nearly impossible to resist.

Investment crowdfunding—being entirely online—changes this calculus entirely. By allowing entrepreneurs to connect with and obtain financing from investors via the internet, investment crowdfunding frees them from geographic constraints. Far-flung entrepreneurs can use investment crowdfunding to find investors without having to physically pick up and move.

Other aspects of our contemporary telecommunications and transportation systems allow entrepreneurs to conduct business in real time with partners and customers around the world. For instance, a company with a single office in South Dakota could connect with employees and contractors across the country using Zoom, have its product fabricated in China, and sell it globally via Amazon. Investment crowdfunding adds the ability to fundraise from afar, thereby encouraging entrepreneurship in every city, town, and county, rather than just the usual hotspots like Silicon Valley.

Beyond geographic inclusivity, investment crowdfunding also seeks to give any and every type of person—regardless of race or gender—the opportunity to raise capital for their entrepreneurial ventures. The challenge of landing business capital via traditional forms of fundraising, such as VC or angel investment, has often been even more pronounced for women and many racial minorities. According to recent reports, only about 9 percent of VC-backed startups had a woman founder, and the figure is only 1 percent for Black founders and 2 percent for Latino founders.[11]

The online nature of investment crowdfunding, however, gives women and minority entrepreneurs the opportunity to present their business idea in a color-blind fashion. Alternatively, such entrepreneurs can emphasize their race or gender as a signal to investors who are specifically seeking to invest in, say, female or Black entrepreneurs—and this is large pool.

In sum, investment crowdfunding offers an inclusive way to bring needed financing to startups all across America, in areas both rural and urban. Further, it

---

[11] RATEMYINVESTOR, DIVERSITYVC REPORT 7–8 (2019), https://ratemyinvestor.com/diversity_report (last visited Sept. 24, 2022) (77% White, 18% Asian, 2% Middle Eastern, 2% Latino, 1% Black); Jennifer S. Fan, *The Landscape of Startup Corporate Governance in the Founder-Friendly Era*, 18 N.Y.U. J.L. & BUS. 317, 389 n.430 (2022) (reporting that "only 11.5% of total venture capital funding went to teams with at least one female founder," and that "approximately 2.6% of total funding went to Black and Latinx founders," in 2019 and 2020, respectively); Paroma Sanyal & Catherine L. Mann, *The Financial Structure of Startup Firms: The Role of Assets, Information, and Entrepreneur Characteristics* 15 (Fed. Reserve Bank of Bos., Working Paper No. 10-17, 2010) ("Consistent with other research, [we find that] startups owned by African-American entrepreneurs have a lower probability of having any type of external finance, especially external equity, and instead finance their firms through personal resources.").

allows entrepreneurs of every race, gender, ethnicity, and religion, rich or poor, young or old the opportunity to access necessary startup capital to fund their business ventures. Because it is internet-based and so much less costly than a traditional public offering, investment crowdfunding provides an opportunity for anyone with an idea to go online and seek funding to make it a reality—not just those in Silicon Valley, not just those with wealthy friends, not just those with connections. Crowdfunding is open to anyone and is meant to encourage an inclusive business culture in every state and locality and every field of endeavor that is the subject of active entrepreneurship.

1. Empirical Report

In contrast with the traditional world of VC investing, which is dominated by men, mostly White, and centered in Silicon Valley, investment crowdfunding is designed to be a system that is more inclusive to women and minorities, and regardless of location. Has this actually occurred? The data suggests so.

Let us start with geography. Because investment crowdfunding is conducted entirely over the internet, entrepreneurs in Arkansas or Iowa are in as good a position as those in California or New York to raise capital using this method. This theoretical idea does seem to have translated into the real world. By 2020, the United States had seen investment crowdfunding offerings from companies based in every single state, and in more than 1,300 different cities. In 2021 alone, there were nearly 700 unique cities represented.[12]

No surprise, companies based in California still dominate investment crowdfunding, followed by New York, then Texas and Florida, as these are the states with the largest populations and economies. As time has gone by, though, the proportion of offerings in these states has fallen, meaning that the offerings are being more evenly distributed across the country. In 2017, for instance, these four states accounted for about 60 percent of all offerings, whereas by 2020, this proportion had dropped below 50 percent and has continued to fall. According to one leading American platform, only 13 percent of the entrepreneurs on its site are based in Silicon Valley.[13]

Similarly, female entrepreneurs seem to have found investment crowdfunding to be a more fertile source of funding than VC and angel investing. Different sources have different numbers, but it appears that a much higher percentage of crowdfunding companies are led by a female entrepreneur, compared with those

---

[12] Crowdfund Capital Advisors, Investment Crowdfunding 2021 Annual Report: Time to Celebrate (2022).

[13] *Our Public Benefit Impact Report*, Wefunder, https://wefunder.com/pbc (last visited Oct. 28, 2022).

40 PURPOSE

traditional sources. In the United States, the leading investment crowdfunding platforms report that about one-quarter of the companies on their sites have a female founder.[14] This is double or triple the rate of VC investment described earlier in this chapter.

Take Caribu, for example, an interactive video-calling company founded in 2015 by Maxeme Tuchman, a young Latina in Miami.[15] When Caribu sought early-stage funding, Tuchman initially met with angel investors and VCs in Silicon Valley and elsewhere. She was unable, however, to land the money she needed—at least not on terms she found acceptable. One reason for her difficulty, she thought, was that she was a woman of color, and not "a white dude with a hoodie."[16]

After several years of frustration, Tuchman launched an investment crowdfunding campaign in 2019—on her own terms—and found a highly receptive audience. Caribu ultimately raised over $1 million, which she says was the first time a Latino-led company hit that mark via investment crowdfunding—and she did it, she tells me, "without being sexually harassed." Caribu's small army of enthusiastic users immediately jumped into the offering, and its popularity attracted other investors, who had never used the product before. Ultimately, more than 1,500 people participated in the offering, which maxed out at the legal limit (which was then roughly $1 million).

Women entrepreneurs are using investment crowdfunding to good effect in other jurisdictions too. A recent UK report comparing VC, angel, and other sources of startup capital in the United Kingdom concluded that investment crowdfunding "incontestably comes out on top as the most gender equitable investor type, with 24% of deals going to companies with a female founder."[17]

---

[14] Anne Burke, *Leveling the Playing Field: Startup Funding Without the Golden Handcuffs*, STARTENGINE (July 2, 2021), https://www.startengine.com/blog/venture-capital-vs-equity-crowd funding (27% of companies have a female founder or co-founder); *Our Public Benefit Impact Report*, WEFUNDER, https://wefunder.com/pbc (last visited Oct. 28, 2022) (22% of founders are female).

[15] Barry Samaha, *How Women of Color Are Using Equity Crowdfunding to Achieve Success in the Tech World*, HARPER'S BAZAAR, July 28, 2021; Maxeme Tuchman, *Maxeme Tuchman '00, Award-Winning Entrepreneur and New College of Florida Alumna, Shares her "10 Pieces of Advice" with Graduates at Commencement 2022*, NEW COLLEGE OF FLORIDA (May 21, 2022), https://www.ncf. edu/news/maxeme-tuchman-00-award-winning-entrepreneur-and-new-college-of-florida-alu mna-shares-her-10-pieces-of-advice-with-graduates-at-commencement-2022. I also spoke personally with Tuchman.

[16] Barry Samaha, *How Women of Color Are Using Equity Crowdfunding to Achieve Success in the Tech World*, HARPER'S BAZAAR, July 28, 2021 ("'I realized there was a false assumption placed on me that didn't expect me to know how to run a business,' she says. 'People were looking at me and thinking, '[S]he's a woman. She probably doesn't understand how the numbers work.' I was more than prepared, and still VC investors were telling me that they need to see more numbers. Then I started wondering, "Is it me? Is it my background? Is it the assumptions that they're making? Or is it the business?" You just never know.'") (quoting Maxeme Tuchman).

[17] NEWABLE BEAUHURST, FEMALE ENTREPRENEURS 38 (2019).

In New Zealand, one of the two leading crowdfunding platforms in the country (PledgeMe) was itself founded by a woman and takes pride in the fact that a majority of its offerings have been female-led. On the other top Kiwi platform (Snowball Effect), one of its most successful offerings of all time was for The Hello Cup, a female-led company that sells reusable menstrual cups that serve as a replacement for tampons.

Investment crowdfunding likewise has created a more inclusive playing field for minority entrepreneurs, with one leading platform reporting that more than 30 percent of crowdfunding companies have a minority founder or co-founder.[18] With respect to Black entrepreneurs, specifically, another leading platform has said that roughly 4 percent of its companies have Black founders, compared to about 1 percent in the VC world.[19]

Crowdfunding companies commonly describe themselves as "minority founder," "female-led," and other such adjectives. This appears to have an effect on the investors, especially since many of them actively seek to spread startup capital to the traditionally underfunded. As a convenience to these investors, crowdfunding platforms often have functions that allow them to easily search and sort offerings using keywords like "Black Founders," "Women Founders," "LGBTQIA+ Founders," and the like. The investors, for their part, sometimes post messages on the platform indicating their support for Black and other minority entrepreneurs. A couple of real-life quotes: "It was important for me to invest in another Black woman owned business." "I invested because I believe in young black female entrepreneurship."

In sum, it does appear that investment crowdfunding is actually achieving this second goal of creating an inclusive market where entrepreneurs of all types, and from all over, have an opportunity to get funded.

C. INCLUSIVE INVESTING

The final objective of investment crowdfunding is to democratize the market for investing in startup and small businesses. For decades, the chance to invest in private companies was legally available only to wealthy investors and those who knew the founders personally. Investors without wealth or connections have been legally limited to investing in "public" companies, meaning those

---

[18] Anne Burke, *Leveling the Playing Field: Startup Funding Without the Golden Handcuffs*, STARTENGINE (July 2, 2021), https://www.startengine.com/blog/venture-capital-vs-equity-crowd funding (reporting that, "[t]hrough the first five months of 2021, 33.3% of campaigns had a minority founder or cofounder").

[19] *Our Public Benefit Impact Report*, WEFUNDER, https://wefunder.com/pbc (last visited Oct. 28, 2022).

42 PURPOSE

who registered their securities and are listed on a major stock exchange like the New York Stock Exchange or NASDAQ.

This differential treatment for the wealthy and well connected is an artifact of two exemptions—meaning exceptions to the registration requirement—embedded in federal securities law. First, the law has always exempted private offerings from the registration requirement—that is, offerings made available to an exclusive group of known people and not the general public. If your brother-in-law buys half the shares in your small business, you do not need to register those securities. The securities laws are designed to deal with offerings of securities made to the public, such as those in an advertisement or on a commercial, rather than an intimate, private deal between a small number of people who know each other well.

Second, there is also a longstanding registration exemption for offerings made only to investors that are "accredited" by the SEC to make such investments. This latter exemption has been used regularly since the SEC adopted a regulation in 1982 that clarified that all wealthy people—those with a net worth of more than $1 million or an income north of $200,000—were deemed to be accredited. The theory is that wealthy people have the capacity to absorb the loss if their investment in unregistered securities goes down the drain, whereas people of modest means lack that cushion. Beyond wealthy individuals, banks, VC funds, pensions, and endowments are also considered "accredited" investors, and many other countries have similar rules. (In a recent move, the SEC has expanded the definition of "accredited investor" to include people who hold certain stock-broker certifications—for example, Series 7—regardless of wealth or income.)

Because registration is expensive and burdensome, prior to investment crowd-funding, entrepreneurs generally tried to sell securities using either or both of the private-offering and accredited-investor exemptions. That is, the only people invited to invest in private startups or small businesses were those who came within the private-offering exemption (family and friends) or the accredited-investor exemption (the wealthy). In effect, nonmillionaires were left out, effectively barred from investing in strangers' startups and small businesses, thanks to this well-intentioned regulatory apparatus.

Investment crowdfunding is designed to break down this barrier by empowering ordinary nonaccredited investors to take a chance and invest in private companies' unregistered securities. This is an inclusive vision of investing that welcomes all people, regardless of wealth, certifications, connections, or anything else. Anyone with an internet connection is invited.

While it is true that many crowdfunded companies will surely fail (a subject explored in the next chapter), it seems only fair to give everyone—not just the wealthy and connected—the freedom to take their chances and invest a small amount in what they hope will be the next Facebook. Furthermore, ordinary people are permitted to spend their money in other ways that may seem foolish, such as buying a lottery ticket or an expensive SUV. Why shouldn't they be allowed to buy into a fledgling private business too?

In conclusion, investment crowdfunding seeks to democratize the market for financing speculative companies by inviting ordinary people to make investments that have long been offered to connected and accredited investors. Previously, as President Obama said when he signed the federal investment-crowdfunding bill into law, entrepreneurs could "only turn to a limited group of investors—including banks and wealthy individuals—to get funding." However, thanks to the new law, "start-ups and small business will now have access to a big, new pool of potential investors—namely, the American people. For the first time, ordinary Americans will be able to go online and invest in entrepreneurs that they believe in."[20]

1. Empirical Report

The third goal of investment crowdfunding is to democratize the investor pool for startup capital by inviting everyone to participate, not just the wealthy and connected. This has happened, as the market is indeed open to all, and while the number of investors started out rather small, it is growing quickly, as shown previously in Table 2.1. The story is similar in the other countries we will review in Chapter Six.

There were fewer than 100,000 investments per year for the first several years of investment crowdfunding in the United States. In 2019, however, that number doubled to roughly 200,000, and then nearly doubled again twice more. The year 2020 saw approximately 350,000 individual investments, and that grew to 530,000 in 2021. All told, more than one million people have participated in investment crowdfunding, hailing from every state in the country.

The average amount each individual invests in any given company is roughly $1,000. Anecdotally, it seems that this average hides a large standard deviation; in other words, the $1,000 average comes from many people investing a couple of hundred dollars, and a few putting in several thousand or more. Furthermore, that number has drifted down over the years, which seems to be a result of more people participating and each of them putting in a smaller amount.

* * *

[20] Barack Obama, Remarks by the President at JOBS Act Bill Signing (Apr. 5, 2012), https://obamawhitehouse.archives.gov/the-press-office/2012/04/05/remarks-president-jobs-act-bill-signing.

44 PURPOSE

Investment crowdfunding thus presents a compelling vision of inclusive and expanded entrepreneurship. Like any form of financial contracting, however, it must overcome three fundamental challenges if it is to function effectively. Those three challenges are the subject of the next chapter.

Chapter Three
Challenges

Investment crowdfunding, like many new technologies, is both useful and dangerous: early-stage ventures commonly fail, for one reason or another, leaving the investor with a large or even total loss. The entrepreneur may be tempted to spend the investors' money on a high salary and a lavish office for himself. He may even be a con artist who swipes the money and runs off. Even a good business can be a bad investment if you overpay for it. Maybe only low-quality businesses will even participate in crowdfunding, as the best ones will get VC funding.

These and other concerns may lead one to wonder if investment crowdfunding can actually succeed. Or, is it just a way to give "middle class families the same opportunities that millionaires have always had to lose their money"?[1]

Stepping back, the question is broader than crowdfunding and really goes to the fundamental principles of entrepreneurial finance. These risks—of business failure, fraud, and the rest—are not unique to investment crowdfunding but rather are ubiquitous features of investing in startup companies. VCs and angel investors have to deal with these same risks, as do "rich uncles" who invest in their relatives' companies.

In fact, one might wonder how anybody ever gets up the courage to invest in a startup company in the face of all these challenges and risks—but we know they do, especially in places like Silicon Valley. Why? How?

These are important questions, and they have been carefully analyzed by scholars in law, economics, and business over the past several decades. The fruit of this work is a simple theory, crystallized by Stanford professor Ronald Gilson and widely accepted in the literature.[2]

The idea is that there are three fundamental challenges that all systems of finance must confront and overcome: (1) uncertainty: the future performance of a company is uncertain, especially for startup companies; (2) information asymmetry: entrepreneurs necessarily know much more than investors about their business; (3) agency costs: once they get the money, entrepreneurs will be

---

[1] 157 Cong. Rec. H7286 (Nov. 3, 2011) (statement by Rep. Jared Polis, who ultimately supported the bill that became the JOBS Act).

[2] Ronald J. Gilson, *Engineering a Venture Capital Market: Lessons from the American Experience*, 55 STAN. L. REV. 1067 (2003).

Investment Crowdfunding. Andrew A. Schwartz, Oxford University Press. © Andrew A. Schwartz 2023.
DOI: 10.1093/oso/9780197688526.003.0004

46 CHALLENGES

tempted to shirk and enrich themselves at the investors' expense.[3] If these three challenges are not addressed effectively, investors will pick up their ball and go home, and the whole market will collapse.

Using this theoretical perspective, we can see that the various risks and dangers listed at the outset of this chapter can each be understood as falling within one or another of the "trio of problems." Fraud, for example, is one type of information asymmetry. Similarly, the likelihood of business failure is an aspect of uncertainty. And a high salary for the entrepreneur is a species of agency costs.

This chapter will take a close look at the three fundamental challenges of startup investing and how they express themselves in the distinctive context of investment crowdfunding. This will set up the next several chapters, which will describe the private and legal responses to these three challenges.

A. UNCERTAINTY

If future financial performance were perfectly predictable, investing would be a cinch. But the real world is inherently unpredictable, and we are constantly surprised by what happens next. The global financial crisis, the COVID-19 pandemic, streaming video, cochlear implants—who knows what will happen next? This makes investing challenging and risky, not simple and safe, like keeping your money in government bonds. This inherent uncertainty makes rational people reticent to invest at all—and especially fearful of startup companies.

First consider the (imaginary) world of perfect certainty. Imagine that Company X, with one million shares outstanding, is certain to make a steady profit of $1 million per year, every year, forever. If Company X offers shares of stock for $200 each on an investment crowdfunding platform, should you invest? Or, in the parlance of startup finance, is $200 a fair "valuation" for Company X?

In the imaginary world of perfect certainty, this is an easy question. Since there are one million shares and $1 million of profits each year, then each share is sure to generate $1 per year for its holder. What is it worth to have a stream of $1 sent your way every year, forever? This year's $1 is worth $1, but next year's is worth less, maybe 95 cents, due to inflation and the "time-value" of money. The year after that, that future $1 is worth even less to you today, maybe 90 cents, and if we go out ten or twenty years, those future cash flows are worth effectively nothing to you right now.

---

[3] Ronald J. Gilson, *Engineering a Venture Capital Market: Lessons from the American Experience*, 55 STAN. L. REV. 1067, 1076 (2003); *see* Robert P. Bartlett III, *Venture Capital, Agency Costs, and the False Dichotomy of the Corporation*, 54 UCLA L. REV. 37, 41 n.9 (2006) (collecting sources).

UNCERTAINTY   47

If we add each of these values ($1 + $0.95 + $0.90 + . . .), they will sum up to around $12. That tells you that each share in Company X is worth roughly $12—and that the $200 share price you were offered is obviously way too high. This technique is called the "discounted cash flow" analysis because we are discounting the future cash flows to today's dollars, and it is the lodestar of corporate valuation on Wall Street and everywhere else.

The discounted cash flow calculation is highly dependent on the so-called "discount rate," and reasonable people can differ over which number to use, from as low as a few percent to as high as 20 percent. In the example of Company X, if we use a 5 percent discount rate, each share is worth $20; if we were to change to a 3 percent rate, each would be worth about $33; if we used a 10 percent rate, each share would be worth $10. With any reasonable figure, Company X would be a bad investment at $200 per share, as the real money-making power of the company is only worth one-tenth that amount.

By the same token, if Company X were offering shares at $5 per share, rather than $200, it would be a screaming bargain and you should definitely invest. You would be getting a stream of $1 annual earnings, and only pay an attractive "five times earnings" for the share, as opposed to a ridiculous "two-hundred times earnings."[4] Another way to look at it is that, at $200 per share, it will take 200 years of $1 per year just to make back your initial investment in Company X. At $5 per share, it's pure profit after five years—for the rest of the imaginary universe.

The key takeaway is that valuation is everything. Company X is a great investment at a low valuation ($5 per share), a fine investment at a reasonable valuation per share ($20, say), and a terrible one at an outrageous valuation ($200 per share). This is universal: a great company can be a poor investment, and a terrible company can be a great investment. It all depends on what you pay, that is, the valuation. In the fictional world of perfect certainty, a reasonable valuation can easily be deduced for any company, making it very easy to be a successful investor.

Now let us shift from the imaginary world of certainty into the real world of uncertainty. There is no such thing as Company X with perfectly predictable, risk-free returns that go on forever. The real world doesn't work that way. Nothing is certain, especially not financial performance, and especially *especially* the financial performance of young startup companies.

Uncertainty is not limited to startup companies, as the performance of even well-established companies is also unpredictable. Consider Blockbuster Video.

---

[4] In the real world, investors sometimes do pay two-hundred times earnings—but only for companies whose earnings are expected to grow rapidly in the coming years; our example is for a static stream of earnings.

48 CHALLENGES

As of 2005, say, Blockbuster Video was a longstanding national chain with decades of growth and profits. Even so, its future performance was uncertain—as we now know, since it ended up going out of business at the hands of internet-based streaming services like Netflix. For another example, consider the century-old company U.S. Steel; over the past few years its stock price has been as low as $5 and as high as $45—suggesting that its expected earnings power is unclear to the professionals trying to predict it.

All that said, investment uncertainty is surely greatest when dealing with startup companies. By definition, startup companies have little or no track record from which to extrapolate, so future performance is entirely speculative. Unlike my fictional Company X, startup companies often have no profits or, if they do, they are almost never a steady stream that lends itself to a simple discounted-cash-flow analysis.

Whether a startup company will succeed depends on the uncertain future. Will the company be able to produce and market its product? Will people want to buy it? Will the CEO be an effective leader and manager? We cannot know, and can only make predictions and guesses.

Startup companies are often based on developing some form of technology, like software code, or a new invention. This adds an additional layer of uncertainty, as the nature of new inventions and new technology is that their utility, value, and popularity are always and necessarily unpredictable. If Apple knew that the Newton would be a failure and the iPad a success, it would have skipped the former and gone right to the latter. But it did not, and could not, know how the future would play out.

The point is that the performance and proper valuation of startup companies is more of an art than a science, making it especially uncertain. For these reasons, crowdfunding investors are at significant risk of buying into companies that fail entirely. They are also at risk of buying into companies that do well, but at an unreasonably high valuation. In such circumstances, the investors can lose money even if the company survives.

Consider, for example, a UK company called Sugru that sells a moldable glue invented by the founder. With a useful product and a strong social media presence, Sugru conducted two highly successful crowdfunding offerings, raising £5 million in 2015 and 2017, at a valuation of £33 million. In 2018, however, the company was sold to a larger player in the adhesive industry for less than £8 million, representing a 90 percent loss for the crowdfunding investors (as well as several VC funds).[5] Valuation is key—and so easy to get wrong.

All this uncertainty makes it plain to see why startup companies have a hard time raising capital. Investors are asked to hand over their money based on their

---

[5] Ciara O'Brien, *Investors in Sugru Lose Up to 90% of Their Money*, IRISH TIMES, May 17, 2018.

best guess about how the future will play out for this company, in light of the industry, the economy, and a thousand other things. Unless the investors can get some measure of certainty, they may well be too scared to put their hard-earned money at risk, and the market will fizzle out. In other words, uncertainty, left unchecked, has the capacity to destroy the investment crowdfunding market.

As we will see in the next few chapters, investment crowdfunding has numerous structures designed to reduce the amount of uncertainty to a level that investors find acceptable. Perfect certainty is impossible, of course, but various forms of private ordering and legal rules do serve to lower uncertainty for crowdfunding investors. For one thing, crowdfunding platforms generally research and vet companies before listing them, thus presenting a curated set of offerings to investors. For another, crowdfunding companies are often required by law to provide mandatory disclosures about their business to potential investors, and even do so when not required; this likewise reduces uncertainty. For a third, investors share information with one another on crowdfunding platforms' communication channels, again reducing uncertainty.

There is one useful empirical data point suggesting that crowdfunding company valuations are, if not accurate, at least rational. In the United States, valuations for post-revenue companies (those that have customers and cash flow) are higher, on average, than the valuations for pre-revenue companies (those that have yet to sell a product or bill a customer). In 2021, for instance, post-revenue companies that raised money through investment crowdfunding were valued at $28 million, on average, while pre-revenue companies were only valued at $18 million, on average.[6]

Still, uncertainty is a significant challenge for investment crowdfunding that must be effectively cabined if the market is to function.

B. INFORMATION ASYMMETRY

"Information asymmetry" simply means that an entrepreneur soliciting investment always knows more about the company than do potential investors. Consider an investment in a small farm. The relevant information about the farm and its prospects—whether the fields have good drainage, whether the tractor is rusty, and so forth—is not known equally to both the farmer and the potential investors. Rather, the farmer knows a great deal, and the investors very little. In other words, this information is distributed asymmetrically.

---

[6] Crowdfund Capital Advisors, 2021 Annual Report: Time to Celebrate Success 67 (2022).

50   CHALLENGES

This problem of information asymmetry is inherent in all forms of investing, although sometimes the information can be made more symmetric with little effort, as in the case of the farm. The investors can physically go to the farm—maybe they live nearby, and have farming experience—and inspect the drainage, the tractor, and the like for themselves. This can resolve the problem of information asymmetry and embolden the potential investors to buy in.

The quality of most real-world investments is more difficult to judge than that, however, especially if the company's success depends on some sort of technological component, as is often the case for startup companies. Computer code, for example, is not easy to read or review; the programmer himself will surely know her code better than anyone on the outside looking in.

Left unresolved, information asymmetry can destroy a market entirely, thanks to a devilish dilemma called "adverse selection" or, more colorfully, the "lemons problem."[7] The lemons problem is this: potential investors are aware that entrepreneurs and other company insiders hold important information that they (the investors) can never truly know. This makes it difficult to distinguish between good investments and bad ones (lemons). To protect themselves, investors will only offer a low price for all investments, including the good ones; this accounts for the risk that they might pick a lemon. Any entrepreneur with a good opportunity will depart the market since he doesn't want to sell for a low price, leaving only the bad ones behind. Investors recognize all this and walk away rather than invest in a market full of lemons. The end result is that the market unravels and everybody goes home.

Information asymmetry, and the lemons problem it can cause, is of particular concern for investment crowdfunding, as it is conducted entirely online. Crowdfunding investors do not take a trip out to the company office and do not personally interview the entrepreneur behind a venture. Moreover, crowdfunding investors are regular people, not experts in the field.

Finally, the very availability of VCs and angels has led some to worry that investment crowdfunding is doomed to be a market full of lemons. The idea is that if a company were poised to be the next Facebook, it would have been funded by VCs or angels and would not have had to resort to investment crowdfunding in the first place.

Startup companies are known to welcome VC and angel investment because they invest more than just money. They provide valuable advice and introductions, as well as a sort of "seal of approval" that can itself attract employees and customers. For an entrepreneur, having an experienced VC or

---

[7] George A. Akerlof, *The Market for "Lemons": Quality Uncertainty and the Market Mechanism*, 84 Q.J. ECON. 488, 488–91 (1970).

angel in your corner financially motivated to help the company grow and succeed may be just as valuable as the capital itself.[8]

In crowdfunding, by contrast, the company gets the money but none of these value-added services. This suggests, in turn, that any rational entrepreneur with a promising venture would pursue VC or angel funding, not crowdfunding. Hence the very fact that a company is raising money via investment crowdfunding may act as a signal of poor prospects.[9]

At first blush, this seems a strong argument, but it is not ultimately as powerful as it first appears, simply because its core assumption is wrong: it is not actually true that a rational entrepreneur would always prefer VC funding over crowdfunding.

For one thing, the advice and other services provided by VCs are not always valuable in the real world. Some such investors are more meddlesome than helpful, or even compromised by a conflict of interest between the VC fund as a whole, on the one hand, and the individual company, on the other.[10] For another, investment crowdfunding offers an advantage that VC and angel investing cannot match, in that it allows a company to get a sort-of "double return" on their fundraising efforts because every dollar spent is both advertising for consumers as well as solicitation of investors. Going forward, the investors who are now customers, and the customers who are now investors, can form an army of "brand ambassadors" with a financial stake in buying the company's products and getting their friends to do the same.

Taking it all into account, we must conclude that at least some rational entrepreneurs would actually prefer crowdfunding over VC or angel investment, so the lemons problem is not fatal to the form, as feared by some commentators. As a matter of fact, it seems that the "stigma" of raising money though crowdfunding has greatly abated over the years as the market has grown and no longer seems so novel and untested. Indeed, VCs and angels have warmed to the field and now sometimes invest directly in, or in parallel with, crowdfunding offerings. This is particularly true in the more mature markets of the United Kingdom and New Zealand, but is also starting to happen in the United States and elsewhere.

Even so, information asymmetry is a real issue for investment crowdfunding, and the problem is heightened by the availability of a prestigious and private alternative, namely, VC and angel financing. If it cannot be addressed, investors will stay away and the market will fall apart.

---

[8] Ronald J. Gilson, *Engineering a Venture Capital Market: Lessons from the American Experience*, 55 Stan. L. Rev. 1067, 1072 (2003).

[9] Darian M. Ibrahim, *Equity Crowdfunding: A Market for Lemons?*, 100 Minn. L. Rev. 561, 589 (2015); Michael B. Dorff, *The Siren Call of Equity Crowdfunding*, 39 J. Corp. L. 493, 497 (2014).

[10] *In re* Trados, 73 A.3d 17, 48–50 (Del. Ch. 2013); Ronald J. Gilson, *Engineering a Venture Capital Market: Lessons from the American Experience*, 55 Stan. L. Rev. 1067, 1085 (2003).

52 CHALLENGES

Fraud is probably the worst type of information asymmetry. Fraud is where the entrepreneur lies to the investors about something important; the entrepreneur knows the truth, but the investors do not, hence the asymmetry of information. When investment crowdfunding was under development in the early 2010s, fraud seemed to be the number one concern among the commentariat.[11] Yet fraud has not developed into a major problem in the investment crowdfunding market.

In the United States, there has only been a single formal allegation of fraud on the part of crowdfunding entrepreneurs.[12] In that case, the SEC alleged that the people behind two offerings that raised nearly $2 million on an obscure investment crowdfunding platform committed fraud by hiding the fact that the real "driving force" behind the venture was an unmentioned party who had a criminal conviction on his record. The SEC also alleged that the defendants diverted investor funds for their own use.

This is the only example of fraud in the American investment crowdfunding market to date. On the one hand, it is disappointing to see these allegations. On the other hand, it is heartening that, after more than 4,000 offerings, this is the only known example of alleged fraud. Hopefully this represents the exception that proves the rule, but we will not know for sure until more time has passed. One thing we do know is that the SEC has not identified investment crowdfunding as a particular problem; of the nearly 3,000 enforcement actions it filed from 2016 to 2021, there was only one (the one just mentioned) that related to investment crowdfunding.[13] By contrast, the SEC brought more than eighty enforcement actions related to fraudulent and unregistered cryptocurrency offerings and platforms during that same time period.[14]

The low apparent level of fraud in the investment crowdfunding market makes sense, because the gravity of the consequences and the chances of detection are both relatively high, while the potential returns are rather modest. The law, in the United States and elsewhere, includes effective antifraud provisions, and it also empowers state authorities as well as jilted investors to sue issuers and other parties who engage in wrongdoing such as this. Furthermore, everyone who posts information will be logged in, making it easy to track down exactly who said what and when. Given all this, it seems that issuers with fraudulent intentions would have better luck elsewhere.

---

[11] *E.g.*, Joan MacLeod Heminway & Shelden Ryan Hoffman, *Proceed at Your Peril: Crowdfunding and the Securities Act of 1933*, 78 TENN. L. REV. 879 (2011); Thomas Lee Hazen, *Crowdfunding or Fraudfunding? Social Networks and the Securities Laws—Why the Specially Tailored Exemption Must Be Conditioned on Meaningful Disclosure*, 90 N.C. L. REV. 1735 (2012).

[12] Complaint, Sec. and Exch. Comm'n v. Shumake, No. 21-cv-12193 (E.D. Mich. Sept. 20, 2021).

[13] Press Release, *SEC Announces Enforcement Results for FY 2021* (Nov. 18, 2021).

[14] Press Release, *SEC Nearly Doubles Size of Enforcement's Crypto Assets and Cyber Unit* (May 3, 2022).

As we will elaborate in the next few chapters, investment crowdfunding has multiple structures to reduce information asymmetry and root out fraud. Most basically, the entire system is based on entrepreneurs posting information on crowdfunding platforms to educate investors about themselves and their company. In most jurisdictions, entrepreneurs are legally required to share certain types of information as a matter of mandatory disclosure, but they commonly go above and beyond the legal minimum. Entrepreneurs actively engage in questions and answers with investors on the platform and provide updates and interviews, all of which are posted there for their benefit.

More will be said in the following chapters, but suffice it to say that crowdfunding companies can be expected to, and do, reduce information asymmetry and encourage investors to take the plunge.

C. AGENCY COSTS

The third fundamental challenge of financial investing relates to opportunistic behavior, also known as "agency costs." This idea has its origins in the general law covering "principals" and "agents." An agency relationship is one in which one party, the principal, hires another party, the agent, to perform some service for the benefit of the principal. By way of example, a Hollywood talent agent negotiates contracts on behalf of a movie star, who is the principal. Agency relationships can be tremendously valuable, for instance, when an agent has specialized knowledge or skills.

The foundational rule of agency law is that an agent is supposed to selflessly advance the interests of the principal—but agents have interests of their own, and they are often in a position to advance them. This divergence of interests is formally known as "agency costs," and they arise when an agent falls short of the ideal and advances his own interests, rather than those of the principal.

For example, a bartender is an agent for the bar owner. This means he is legally bound to advance the latter's interests by promptly serving up drinks to the customers with a smile and maintaining a clean environment. But in real life, a bartender may prefer to further his own interests. He might be surly, even if it means customers buy fewer drinks. He might not be too eager to wipe down every spill the moment it happens. He might even take customer's money and put it right in his own pocket, rather than the cash register. All of these are agency costs and harm the bar owner.

One might say, can't the bar owner just monitor the bartender, such as by video surveillance? Sure, he could, and that would reduce the chances for the latter to make mischief. Yet it is important to recognize that the costs of installing and using any monitoring system is itself a type of agency cost. Thus the key

54 CHALLENGES

question is how to minimize the combination of agency misbehavior and monitoring costs.

Agency costs are an important concern for investment crowdfunding. In a company financed in this way, the investors stand in the position of principal, while the CEO, board of directors, and other managers of the company (known collectively as "management") play the role of agent.[15] This will surely lead to the same sort of agency costs we have long observed in other contexts.

Moreover, crowdfunding investors each have a small amount at stake, akin to the traditional public company with widely dispersed, passive shareholders. Management is in control of the company on a day-to-day basis and would seem to be just as prone to shirking, stealing, and generally acting against the investors' interest as any other agent would be.

In real life, investment crowdfunding has seen a few instances of managerial misbehavior, yet it does not seem particularly beset by the problem. Agency costs are hard to spot from the outside—indeed that is part of their devilish nature— but they seem to be no worse among investment crowdfunding companies than traditional public companies.

Dealing with agency costs in the crowdfunding context is in the interest of all parties. For investors, the reason is obvious: they want the founders, promoters, and managers to do a good and faithful job running the company. As for entrepreneurs, they realize that no one will invest in the company (or will only do so at an insultingly low price) unless they can assure potential investors that agency costs will be sufficiently cabined. In short, agency costs must be addressed for crowdfunding to function.

We will discuss in the following chapters the many ways through which investment crowdfunding tries to address agency costs, but here are three key methods. One, because crowdfunding investors are also often "brand ambassadors," management has an incentive to treat them fairly. Second, entrepreneurs have their personal reputation literally linked to the crowdfunded company; if they engage in opportunistic behavior, their online reputation will be permanently sullied, so they might think twice before doing so. Third, crowdfunding investors can use technological means, like Zoom, to monitor and keep tabs on company management.

* * *

Uncertainty, information asymmetry, and agency costs are the three fundamental problems of all types of investing. VCs and angel investors have developed a set

---

[15] The analogy is not technically accurate, since corporate managers are not really agents of individual shareholders; rather, "they stand in a fiduciary relation to the corporation and its stockholders." Guth v. Loft, 5 A.2d 503, 510 (Del. 1939). Nevertheless, it serves as a useful, if rough, model of corporate governance.

of powerful techniques to address them—but they do not translate to investment crowdfunding's distinctive online context. Traditional public stock markets depend primarily on heavy regulation, especially mandatory disclosure, to respond to the trio of problems—but crowdfunding is, by definition, exempt from those regulations and disclosures.

Hence investment crowdfunding needs a distinctive set of tools to address the three fundamental challenges. These tools, both legal and private, will be described in the next few chapters.

Chapter Four
Private Ordering

In the last chapter, I explained that investment crowdfunding needs to effectively address the three fundamental challenges of uncertainty, information asymmetry, and agency costs—or it just won't work. There are essentially two ways that investment crowdfunding can respond to these fundamental challenges. The first is through legal methods, including both statutes and regulations. The second is through the actions of individuals and private organizations, known as "private ordering."

We will get to the law in Chapters Five and Six, but this chapter is devoted to private ordering. I begin here, rather than with the law, for several reasons. For one thing, there are sound theoretical reasons to think that private ordering is particularly effective in this area, as I will explain in this chapter. For another, the two leading crowdfunding jurisdictions in the world—namely, the United Kingdom and New Zealand—rely primarily on private ordering, not legal regulation, to govern their investment crowdfunding markets.[1] So it makes sense to examine closely how private ordering operates in this sphere.

Finally, legal regulation is the more obvious method—at least for a lawyer like me—and so I want to call particular attention to private ordering. Statutes and regulations are overt and express, available for anyone to observe. You can look them up in a book. Private ordering, by contrast, is often invisible, or at least opaque—but it may be even more important than law in the context of investment crowdfunding. My goal in this chapter is to enumerate and describe the methods of private ordering that are most vital to the effective functioning of the investment crowdfunding market.

The private ordering methods I describe in this chapter are independent of any particular set of regulations and will function in essentially any legal environment. The reader might object that many of these methods that I call "private" actually have a public aspect to them, as they depend on certain basic background rules of law and procedure, such as those of contract and property and the ability to sue in public courts.

I take the point, but it's merely a semantic one. There is a meaningful difference between private parties voluntarily arranging their affairs in any way they

---

[1] In Chapter Six, I will describe such a reliance on private ordering as the "liberal model" and contrast it with the "standard model," which depends mainly on laws and regulations.

Investment Crowdfunding. Andrew A. Schwartz, Oxford University Press. © Andrew A. Schwartz 2023.
DOI: 10.1093/oso/9780197688526.003.0005

58 PRIVATE ORDERING

wish, knowing that the courts stand ready to enforce them as needed, on the one hand, and the government dictating to those parties how they must arrange their affairs, on the other. As a convention, we often refer to the former as private ordering and the latter as government regulation. But it's only a convention, and the reader ought not to be overly distracted by the language.

I separate this chapter's discussion of private ordering into three parts, corresponding to the three primary actors in the investment crowdfunding market: investors, entrepreneurs, and platforms—though not in that order. I begin with platforms, and their role as intermediaries standing between entrepreneurs, on the one side, and investors, on the other, a structure known as *gatekeeping*. After that, I examine three methods of private ordering relating to entrepreneurs: *voluntary disclosure, online reputation*, and *digital trail*. Finally, I describe three methods of private ordering that focus on investors: *wisdom of the crowd, syndication*, and *remote monitoring*.

Some of the private methods discussed in this chapter, like syndication, have their origins in the practices of VCs and angel investors. Others, such as gatekeeping, come from the world of traditional stock exchanges. Still others, like the wisdom of the crowd or remote monitoring, are distinctive to crowdfunding and its online nature. This suite of seven private methods is well suited to address the trio of problems described in Chapter Three.

Any one of them standing alone has an impact, and collectively they represent a powerful web that can facilitate the market and protect investors—all at a very low cost. This is not to say that private ordering can create a perfect market, full of promising companies at a fair price and free of fraud—but perfection is not really our goal because it is too expensive to achieve.

We could put an end to cars speeding on the highway by assigning every police officer to that task, installing radar guns along every mile of highway, and sentencing speeders to life in prison—but that would not be a sound policy. Better to allow some speeders to get away with it than to expend the resources, and impose the harms, that it would take to achieve 100 percent compliance.

So too with investment crowdfunding. Our goal is to have an effective market, and that means acknowledging that the trio of problems will not be totally obliterated, but reduced in an efficient manner.

So far, this seems to be working fairly well. Experience over the past decade suggests that the private ordering methods I identify in this chapter are actually used in practice, and to generally good effect. This is true in the United Kingdom and New Zealand, the two countries that follow the "liberal model" and rely most heavily on private ordering, but it is also true in the United States and other jurisdictions that follow the "standard model" and rely primarily on government regulation. Throughout the chapter, I will offer reports and anecdotes from the real world.

As stated, this chapter is organized in three parts, one relating to platforms, one to entrepreneurs, and one to investors. Before getting there, however, permit me to first explain just what I mean by "private ordering."

The term "private ordering" may be foreign, but the concept is familiar. Imagine attending a general-admission concert, one with no assigned seats. Where would you seat yourself? Without an usher to guide you, you are free to choose a seat based on your own private interests: you want to be close to the stage, but not too close, and not directly behind a tall person, and it's important to get seats together with your friends, but not absolutely vital, and so on and so on. As more and more people enter the concert hall and make their own private choices, the crowd will usually arrange itself, not in random clumps, but in a nearly perfect mathematical arc emanating from the front center of the stage. The shape of such a crowd—it often looks like a baseball field—is highly ordered, but its order comes from the private choices of individuals, not an intentional plan or a set of rules.

Nobel laureate Friedrich von Hayek referred to this phenomenon as "spontaneous order," and contended that it is generally superior to central planning, such as by a committee of experts or government agency.[2] The reader may already see the relevance of Hayek's ideas, and we shall return to them throughout this chapter and beyond.

For another example of private ordering in the real world, think about how parents hire babysitters to watch their children. The babysitting market is, like the crowdfunding market, subject to three fundamental challenges: Uncertainty (what will happen after the parents go out?); information asymmetry (it's hard for parents to assess the qualifications of a prospective babysitter); and agency costs (the babysitter might text her friends rather than keep a close eye on the kids).

Given the importance of picking a good babysitter and the risk of grave consequences from picking a bad one, we could use legal regulation to respond to this trio of problems. We could enact a state or even federal law requiring all babysitters to be licensed with a government agency, and mandate that they hold certain certifications, such as in CPR. We could make it illegal to hire an unlicensed babysitter and impose fines or even imprisonment on any violators.

Laws of this type would likely reduce the risk of hiring an irresponsible babysitter and enhance the safety of our children. At the same time, they would surely add to the cost of babysitting services, as babysitters would have to cover the costs of obtaining and maintaining their licensure. In the real world, as the reader well knows, laws of this type have not been adopted. Does this suggest that we don't care about our kids? Hardly. It means that parents use methods of private ordering that help them overcome the trio of problems and select a

---

[2] F.A. Hayek, *The Use of Knowledge in Society*, 35 AM. ECON. REV. 519 (1945).

60 PRIVATE ORDERING

responsible babysitter and that these methods are more cost-effective than legal regulation would be.

We see many forms of private ordering in the babysitting market. To offer a handful: (1) People hire babysitters from their neighborhood, rather than from far away; the babysitter's interest in maintaining a good local reputation lowers agency costs. (2) Parents swap babysitting services, placing each at the mercy of the other and reducing agency costs. (3) Parents monitor their babysitters using inexpensive technological means, such as a digital video camera ("nanny cam"), again reducing agency costs. (4) Parents recommend specific babysitters to each other based on personal experience; this reduces uncertainty and information asymmetry. (5) Private agencies vet babysitters and charge parents for access to their list of recommended providers; this likewise addresses uncertainty and information asymmetry.

We don't usually think in these terms, but countless parents rely on these sorts of private methods, rather than legal regulation, to select and monitor babysitters. If we passed a law creating a babysitting licensure system, it might well work to protect our children, but the cost of compliance could push the price of babysitting services to unreasonable heights. Private ordering achieves the same goal at a lower cost.

Private ordering does not always work perfectly, of course. There are certain situations known to cause a "market failure," which means that leaving individuals alone, free to do as they wish, will produce a bad collective outcome. Monopoly is a good example of a market failure. If there is only one power plant in a town, you can't really allow a free market for electricity there. The plant can charge any price it wants, and the locals will be forced to pay it, as they have no other choice. To address this market failure, we have enacted a set of antitrust laws and created regulatory bodies to enforce them.

Pollution is another type of market failure; we have special environmental laws that respond to this. More generally, we can deploy legal regulation of various types to resolve different types of market failures. To this end, Chapters Five and Six will describe investment crowdfunding's regulatory regime, highlighting where it responds to a potential market failure.

Despite the foregoing, market success, not market failure, is the more common case. Markets work quite well most of the time, and our economy is overwhelmingly organized through market prices and the private choices of individuals, not regulatory fiat. McDonald's decides how much to charge for a hamburger based on consumer demand, competition from Wendy's, and other factors; there is no Bureau of Beef Pricing that determines the price. Same for haircuts, houses, and almost everything else—including startup companies.

VCs and angels rely on private ordering, not the law, to overcome the trio of problems described in Chapter Three. They generally invest locally, allowing them to personally meet with an entrepreneur and get to know the company well, before they invest. This reduces uncertainty and information asymmetry, and it also responds to agency costs, as the entrepreneur's reputation will be on the line. VCs and angels are typically experts in a given field of technology, and have often founded a related company themselves, further reducing uncertainty and information asymmetry. VCs often take a seat on the board of directors, and angels physically come in to the office on a regular basis. They really do stand over the shoulder of the entrepreneur—and he knows it—and this reduces agency costs.

The friends and family of an entrepreneur have their own nonlegal methods for addressing uncertainty, information asymmetry, and agency costs. Compared with strangers, they can be more certain of a venture's prospects because they know the entrepreneur personally and are familiar with his past successes and failures. Their personal relationship also reduces information asymmetry and agency costs. If your old college buddy was a straight-A student and was constantly being promoted at work, you know a lot about his chances of success. Also, he is likely to work hard for his investors—serve as a faithful agent—since they are also his family and he has to see them on Thanksgiving. All of this explains the good sense behind the registration exemption for private placements that I discussed in Chapter One.

These methods of private ordering work well in their contexts, but they do not translate to investment crowdfunding. Most obviously, crowdfunding investors cannot all join the board of directors or regularly pop in the office, and inherent to the nature of crowdfunding, most crowdfunding investors do not have personal relationships with the founders they support.

This chapter thus presents seven categories of private ordering that are tailored to the distinctive online context of investment crowdfunding. The first is probably the most important; I call it "gatekeeping."

A. PLATFORMS

1. Gatekeeping

Companies do not solicit crowdfunding investments directly from individual investors the way that they might from angels or venture capitalists. Under the definition of the form I provided in Chapter One, there is always an intermediary website—often called a "platform" or a "portal"—that stands between the company and the public. They are new and entirely online, but their role as middleman is similar to that of a traditional stock market, like the New York Stock Exchange. Platforms act as "gatekeepers" that only allow some companies to participate and list on their platform, and reject others.

62   PRIVATE ORDERING

Gatekeeping serves to reduce uncertainty and information asymmetry. In contrast with the crowd of investors, the people who operate investment crowdfunding platforms possess knowledge and experience in raising startup capital and investing in startup companies. This gives them the expertise to stand at the gate and select promising companies to list on the site, and to reject the weak, the overoptimistic, and the fraudulent. To make this delineation, the platform may demand information from the companies that want to participate and conduct its own research and analysis as well. All of this redounds all to the benefit of investors, as it reduces both uncertainty and information asymmetry: investors trust that the platforms have vetted the companies and are only presenting ones that have some chance of success.

In addition, platforms can—and do—"groom" companies such that they present themselves to the crowd in the best light possible. On Seedrs, a UK platform, entrepreneurs can go through the "Seedrs Academy," a set of "guides, tools and resources to help founders grow their business, raise capital and successfully crowdfund."[3] SeedInvest, an American platform, boasts that its "stringent" due diligence process "allows entrepreneurs to ready themselves, and their materials, for future meetings with investors."[4] Snowball Effect, a platform in New Zealand, takes companies by the hand and leads them through every step of the process, including a sort of "mock" pitch to experienced investors, who provide feedback.

One of the most important aspects of this sort of grooming is that platforms can help entrepreneurs decide upon a reasonable valuation for the company. An entrepreneur may come in claiming that her two-month old company is worth $100 million, but the platform can educate her about the valuation process and help guide her to a more reasonable figure, perhaps using recent comparable transactions. The entrepreneur always decides upon the final figure—but, if she stubbornly sticks to an unreasonably high value, the platform can simply decline to list the company on its site. This is another way that platforms work for the benefit of investors.

Importantly, the platforms are constantly learning from experience. Each time a platform lists a company, it can observe how it performs, both during the campaign and afterward. With each company that a platform lists on its site, it learns new things. This includes broad lessons, such how to value seed-stage companies, which types of companies are popular with investors, and how they perform after raising money through investment crowdfunding. But platforms also learn many fine-grained details, such as how many Facebook followers a company needs to have a realistic chance to raise $1 million. With each company

---

[3] SEEDRS ACADEMY, https://www.seedrs.com/academy/ (last visited Sept. 24, 2022).
[4] James Han, 5 things you need to do to get ready for due diligence, SEEDINVEST, Apr. 2, 2015.

that they analyze and either list or don't, they learn more and more, and this iterative process hones their capacity to act as gatekeepers.

But is it realistic to expect platforms to act as responsible gatekeepers in the real world? Why should they go to all this trouble to curate, vet, and groom the companies they list? After all, it may be a competitive advantage to be lax and just let any company participate. It costs time and money to select which companies to allow on a site, and a platform that skimps on its gatekeeping responsibilities will avoid those costs and thus increase its profits.

This is a fair concern, but platforms have strong economic incentives that push them to serve as responsible gatekeepers. The main way that a platform makes money is by listing companies, attracting investors, and putting the two groups together, then taking a percent of the amount raised as a commission. (In the United States, the typical rate is 6–9 percent of the amount raised, and other countries are similar or higher.) Crowdfunding platforms are private businesses trying to turn a profit over the long term. As such, they have a strong self-interest in establishing and maintaining a reputation as a reliable place for investors to put their money. If they fail in this endeavor and acquire a poor reputation, investors will not come back, and they will go out of business.

Notably, the incentives of the platform differ from those of an entrepreneur. Unlike an entrepreneur, who may seek to raise funds just once, platforms are "repeat players" with a long-term financial interest in keeping investors happy. If a single entrepreneur tricks the crowd and runs off with the investors' money, the entrepreneur may be pleased, but this is bad news for the platform, since the investors who lost their money are unlikely to return to the hosting platform for future offerings. Fraud, in other words, is bad for business. Hence, platforms have an economic incentive to vet and review companies that seek to list on their sites, in a manner analogous to "listing standards" on a traditional stock exchange.

In addition, many (but not all) of the leading investment crowdfunding platforms take a financial interest in the companies they list, sometimes called a "carry." This gives them a direct self-interest in taking the time to find high-quality companies to list on their platform. American platform Republic, for instance, takes for itself 2 percent of the securities that are sold on its site (in addition to a 6 percent commission). For an alternative model, Seedrs in the United Kingdom charges its investors a 7.5 percent "carry" on any profits they make (in addition to a 7.5 percent commission). These structures put the platforms' own "skin in the game," giving them a reason to care whether the companies they list are likely to succeed.

In sum, as a matter of their own survival and self-interest, platforms have clear incentives to act as gatekeepers that keep fraudulent and undesirable companies out of the market, so that only legitimate companies with reasonable prospects are presented to investors.

64 PRIVATE ORDERING

There are, nevertheless, countervailing forces that may undermine this salutary system. First and foremost, the incentive to act as a strict gatekeeper may only work over such a long time frame as to be ineffective. A crowdfunding platform that takes a lax approach to its gatekeeper role and lets practically anybody list on its site might not be discovered until years have passed and most of the companies it listed have gone down the tubes. By that time, the platform will have collected years' worth of fees (which are rather rich) while putting in only minimal resources and effort. At that point, its operators may not care that their platform will henceforth be a pariah—they are too busy sailing on their yachts.

There is also a glass-half-full version of this same story. A platform that allows any company that fits a certain set of objective criteria to participate is also doing its part to develop an "inclusive" system where all entrepreneurs can have a chance to get funded. As long as a platform takes reasonable steps to making sure its listings are nonfraudulent, it may be a reasonable policy to post all companies, regardless of their apparent business merit. This would certainly promote an inclusive environment for entrepreneurs, and it would recognize all of our inabilities to predict which businesses will thrive and which won't.

Another cause for concern is that most crowdfunding investors, at least so far, make a single investment and never return to the market. Platform operators have told me that roughly three-quarters of investments come from first-time investors—these are typically the loyal customers I call "brand ambassadors" and discuss later—yet the gatekeeping idea depends on investors returning again and again.

These points are well taken. In practice, however, platforms claim to take their gatekeeping role very seriously and, by all appearances, they actually do, especially when it comes to preventing fraud. In my research over the past decade, which includes speaking personally with founders and senior executives at multiple leading platforms around the world, I've found that they focus intensely on their role as gatekeepers. The platforms understand perfectly well how vital it is to protect their reputation and accordingly try to exclude companies that have any chance of being fraudulent. Leading platforms generally conduct significant due diligence and are highly selective in deciding which companies to allow to list on their site. They judge the business plan, review the finances, often interview the entrepreneur, and only accept the companies that meet their own standard.

Putting fraud to one side, platforms differ in how they approach their role. Some are highly selective and seek to present just a slice of the best opportunities they can find. Others are more willing to list anyone who wants to participate and therefore list a much higher volume of offerings. As the market has developed, different platforms have started to establish reputations in one direction or the other. American platform SeedInvest, for instance, sees itself as a strict gatekeeper, stating on its home page: "Only a small selection of companies make it through our due diligence process. We're not an open marketplace where anyone can just click and raise."[5]

Most of the leading sites take a strict approach to gatekeeping, and list only a small percent of companies that seek to participate. Republic, one of the top American platforms by deal volume, says that it only approved about 300 of the roughly 7,000 applications it received in 2020, representing an acceptance rate of 4 percent.[6] StartEngine, another leading American platform, reports a 1 percent rate.[7]

This is true around the world, not just in the United States. New Zealand platform Snowball Effect, the largest platform in that country, reportedly rejects 98 percent of the hundreds of companies that seek to crowdfund on its site.[8] Snowball Effect is selective because, according to the company, "we've got our own reputation [to protect and because] we want investors to get what we think are interesting opportunities that are ready for public investment."[9] Exactly.

Many platforms loudly tout their role and diligence as gatekeepers. For instance, Canadian platform FrontFundr has an entire page on its website ("Due Diligence") that explains its role and process as gatekeeper: "Our Due Diligence team performs a thorough review of all the companies we list on our platform. This not only creates confidence among our investors, it also ensures entrepreneurs are well equipped for a capital raise."[10] Some platforms, by contrast, play down their role and the level of due diligence they perform, presumably to avoid making investment recommendations, which they are not allowed to do.[11]

---

[5] *Seedinvest: Startup Investing. Simplified.*, https://www.seedinvest.com (last visited Aug. 1, 2022).

[6] Jacob Gallagher, *Investment Crowdfunding: Is Buying $100 in Equity in Your Favorite Shoe Brand Worth It?*, WALL ST. J., May 3, 2021.

[7] Anne Burke, *Leveling the Playing Field: Startup Funding Without the Golden Handcuffs*, STARTENGINE (July 2, 2021), https://www.startengine.com/blog/venture-capital-vs-equity-crowd funding.

[8] Calida Smylie, *Are Equity Crowdfunding Regulations Too Light Handed?*, NAT'L BUS. REV., June 12, 2017 ("98% of companies we point in another direction") (quoting Snowball Effect co-founder Josh Daniell).

[9] John Anthony, *New Zealand Crowdfunding Platforms Gearing Up for Big 2016*, STUFF, Jan. 24, 2016 ("We need to make sure that companies are suitable for our offering and a lot of companies aren't.") (quoting Snowball Effect chief executive Simeon Burnett).

[10] *Due Diligence*, FRONTFUNDR, https://info.frontfundr.com/due-diligence (last visited June 18, 2022).

[11] *E.g.*, Terms of Service Policy ¶ 4.3.1, WEFUNDER, https://wefunder.com/terms (updated Oct. 17, 2022) ("Wefunder Portal performs a limited review of the information provided by each Startup to determine whether it is appropriate for inclusion on the Site . . . . This review is not intended to verify any information provided by the Startups regarding their operations, assess the likelihood that a Startup will succeed or generate investment returns, or otherwise inform or influence any investment decisions by investors. Neither Wefunder Portal nor its affiliates performs any separate due diligence on the Startups.").

66   PRIVATE ORDERING

In most jurisdictions (but not the United Kingdom), there are certain minimal levels of gatekeeping that are required by law, such as specific due diligence obligations. Even in those jurisdictions, we still see private ordering, with many platforms touting the fact that they go above and beyond the legal minimum. For example, Australian platform Equitise states on its website that it has "a very high standard of due diligence over and above the level imposed by our regulatory authorities."[12]

For another example, Republic, a leading American platform, says that it does an "initial screen" of the companies that seek to list on its platform, followed by "the formal due diligence process": "We review each startup's pitch deck, conduct screening calls, and complete independent research to better understand the startup's business and, if necessary, tap into our networks" to evaluate the business and its prospects.[13] This sort of independent research is not mandated by law, as we shall see in the next chapter.

Where there is no minimum level of due diligence, as in the United Kingdom, the leading platforms have established and published their own gatekeeping and due diligence standards entirely as a matter of private ordering. Seedrs uses "The Seedrs Standard: Guide to Due Diligence," and Crowdcube uses its own "Due Diligence Charter." These documents define and describe the standard due diligence procedures at each platform and are written in plain English.[14] Both platforms pledge to conduct background checks on key personnel, fact-check statements and claims made by companies on its site, and more. They also make clear what they do not do, and where investors have to take responsibility. This is private ordering at its most pure: Crowdcube and Seedrs developed these standards on their own, without any law or regulation directing them to do so, as a way to attract investors and companies to their platforms.

In fairness, we might note that Crowdcube beefed up its due diligence process following the demise of Rebus, a company that raised over £800,000 on the platform in 2015, only to go bust less than one year later due to insufficient cash flow.[15] There were news reports at the time suggesting that the offering may have been misleading because it omitted certain information and that the pitch featured someone who had previously been legally banned from serving as a financial advisor. This episode generated negative publicity for Crowdcube—and

---

[12] Stewart Na, *Equitise's Capital Raising Process*, Equitise, https://help.equitise.com/en/articles/5899800-equitise-s-capital-raising-process (last visited Oct. 28, 2022).

[13] *How we select startups*, Republic, https://republic.com/help/how-we-select-startups (last visited June 18, 2022).

[14] The Seedrs Standard: Guide to Due Diligence (2022), https://newsroom-cdn.seedrs.com/newsroom/wp-content/uploads/2022/07/05100808/SeedrsDueDiligenceGuide2022.pdf; Crowdcube, Due Diligence Charter, https://www.crowdcube.com/explore/investing/due-diligence-charter (last visited Oct. 28, 2022).

[15] Oscar Williams-Grut, *Crowdcube Defends the UK's Biggest Crowdfunding Failure: "They Weren't Trying to Pull a Fast One,"* Bus. Insider UK, May 12, 2016.

PLATFORMS 67

indeed for the entire UK investment crowdfunding industry.[16] Crowdcube, under market pressure to respond, expanded the scope of its due diligence, and the platform ultimately regained the trust of the marketplace. This is private ordering in action, once more.

The sort of curation and due diligence just discussed is most true at the leading platforms in each jurisdiction, as they have the best reputations, and thus the most to lose from allowing low-quality companies to list on their sites. Lower-tier platforms, almost by definition, are not as selective, and some of the companies that are rejected by the top sites are able to get listed at one of the less prestigious platforms.[17] Notably, the sole fraud case brought by the SEC involved an obscure platform, not one of the leaders.[18]

These lower-tier sites, however, represent a small fraction of the industry. In all the jurisdictions I have studied, a couple of leading platforms dominate the investment crowdfunding market. In the United Kingdom, for instance, the two leading platforms control more than 90 percent of the market;[19] in New Zealand, the three leaders control more than 95 percent of the market.[20]

In the United States, things are bit more spread out, but not by much. Since Regulation Crowdfunding went live in 2016, the SEC has granted licenses to eighty-five platforms all told, although twenty-four have closed down, leaving sixty-one active platforms as of 2021. Of all these, however, just three leading platforms—Wefunder, StartEngine, and Republic—hosted 84 percent of all crowdfunded offerings from 2016 to 2021. Looking just at 2021, those three leading sites accounted for 75 percent of all the money raised that year across all platforms.[21]

---

[16] James Hurley, *Crowdfunders Misled by Pitch Face Massive Losses*, THE TIMES (UK), Apr. 8, 2016 ("The revelation will raise concerns that ordinary investors are being mistreated because [investment crowdfunding] platforms are failing to meet regulatory demands that pitches are fair, clear and not misleading."); Adam Palin, *Rebus Collapse Increases Demands for Investor Protections*, FIN. TIMES, Feb. 5, 2016.

[17] Oscar Williams-Grut, *Crowdcube Defends the UK's Biggest Crowdfunding Failure: "They Weren't Trying to Pull a Fast One,"* BUS. INSIDER UK, May 12, 2016 ("90% of the businesses that apply to us don't get through to the site. There are lots of business[es] that came to us and for financial reasons we turned them down. . . . Days later they pop up on competitors['] sites which from my point of view is really concerning because a) it takes us weeks to do our due diligence process, not days and b) there were clearly fundamental reasons why we rejected those businesses.") (quoting Crowdcube co-founder Luke Lang).

[18] Final Judgment as to Defendant TruCrowd, Sec. and Exch. Comm'n v. Shumake, No. 21-cv-12193 (E.D. Mich. Dec. 23, 2021) (entering final judgment against investment crowdfunding platform TruCrowd, operating under the name Fundanna).

[19] COMPETITION AND MKTS. AUTH., ANTICIPATED ACQUISITION BY CROWDCUBE LIMITED OF SEEDRS LIMITED: PROVISIONAL FINDINGS REPORT 7 (2021).

[20] FIN. MKTS. AUTH., PEER TO PEER AND CROWDFUNDING SECTOR SNAPSHOT (2021), https://www.fma.govt.nz/library/reports-and-papers/peer-to-peer-and-crowdfunding-sector-snapshot.

[21] CROWDFUND CAPITAL ADVISORS, 2021 ANNUAL REPORT: TIME TO CELEBRATE SUCCESS 80–82 (2022).

68 PRIVATE ORDERING

The markets seem to get more concentrated as time goes by since, as crowd-funding develops, the smaller and less-reliable platforms fall by the wayside. Thanks to "network effects," companies and investors flock to the largest and most heavily trafficked platforms, putting the rest out of business.[22] In the United States, for instance, the share of funds raised by the three leading platforms just cited was 53 percent in 2018, 69 percent in 2019, 78 percent in 2020, and 84 percent in 2021.

The value of gatekeeping can be demonstrated by the fact that lower-tier platforms are generally less strict gatekeepers than the leaders—and it is on these lower-tier sites where we have seen the rare instance of fraud. In the United States, the sole enforcement action brought by the SEC in the context of investment crowdfunding related to an offering posted on a minuscule platform with less than 1 percent of the market.[23] For that platform, there was not much to lose by allowing the dodgy offering that led to SEC action. But for a leading site, a similar story could be devastating and drive business to the competition. This inspires them to guard the gate vigilantly.

For all its value, gatekeeping does have an unavoidable downside. The high level of diligence and selectivity of leading platforms does a good job of responding to the three fundamental challenges of capital finance. But the presence of powerful and strict gatekeepers makes the system much more exclusive than inclusive—think of bouncers behind the velvet rope at a nightclub—and yet inclusivity is one of the essential goals of the form (as discussed in Chapter Two).

Because of the gatekeepers, entrepreneurs cannot go directly to the crowd and solicit funds; rather, they first have to impress the platform's management (many of whom wear fleece vests). This is clearly contrary to the radically inclusive vision found in reward crowdfunding and the original version of Regulation Crowdfunding. Recall from Chapter Two that one of the fundamental purposes of investment crowdfunding is to foster an inclusive system where any and all entrepreneurs, regardless of who they know or where they are from, are invited to pitch their company directly to the public. This followed the tradition of reward crowdfunding on websites like Kickstarter, which does not screen, curate, or vet the projects before presenting them to the crowd. The upshot is that anyone with an idea can go on the platform and present it to the crowd.

This radically inclusive model has not translated directly to investment crowdfunding, which has rebuffed it in favor of gatekeeping. This can be seen most plainly in the regulatory history of Regulation Crowdfunding, which we will

---

[22] COMPETITION AND MKTS. AUTH., ANTICIPATED ACQUISITION BY CROWDCUBE LIMITED OF SEEDRS LIMITED: PROVISIONAL FINDINGS REPORT 7 (2021) (noting that Crowdcube and Seedrs' market share had increased since 2018).

[23] CROWDFUND CAPITAL ADVISORS, 2021 ANNUAL REPORT: TIME TO CELEBRATE SUCCESS 80–82 (2022).

cover in the next chapter. In summary, the SEC's first set of proposed regulations would have required platforms to list any and every company that wished to participate. But its final version of Regulation Crowdfunding, which is now in place, expressly allows platforms to act as gatekeepers that pick and choose which companies to accept.

Across jurisdictions, not just in the United States, the radically inclusive model has been rejected in favor of gatekeeping, which necessarily implies including some companies and excluding others—a direct affront to the goal of inclusivity and unmediated access to the crowd. Platforms, as we have seen, have a fundamental business need to cultivate and protect a sound reputation among investors, otherwise people may not be willing to invest their money on the site. This would be impossible if they listed any and every business that asked to be included. Some sort of gatekeeping function seems vital for the system to function effectively—or maybe at all. A gate-free system would have led to anarchy and had to be avoided.

The platform operators are themselves aware of the tension between efficiency and inclusivity and try to balance them. The point is that there is a tension within investment crowdfunding between inclusivity and effectiveness. While inclusivity is important, it cannot be given free rein, or the entire project is prone to failure. Some level of gatekeeping is necessary. That said, in balancing inclusivity and effectiveness, platforms lean one way or the other, depending on their mission and goals. Some are more focused in one direction, some are more focused in the other.

At the very least, and without infringing on inclusivity, all platforms must reject companies that engage in fraud. That much is clear. Beyond suspicions of fraud, platforms can try to analyze which companies have reasonable prospects for financial success, and exclude those that seem unviable. Some platforms will take a more active role in trying to strictly present only "winners," while others will be more liberal with who they allow to participate.

Also, many crowdfunding investors have nonfinancial motivations for investing. Perhaps they want to support a local company to enhance their community, or invest in a company committed to certain environmental or social goals, or one founded by a member of an underrepresented demographic group. A decision to exclude such companies because they stand little chance of generating financial returns for investors would not be welcomed by the crowd— even if it would protect them from a financial loss.

Strict platforms are probably more protective of investors, but they will surely misjudge and exclude at least some companies that should be given a chance. A major theoretical premise of crowdfunding is that a large crowd can recognize promise where a small group—like a platform's management team—might see none. Liberal platforms humbly recognize their own inability to make perfect

70 PRIVATE ORDERING

predictions and give the crowd a chance to make their choices. This is, on balance, riskier for investors, but it is a question of degree—and different platforms come down at different points on the spectrum.

B. ENTREPRENEURS

Now let us turn to three forms of private ordering centered on entrepreneurs: voluntary disclosure, online reputation, and digital trail.

1. Voluntary Disclosure

The essence of "information asymmetry"—one of the three challenges from Chapter Three—is the common sense idea that entrepreneurs always and necessarily know much more about the business than outside investors do. But entrepreneurs can reduce this asymmetry in a straightforward way: they can tell investors about the business and share key information with them. In the parlance, this is known as "disclosure."

Because investment crowdfunding is conducted via online platforms, entrepreneurs can give all potential investors the same information and data at the same time, cheaply and easily, just by posting it to the web. Time-strapped entrepreneurs don't have to repeatedly present the same slide deck to multiple audiences; they can create a single video and post it on the internet for all to click on.

An entrepreneur can describe the company's business, what it does, for how long, and what its future plans may be, and post this all to a crowdfunding website. She can disclose financial data, like the company's assets, debts, sales, profits, and cash flow. She can recount who founded the company, who is running it, the identity of the board of directors and major shareholders, and how many employees it has. These sorts of disclosures plainly reduce information asymmetry, as well as uncertainty, two of the three fundamental challenges recounted in Chapter Three.

But will this actually happen—voluntarily? Should we expect entrepreneurs to willingly disclose all this information to potential investors—both the bad and the good—and thereby reduce information asymmetry? Or do we need to impose "mandatory disclosure," meaning a legal obligation to disclose certain information?

Economic theory, as well as common sense, suggests that crowdfunding entrepreneurs should be expected to disclose a great deal of information to investors, freely and voluntarily, and include both the negative and the positive.

The idea is simple: unless an entrepreneur voluntarily discloses at least some information about her business, no one would invest. Or they might invest, but only a little bit, and at a low valuation.[24]

Consider the simple situation where a stranger (or even your sister-in-law) calls you up and asks you to invest in her business. If she refuses to tell you anything about the business—what it does, how it's going, plans for the future—there is no way that you would hand over your money. To get you to invest in the first place, she essentially has to provide at least some basic disclosure about the company—and she knows it. If she replies "no comment" to all your questions, you are not going to buy in. Even if it's your sister-in-law and you want to help her out, you would only invest a very small amount—and strangers won't even go that far. In short, it is in her interest to voluntarily disclose information about her company; she will not be silent.

This phenomenon—formally known as "signaling"—suggests that crowdfunding entrepreneurs have an incentive to voluntarily disclose information to potential investors. This is most obvious with regard to good news. If your sister's company recently won a $10 million government contract, she would be sure to mention it in her pitch. She wants you to invest, and so she has every reason to tell you about the contract—in fact, she may well talk your ear off about it.

But the incentive to disclose is not limited to good news. Importantly, signaling theory holds that entrepreneurs feel pressure to disclose even bad news and negative information about the company. This incentive exists because, if an entrepreneur stays silent, investors will presume that things are actually even worse than they really are.

For this reason, a company seeking to raise money via crowdfunding has a private incentive to disclose all relevant information, both the good and the bad. Potential investors will presume a company that discloses nothing has something to hide (such as poor business performance) and refuse to invest. Thus, a company that is performing well (or even just fine) has an incentive to voluntarily disclose relevant information to distinguish itself from those poor prospects that remain silent. Even a company that is doing poorly will say so, to avoid being viewed as a total disaster.

Beyond entrepreneurs, crowdfunding platforms also have an economic incentive to encourage voluntary disclosure from the companies that they present to investors. The way that platforms make money is on transaction fees generated each time an investor buys into a company. Since revenues rise in tandem with the volume of transactions, an exchange has a financial incentive to retain investors, with the result that platforms want investors to be—and feel that they

---

[24] Frank H. Easterbrook & Daniel R. Fischel, The Economic Structure of Corporate Law 288–89 (1991).

72 PRIVATE ORDERING

are—sufficiently informed. Platforms are long-term players that depend on investors coming back again and again for years, but they are not likely to return if they feel that they were misled or that important information was kept from them.

For this reason, a platform can be expected to require an entrepreneur to disclose key information to investors, as a condition of listing on the platform. This sort of contractual arrangement is a classic method of private ordering. Indeed, this sort of voluntary disclosure through "listing standards" is exactly what we saw among the traditional stock exchanges, like the New York Stock Exchange, prior to the passage of the Securities Act of 1933. Requiring entrepreneurs to disclose information to investors is also consistent with platforms' role as gatekeepers—and may even be conceived as a component of gatekeeping.

Depending on the demands of investors and its own judgment, a platform might demand a specific set of disclosures from listed companies, perhaps on a form of its own devising. Alternatively, a platform may give each company more freedom to present themselves and then review each set of disclosures on a case-by-case basis. Either way, the result is that we should expect investors to receive a reasonable level of information about crowdfunding companies, as a matter of voluntary disclosure.

In short, crowdfunding companies have powerful incentives to voluntarily disclose a great deal of information about themselves to potential investors, and this serves to reduce uncertainty and information asymmetry.

Will this information be accurate, or fairly presented? One reason to think it will is that a material misrepresentation in a crowdfunding offer would constitute fraud, which would allow the investors to get out of the deal. In all commercial transactions, from the simplest contract to the most complex collateralized debt obligation, whenever one side communicates with the other, they are bound to be honest. Intentional misrepresentations are not allowed. In the context of crowdfunding, if the entrepreneur lies and tricks you into making a deal, the law allows you to later rescind (tear up) the contract on the basis of fraud and get your money back.

Sometimes, this may call for litigation. In many crowdfunding cases, however, it would not be economically viable to pursue a claim as an individual. For example, if you were duped into investing $200 into a crowdfunding company due to the entrepreneur's lies, you might be sad about the loss, but you won't bring a lawsuit if the attorney's fee will be $10,000. But if the whole crowd of investors were to join together in a class action, the aggregate amount at stake might make that $10,000 fee worth paying.

Beyond private actions brought by individuals or a class of investors, government regulators are also empowered to pursue civil and even criminal charges against those who perpetrate a fraud through crowdfunding. These regulators,

ENTREPRENEURS 73

such as the SEC in the United States or the Financial Conduct Authority in the United Kingdom, can order a company to repay investors who were misled, pay a fine, or make amends in other ways. One way or another, an effective antifraud regime is needed for the system of voluntary disclosure to work.

So far this has all been a matter of theory. But what happens in real life? As I will describe in detail in the next two chapters, the various jurisdictions I studied provide a convenient test of the theory of voluntary disclosure just described. In the United States, Australia, and Canada, the law requires crowdfunding entrepreneurs to provide certain mandatory disclosures. In New Zealand and the United Kingdom, by contrast, the law does not impose mandatory disclosure and expects that private ordering will generate voluntary disclosure.

This distinction provides a good (albeit imperfect) natural experiment. Do companies in New Zealand and the United Kingdom stay mum, since they are free to do so? Or do they disclose, voluntarily? The answer is that they disclose. Entrepreneurs in the United Kingdom and New Zealand do indeed post a significant amount of information on the crowdfunding platforms that host them. They provide key financial information, narrative descriptions, videos, "pitch decks," and more.

Without being required to by law, companies in New Zealand and the United Kingdom do provide basic financial information, descriptions of the business and its key personnel, plans for the money, and the like. It is a matter of private ordering, whereby the platforms, not the regulators, set the standard for required disclosures. Each platform runs things a little differently. They can learn from one another and make changes as needed rather than being bound to a single legal standard, whether they like it or not.

Notably, the United States and other jurisdictions require that crowdfunding companies provide financial statements that conform to generally accepted accounting principles (GAAP)—the same type used by the largest public companies in the world.[25] There is merit in mandating that all companies use the same system, but very few early-stage companies have GAAP-compliant financial statements and therefore must create them for the purposes of crowdfunding. Anecdotally, this is one the most burdensome (and therefore expensive) aspects of Regulation Crowdfunding.

In New Zealand and the United Kingdom, companies always provide financial statements as part of the offering—but they are rarely in the formal GAAP format. More often, companies post an "information memorandum" of their own design, akin to what they would (and often do) show to an angel investor or VC.

---

[25] 17 C.F.R. § 227.201(t) (Instruction 3); Nat'l Instrument 45-110, *Start-up Crowdfunding Registration and Prospectus Exemptions* (June 24, 2021) (Can.) (official instructions to Form 45-110F1 § 3.5).

74   PRIVATE ORDERING

The financial statements are in slightly different formats, making comparisons a bit tougher—but the cost of producing them is very low.

Thus far, it appears that the voluntary disclosure regime has worked reasonably well. The United Kingdom and New Zealand are two of the leading crowdfunding jurisdictions in the world, at least so far, suggesting that investors have been largely (though not entirely) satisfied with the disclosures they have received. In addition, in the extremely rare case where fraud has been alleged in these "liberal" jurisdictions, the investors were effectively protected.

In New Zealand, for instance, there has been only one allegation of fraud, and it was handled quite well. In 2020, a medical marijuana company called Medical Kiwi raised NZ$2 million on one of the leading crowdfunding platforms, PledgeMe, from roughly 1,000 investors. In the information it provided to investors, Medical Kiwi stated that it had a "cannabis license," but did not clarify that the license was limited to research use, not yet active, and that the license actually expired right in the middle of the crowdfunding campaign.[26]

A jurisdiction like New Zealand, which relies entirely on voluntary disclosure, needs to have an effective way to police against fraud. What happened next suggests that it does.

The allegations against Medical Kiwi were reported in the country's leading newspaper[27] and to New Zealand's national securities regulator, the Financial Markets Authority (FMA), which investigated the matter. The company cooperated with the FMA and ultimately settled by admitting that its offering was misleading and thereby breached the "fair dealing" provisions of New Zealand law (the equivalent of "securities fraud" in the United States).[28] The company paid a NZ$250,000 fine, issued a corrective statement, and offered all crowdfunding investors the opportunity to return their shares and get their money back.[29] In the end, the company had to pay back roughly one-quarter of the NZ$2 million it had raised.[30]

This episode is one anecdote of the broader idea that the economic incentives for disclosure, combined with the ancient ban on fraud, serves to encourage

---

[26] Media Release, Financial Markets Authority, Medical Kiwi Admits to Making False and Misleading Statements (Dec. 22, 2021), https://www.fma.govt.nz/news/all-releases/media-releases/medical-kiwi-admits-false-misleading-statements.

[27] Kate MacNamara, *Cannabis Firm Funded on Expired Licence*, N.Z. HERALD, Oct. 16, 2020.

[28] Media Release, Financial Markets Authority, Medical Kiwi admits to making false and misleading statements (Dec. 22, 2021), https://www.fma.govt.nz/news/all-releases/media-releases/medical-kiwi-admits-false-misleading-statements.

[29] Media Release, Financial Markets Authority, Medical Kiwi Admits to Making False and Misleading Statements (Dec. 22, 2021), https://www.fma.govt.nz/news/all-releases/media-releases/medical-kiwi-admits-false-misleading-statements.

[30] *Medical Kiwi Fulfils Undertakings to FMA*, MEDICAL KIWI (Mar. 25, 2022), https://medicalkiwi.com/medical-kiwi-fulfils-undertakings-to-fma (reporting that 136 (of 1,037) investors had opted to return their shares for a refund, leading the company to repay, in total, roughly NZ$460,000).

entrepreneurs to voluntarily and accurately disclose key information about their companies, regardless of legal obligation of mandatory disclosure. They must disclose information if they hope to attract investors, and they must be honest in their disclosures, or they face civil and potentially criminal liability.

2. Online Reputation

Investment crowdfunding is not anonymous, and it does not even take place in private. Rather, the sales pitches, discussions, and disclosures all take place in full view of the public on the internet, and the entrepreneur's personal social media pages are often linked directly from the hosting platform. The effect is that an entrepreneur raising money via crowdfunding puts his reputation on the line, in a very public way.

Entrepreneurs, like all of us, have a powerful interest in maintaining a good reputation as an honest and reliable person. This constrains them from acting opportunistically—in other words, personal reputation is a powerful private method for reducing information asymmetry and agency costs as well.

A person's reputation is a valuable asset that takes years to build up, yet it can be easily tarnished, creating a powerful incentive for good behavior. This has always been true, but it has a special intensity on the internet, the site of investment crowdfunding. On the web, everyone's online reputation is subject to round-the-clock monitoring and review—and the internet never forgets. Any misbehavior can be immediately and widely denounced on social media sites like Facebook, LinkedIn, or Twitter, with immediate and long-term consequences for the alleged offender.

Internet pressure is an exceptionally powerful method of enforcing both the law and social norms. For instance, a slew of teenagers have seen their college admissions offers revoked because they posted racist content online, often in response to online petitions and other internet-based calls for action by students and alumni. "In some cases, the revoked admissions offers are the results of concerted efforts by teenagers who have leveraged large social media followings and created Google spreadsheets to collect and document racist and offensive behavior with screenshots, videos and the names of those involved."[31] It is certainly true, as some privacy scholars emphasize, that there are significant downsides to "internet shaming" and online pressure campaigns, including a lack of due process, and the prospects of mob rule and vigilantism.[32] Be that as it may, it

---

[31] Dan Levin, *Colleges Rescinding Admissions Offers as Racist Social Media Posts Emerge*, N.Y. TIMES, July 2, 2020.
[32] DANIEL J. SOLOVE, THE FUTURE OF REPUTATION 94–102 (2007).

76 PRIVATE ORDERING

works, and the prospect of being shamed online should keep crowdfunding entrepreneurs on (or at least close to) the straight and narrow.

The importance and fragility of one's reputation plays a key role in reducing information asymmetry between crowdfunding entrepreneurs and investors. First, reputations protect investors by reducing the chance that fraudulent or weak companies will pursue crowdfunding. An entrepreneur behind a low-quality or phony company would think twice before putting his name out there, for all to see, as the key person behind such a venture. If, as is likely, the truth will be revealed eventually, such an episode would greatly harm the entrepreneur's future prospects.

Second, the entrepreneur's interest in maintaining a reputation as honest and truthful encourages her to provide full and fair disclosure to potential investors—voluntarily. Whatever she discloses about the company is posted on the platform for all to see and remember. A rational entrepreneur may engage in a bit of puffery, but she will try to provide truthful information and avoid misleading statements or omissions that could look bad in hindsight. In short, reputation is an important method for addressing information asymmetry in investment crowdfunding.

Reputation also serves to directly reduce agency costs among entrepreneurs that raise money via crowdfunding. If it turns out that a set of managers at a crowdfunded company slack off or use company assets for their own benefit, leading to poor returns or total failure of the business, those managers may have their reputations damaged by disgruntled investors who complain on the internet. This is analogous to the longstanding requirement that the names and addresses of the directors be listed on the certificate of incorporation, thus allowing potential investors to see who is behind the company (and whose reputation should suffer if the company is a fraud or if management squanders their investments).

In practice, it does seem that the threat of a besmirched reputation helps keep entrepreneurs honest when raising money via investment crowdfunding. The entrepreneur, board members, and key personnel are always prominently listed on the crowdfunding platform hosting the offer, often with a direct link to their LinkedIn or other social media profile, thereby putting their online reputation on the line.

The concept of "brand ambassadors" enhances the power of reputation as a constraint. Crowdfunding investors often play a dual role with the company: in addition to being financial investors, they are also brand ambassadors, meaning loyal customers or clients that the company can rely upon for word-of-mouth and social media advertising, beta testing, and the like.[33] (The term "brand

---

[33] Darian M. Ibrahim, *Crowdfunding Signals*, 53 GA. L. REV. 197, 220–21 (2018) (discussing the value of "brand advocates"); BIRCHAL, FUNDED!: CROWD-SOURCED FUNDING (CSF) IN AUSTRALIA FY2022, at 28 (2022) (discussing "brand ambassadors").

ambassador" isn't important—others might say "evangelist," "advocate," or "champion.") In addition, the audience finds the brand ambassadors to be particularly credible, because they are their friends and family.

Brand ambassadors are valuable to every type of company, but they are absolutely vital for startup companies. By definition, they are not household names and need to market and promote the company to potential customers, clients, employees, and others. Most of the time, this sort of promotion costs the company money; advertisements are not free. But brand ambassadors promote the company just because they love it.

A core of passionate users and supporters is among the most powerful methods of marketing. For example, brand ambassadors wear t-shirts with the company logo. When the company posts an announcement to social media, brand ambassadors will "like" or retweet it to their online friends. When the company has a new product, brand ambassadors will buy it and sometimes even post a review on the internet.

This is easy to see with a rock band, like the Grateful Dead—which must have sold more t-shirts than records—but it even extends to seemingly ordinary companies doing everyday types of business. Consider the example of Monzo, an online bank in the United Kingdom, whose customers are apparently gaga for the service.

Monzo launched an investment crowdfunding campaign in 2016, and specifically sought to raise money from its banking customers: "We're the first bank to enable customers to become shareholders through a crowdfunding platform," said the founder at the time. "Our customers are already helping us to build the bank from the ground up by alpha testing the mobile app."[34] These brand ambassadors responded in force, and the company raised £1 million within two minutes of the listing going live on Crowdcube.[35]

The company returned to Crowdcube two years later and raised £20 million from its brand ambassadors and others. In its formal prospectus, Monzo specifically called out to its customers and invited them to participate, saying that it "could have raised up to £20 million from venture capital firms, but wanted to give Eligible Monzo Customers a chance to invest" through crowdfunding.[36] The founder again described the importance of brand ambassadors to the company, as both customers and investors:

---

[34] *Mondo Takes Just a Minute to Raise £1 Million*, FINEXTRA (Mar. 3, 2016), https://www.finextra.com/newsarticle/28557/mondo-takes-just-a-minute-to-raise-1-million.

[35] *The Story of Monzo*, CROWDCUBE, https://www.crowdcube.com/explore/raising/success-stories/monzo (last visited June 18, 2022).

[36] MONZO BANK LTD., PROSPECTUS (Nov. 26, 2018), https://monzo.com/static/docs/crowdfunding-prospectus-2018.pdf. Eligible Monzo Customers was defined as all approved customers over the age of eighteen and resident in the United KingdomUK.

Our community is the heart and soul of everything we do, so it was a no brainer for us to [invite] the people who believe in our vision the most to become shareholders. . . . Our shareholders are some of our most valuable and engaged customers. On average they are 43% more active and are nearly 3x more likely to tell a friend about us. It's not why we do it but it's great to be able to include them in our journey.[37]

The value of brand ambassadors to Monzo—and countless other companies—is clear. But there is danger as well. If they feel mistreated as investors, the brand ambassadors could boycott the company and encourage others to do the same. If a company were to mistreat their investors/customers through misvaluation, agency costs, opportunistic exits, misleading behavior, or otherwise, these brand ambassadors could quickly turn into "brand assassins." Instead of extolling the company on Twitter and Facebook, they could write angry missives, causing real damage to the company and its prospects.

The fear of such turnabout by a crowdfunding company's investors/customers serves to protect it from misbehavior on the part of the founders and management. The larger and more passionate the army of brand ambassadors, the more power they hold over management. Thus, gathering a large group of investors through crowdfunding, at least for a consumer company, is a way for management to credibly commit to treating them fairly. Combining this idea with the wisdom of the crowd explored earlier, we see that the larger the crowd, the better protected each member will be.

Brand ambassadors is a real-world phenomenon. Around the world, experience shows that momentum is key to a successful crowdfunding campaign. To generate that momentum, market participants all agree that a campaign needs to have a prearranged set of investors ready to pledge as soon as the listing goes online. One of the best ways to generate this sort of ready-to-go interest is if the company already has a preexisting crowd of brand ambassadors who are willing to invest and spread the word. Platforms count on companies to use Facebook, email blasts, and other methods to get their brand ambassadors to support the offering.

Key evidence of the brand ambassador phenomenon is that most crowdfunding investors make a single investment. This suggests that many of them registered with the crowdfunding platform specifically in order to make that investment, rather than learned of it from the platform. Who would do that? Brand ambassadors. And once they have invested, the company has a double reason to

---

[37] *The Story of Monzo*, CROWDCUBE, https://www.crowdcube.com/explore/raising/success-stor ies/monzo (last visited June 18, 2022).

keep them happy and treat them fairly. This protects all the investors, even those who are not themselves brand ambassadors.

For example, Invivo Wines, the first New Zealand company to hit the NZ$2 million issuer limit, called upon its 20,000 Facebook followers to participate. They responded with pledges of nearly NZ$800,000 before the campaign even began, giving it tremendous momentum and propelling it to the NZ$2 million mark. These are Invivo's key customers—and they are now also investors in the company. The company has every reason to treat them well, for if they feel abused, they might not only stop drinking Invivo wine, but they may well vent their dissatisfaction on social media, relentlessly.

There are limits to the effectiveness of reputation as a means of reducing agency costs. For one thing, crowdfunding investors may not be able to detect shirking or mismanagement that does not lead to disastrous results. If the company does fine, but could have done great, the managers and promoters are unlikely to pay a reputational fine. As such, reputation may be more effective at preventing egregious opportunism, rather than modest slacking.

Another limitation is that reputation is most constraining for "repeat players" ' but many, perhaps most, crowdfunding entrepreneurs will be one-time players, seeking funding just once and never returning to the crowdfunding market. Like a traveling salesman from the railroad days, they may be willing to stretch the truth and not care much about their reputation over the long term, since they'll be long gone by then.

That said, at least some crowdfunding entrepreneurs may well be repeat players. An entrepreneur who successfully finances a startup through crowdfunding may well be back months or years later to seek a new round of funding, or even solicit capital for a different company entirely. (As a matter of fact, this does happen; certain companies have even come back three and four times to raise additional money from the crowd.) More importantly, though, is the fact that an entrepreneur's online reputation is not limited to the crowdfunding arena. Misbehavior as a crowdfunding entrepreneur could adversely affect one's reputation for future job opportunities, or even romantic ones.

To summarize, the value to an entrepreneur of maintaining a good reputation—especially with her company's brand ambassadors—is an important force that serves to reduce information asymmetry and agency costs in investment crowdfunding.

3. Digital Trail

Because investment crowdfunding takes place entirely on the internet, every action and utterance is monitored and tracked in a digital format. This indelible

80 PRIVATE ORDERING

data trail ties a person to their online crowdfunding activity forever, thereby reducing information asymmetry and agency costs.

Fraud, misbehavior, and opportunism can happen anywhere, but there is
reason to believe that investment crowdfunding is a less fertile ground for
con artists than many other locations, both in the physical world and online.
Consider first the former. The original securities laws were enacted in the early
1900s, at a time when aggressive salesmen roamed the land, offering deals that
were sometimes too good to be true. These men used aliases and tended to "fly
by night" from one town to the next, making it difficult to track them down
when the investment turned out to be a sham. Even today, there is no shortage
of smooth talkers at golf courses, churches, and elsewhere who trick people into
participating in phony investment schemes.

The social circumstances of investment crowdfunding are very different. Unlike those anonymous salesmen from a century ago, crowdfunding
entrepreneurs are all individually identified by their social media presence. Moreover, there is nowhere to run off to, as the internet is everywhere.
Entrepreneurs and investors alike must create a user name and password, link
a bank account, and so forth before participating on a crowdfunding platform.
The result is a very clear digital trail of precisely who said what when. This deters
misleading claims, market manipulation, and other misbehavior, since it can be
traced back to a person so easily.

To demonstrate the power of the digital trail, consider the case of urban
bicycle-sharing programs, which originated in European cities in the 1960s.
These early systems were free and anonymous; there was no record of who
checked out which bike, making it impossible to monitor their behavior. These
early systems failed because the bicycles were promptly stolen or destroyed, as
might have been expected with no way to place responsibility for a given bike on
a specific person. Even as late as the 1990s, free and anonymous bike-sharing systems were launched in cities including Cambridge (UK) and Boulder, Colorado.
In both places, the systems had to be canceled due to bike theft.

In the 2000s, however, bike-sharing became a well-functioning phenomenon
in many cities around the world, including Paris, New York, and Washington,
D.C. What changed from the 1990s to the 2000s? People did not get more an-
gelic. Rather, there was a revolution in information technology that allowed for
effective and inexpensive monitoring of bike sharers. These new systems used
computer-based systems that generally require people to swipe their personal
credit card to release a bike, thereby creating a digital tether between the renter
and the bike. Thanks to this digital tracking, people take better care of the bikes,
knowing that they can easily be found, and their credit card dunned, if they steal
or damage them.

For another example, consider plagiarism. In the predigital era, it was very difficult to determine whether a given book or article was plagiarized, as it required a careful comparison of the two hard copies. In the digital age, by contrast, plagiarism is exceedingly easy to detect thanks to the availability of electronic methods such as the "compare" function on Microsoft Word. This has led to numerous instances in recent years where high-profile authors were revealed as plagiarists.[38]

The experiences of bike-sharing and plagiarism apply by analogy to investment crowdfunding. Because all investment activity takes place on the internet, the resulting digital trail can be easily monitored, thereby reducing agency costs and information asymmetry.

All that said, it is certainly true that the internet has seen its fair share of investment scams, such as regarding ICOs and NFTs, as well as email phishing, and much else. But investment crowdfunding is fundamentally different from these other forms of online activity. In these other fraud-prone arenas, bad actors generally communicate and deal directly with the investors, without any sort of middleman or independent oversight. Investment crowdfunding, by contrast, is always conducted through an independent platform that stands between entrepreneurs and investors. The platform oversees the deal, with the result that a fraudster would need to pull the wool over the eyes of two parties, not just one. And, as mentioned previously in this chapter, it behooves platforms to vet companies carefully before putting them in front of potential investors, as their gatekeeping function is closely tied to their success.

C. INVESTORS

Finally, let us move to three methods of private ordering that relate to investors: wisdom of the crowd, syndication, and remote monitoring.

1. Wisdom of the Crowd

Crowdfunding represents a leap into the unknown. Of all the companies seeking funding, how should a potential crowdfunding investor pick which one to buy into? She would obviously want to invest in one that will turn out to be successful. But it is challenging, perhaps even impossible, for any given individual to

---

[38] *E.g.*, Jonathan Martin, *Senator's Thesis Turns Out to be Remix of Others' Works, Uncited*, N.Y. TIMES, July 23, 2014, at A1; Steven Levingston, *Portions of Goodall's "Seeds" Were Lifted from Other Works*, WASH. POST, Mar. 20, 2013, at C1.

82   PRIVATE ORDERING

accurately predict which will grow and which will fail. Fortunately, investors are not all on their own—they have the whole crowd to guide them.

a. Theory of the Wisdom of the Crowd

Research from many areas shows that large groups of people—crowds—can collectively do a better job at finding facts and forecasting the future than lone individuals, even experts. This phenomenon is enhanced when people have a financial stake in being right, as is the case for investment crowdfunding. Furthermore, the literature shows that it doesn't matter whether the crowd is rational or holds any expertise in the relevant field. This idea of the wisdom of the crowd is a powerful tool to help crowdfunding investors find worthwhile companies to support.[39]

The wisdom of the crowd can be seen in numerous areas. For one example, the Iowa Electronic Markets—an online futures market where traders buy and sell contracts whose payoffs depend on the outcome of elections and other events— have been able to predict presidential and other elections more accurately than traditional polls. For another, consider the Nenana Ice Classic, an annual betting pool dating from 1917 where Alaskans try to predict the exact date and time when the ice covering the Tanana River will break up, marking the start of spring. It turns out that the average of all the participants' predictions is at least as accurate as any expert model in forecasting the ice breakup. Many other examples could be given.

Although it occurs without direct communication between participants, the wisdom of the crowd is not due to some mystical phenomenon or mental convergence. Rather, it is a simple mathematical consequence of averaging.

Take the example of a weight-judging competition at a county fair. Tickets cost $1 and each contestant writes down a guess as to the cow's weight; at the end of the day the cow is weighed and whoever's guess is closest wins $100. Assume that the cow weighs precisely 1,000 pounds. Some contestants guess too low (say, 500, 750, and 900 pounds), others guess too high (1,100, 1,200, 1,800 pounds). None of them are spot on, and the outliers (500, 1,800 pounds) are really way off. But the average of these six guesses is 1,058 pounds, not far from the truth, and better than any of the individual contestants.

Vitally, as more and more people participate, the average response comes closer and closer to the truth. In one real-life example of a weight-judging competition at an English county fair in England in 1905, roughly 800 contestants tried their luck, including butchers and farmers, who had some expertise in guessing animals' weights, and lots of regular folks with only general knowledge

---

[39] JAMES SUROWIECKI, THE WISDOM OF CROWDS: HOW THE MANY ARE SMARTER THAN THE FEW AND HOW COLLECTIVE WISDOM SHAPES BUSINESS, ECONOMIES, SOCIETIES AND NATIONS (2004).

of such matters. The actual weight of the ox in question was 1,198 pounds, and the closest guess by a single contestant was 1,207 pounds—not bad. But the average of all the guesses of all the contestants—the wisdom of the crowd—was 1,197 pounds—practically perfect.[40]

The crowd is not necessarily wise; it depends on the crowd's errors being all in random directions, rather than consistently off to one side or another. In other words, the wisdom of the crowd requires a diverse crowd of people with different knowledge, skills, and perspectives, as they can be expected to make different errors from each other and thereby balance each other out. A homogenous crowd, by contrast, will tend toward the same errors, so even their average answer will be off the mark, like a group of weight guessers who all tend to guess high.

b. Wisdom of the Crowd in Investment Crowdfunding

The wisdom of the crowd suits investment crowdfunding to a T. Crowds are inherent to the form—indeed it is in the name. Moreover, the investors it attracts are as diverse as possible, since it is open to the broad public, with no restrictions based on of wealth, geography, ethnicity, gender, or anything else. This is not to say that the investor body is diverse in every way imaginable, but merely that, by inviting everyone to participate, crowdfunding investors are a particularly diverse group.

Now, deciding which companies to invest in is more complex and open-ended than predicting when the ice will break up. But the wisdom of the crowd theory applies to complex questions too. Moreover, the ultimate question in crowdfunding investing is binary—invest or not—so while the considerations are complex, the ultimate answer is either yes or no.

On crowdfunding platforms, investors select the investments that seem most promising to them. Over time, as the crowd of investors weighs in, some companies will prove popular with the crowd, others not so. The net effect is a collective prediction of which investment opportunities are the most attractive, like a stock exchange with no securities analysts, no CNBC, and no *Wall Street Journal*. One might expect chaos and anarchy, but the wisdom of the crowd theory suggests that the investors can, as a matter of Hayekian "spontaneous order," collectively succeed in separating the wheat from the chaff.

A typical feature of investment crowdfunding platforms is a "progress bar" that shows, in real time, the amount pledged to a given company. As the amount increases, the progress bar fills in more and more, offering a clear visual representation of the popularity of the company and how close it is to its funding

---

[40] James Surowiecki, The Wisdom of Crowds: How the Many Are Smarter Than the Few and How Collective Wisdom Shapes Business, Economies, Societies and Nations xi–xiii (2004) (describing Francis Galton, *Vox Populi*, 75 Nature 450 (1907)).

84 PRIVATE ORDERING

target. The progress bar informs all members of the crowd whether, and to what extent, a given company is supported by their fellows. This sort of information is necessary for the wisdom of the crowd to function.

Few members of the crowd will be experts on any field in which they might invest, but all of them will be able to add something to the collective effort. One key lesson from Hayek is that information is not concentrated in some central repository. Rather, the knowledge required to transact, build companies, and generate economic growth is splintered among countless people, each of whom holds only a small piece of it. By coming together on crowdfunding portals and voting with their dollars, members of the crowd will each effectively contribute a part of the puzzle. Over time, the full picture can emerge.

There are many different indicators of quality investment opportunities, and different members of the crowd will recognize and appreciate them. If a company holds a patent, that is a positive signal, and one that will be widely recognized. But the value of the certain type of patent is a more nuanced signal that may only be understood by certain people, leading them to invest—or not.

Some indicators are widely understood, like if an entrepreneur holds a degree from Oxford University or MIT, that is a positive signal of his intelligence and perseverance. Yet many other clear signals are only familiar to certain people, based on their knowledge and perspective, and would not be perceived by most members of the crowd. Those people, if sufficiently impressed, would invest and perhaps cause others to take note. The latter group would see that some people apparently think very highly of a given opportunity and take that as an endorsement without knowing the rationale for it. This is an illustration of Hayek's core claim that market activity is a powerful way for information to be tacitly shared among many people.

Take for example a crowdfunding company whose founder graduated from Seoul National University (SNU) in Korea. Compared to Oxford or MIT, relatively few members of the crowd would know that SNU is one of the leading universities in the world, as selective as those schools, and on par with them in many other metrics. Those knowledgeable investors, impressed with the entrepreneur's credential, could vote with their dollars and advance the progress bar. Other members of the crowd, who know nothing of SNU's reputation or success in training business leaders, would see that the progress bar is increasing but not know why. But that is the point; they don't have to know why—they only have to appreciate that other investors must know something that they don't, and trust in the wisdom of the crowd.

The wisdom of the crowd benefits crowdfunding companies as well as investors. A startup company that does not appeal to venture capitalists, angel investors, and other traditional sources of startup funding might yet catch the eye of a few members of the crowd. Their willingness to invest may, in turn, influence others to give the company a chance. Notably, the large size and heterogeneity of crowdfunding investors increases the chance that a diamond in the rough will be recognized as such.

There is a potential dark side, however, as the wisdom of the crowd can sometimes transform into a "madness" of the crowd.[41] History abounds with examples where investors have acted with a mob or herd mentality and piled into investments regardless of their fundamental value—with disastrous results. In the seventeenth century, "tulip mania" gripped the Netherlands, with tulip bulbs skyrocketing in price and then crashing to earth, ruining the buyers. A century later, the United Kingdom experienced the "South Sea Bubble," where stock in the South Sea Company likewise soared and then crashed, leading to widespread and devastating losses. More recently, the United States experienced back-to-back dot-com and housing bubbles in the early twenty-first century, again with terrible conclusions. The point is that crowds of investors are not always wise; sometimes they whip themselves into a frenzy and buy in at extraordinary prices that eventually collapse to their fundamental value.

Investment crowdfunding is certainly susceptible to the madness of the crowd. Just as with tulip mania or the dot-com bubble, investors surely may act with a mob or herd mentality and crowd into a poor investment choice. On the other hand, the innate human tendency toward "groupthink" may be less of a problem for investment crowdfunding than in other arenas, such as the traditional stock market or housing.

Compared to those traditional fields of investment, there is relatively little peer pressure to follow the lead of other investors into crowdfunded companies. For one thing, crowdfunding investors are not tied tightly together by the usual social bonds of neighborhood or church membership. They come from all over the country and may not even personally know any of their fellows. The lack of face-to-face contact in crowdfunding may reduce the likelihood of the sort of mimicry that is found among groups of animals and people. Their only connection is over the internet, a place where people feel especially free to disagree with one another. For these reasons, they are likely to feel and act independently of each other, and such independence is anathema to the madness-of-the-crowd effect.

All that said, herding is certainly a significant risk for crowdfunding investors, and it may not be solvable by private ordering alone. This is the sort of issue where legal regulation can be helpful, and, as we will see in the next two chapters, every jurisdiction we will study has indeed responded to this concern by adopting a so-called "issuer limit." This is a dollar-value limit on the amount of money that

---

[41] *See generally* CHARLES MACKAY, EXTRAORDINARY POPULAR DELUSIONS AND THE MADNESS OF CROWDS (1841).

86 PRIVATE ORDERING

a company may legally raise through investment crowdfunding each year. In the United States, the limit is $5 million, in Canada it is C$1.5 million.

The precise level does not matter; the key for present purposes is that the issuer limit prevents herding from taking off to the level of tulip mania or the dotcom bubble. No matter how excited people get about a given company, only a limited number can herd in before the issuer limit is reached and the platform has to conclude the offer.

In practice, investment in crowdfunding companies appears to follow a "power law," not a normal distribution, though it is too soon to know whether this represents the wisdom of the crowd (good) or herding (bad). Let me explain.

If crowdfunding investors all did their homework and acted independently, without regard for what the others are doing, they should be expected to allocate their investments in a "normal" distribution, whereby the best companies get the most capital, medium companies get a medium amount of capital, and low-quality companies get a little bit of capital. With enough companies of differing quality, and enough investors participating, we would see a smooth distribution where, say, and one-third meet or exceed their target, one-third raise half of their funding target, and one-third raise almost nothing.

But that is not at all what happens in real life, which is more like feast or famine. If a company can reach a certain level—maybe 50 percent of its funding target—it is almost certain to reach and probably exceed its goal. This is because investors tend to congregate in the companies that seem popular with the crowd, and this effect has momentum that cascades on itself (leading to the formal name "information cascade") and accelerates as it grows.[42]

For example, online education startup Everydae launched an investment crowdfunding campaign in January 2020 with a $200,000 funding target and a three-month deadline. The company hit that target in March, and kept going, accelerating all the way to the finish line. In late April, one week to go before the deadline, investors had pledged roughly $600,000. A few days later, the number was $800,000, and the day after that $1 million.[43] The chart went vertical, in other words, and it only stopped because the offering was abruptly cut off by the legal issuer limit (roughly $1 million at the time).

If a company cannot capture those first batch of investors, however, and get the ball rolling, its campaign is unlikely to succeed. Unpopular listings tend to remain unpopular. Unless a company can catch the attention of the crowd, it will

---

[42] Silvio Vismara, *Information Cascades Among Investors in Equity Crowdfunding*, 42 ENTREP. THEORY & PRAC. 467, 487 (2018) (An "information cascade" happens when "late investors base their decision to invest on their own information, but also try to infer extra information from other investors' behavior. This leads to an acceleration of investments if early investors committed money.").

[43] EVERYDAE, www.wefunder.com/everydae/updates. I also spoke personally with the CEO.

almost certainly stay in the doldrums and never even come close to hitting its funding target.[44] I don't need to embarrass anybody by offering examples—but there are many.

In the end, we have a distribution where many companies raise almost nothing, while many other companies go all the way to their funding target and then often far beyond it.[45] Very few companies fall between these extremes, however, since any company that raises some significant portion of its target will almost certainly reach that target, due to cascading behavior. No company raises 90 percent of its target and then falls short. It just doesn't happen.[46] This is an example of what is known as a power law distribution, and it appears to be inherent to investment crowdfunding, regardless of jurisdiction.

The power law distribution suggests one of two things. First, à la Hayek, it could mean that the crowd of investors are, through their crowdfunding pledges, effectively sharing their individual knowledge and creating a collective wisdom of the crowd that can effectively choose the best opportunities available on the platforms. Second, it could mean that investors are mindlessly herding into investments simply because others are doing so.

Which of these scenarios is more accurate? We don't really know, at least not yet, but there is some reason to think that the crowd is more wise than mad. For one thing, investors have proved much more likely to pile in to an offer when it has a known, or at least public, "lead investor," a subject we will return to later in the chapter. These lead investors may not be perfect, but their participation is a legitimate signal of quality.

For another, the companies that fail to capture the attention of the crowd seem, anecdotally, like poor prospects. You can't prove a negative, but I have yet to see a case of a company that seems absolutely wonderful but cannot catch a bid on a crowdfunding platform. All of this suggests that the crowd is making decisions that are at least roughly coherent.

c. Lay Expertise

Crowdfunding investors, unlike angel investors or VCs, are ordinary people from all walks of life. When selecting investments, they lack the sort of technical expertise that angel investors and VCs possess, often from a prior career in a given field. An angel who herself invented and commercialized a medical device might seek to finance up-and-coming entrepreneurs who are doing the

---

[44] Unless the funding target is set absurdly low, which it often is, as we'll see in the next chapter.

[45] For empirical support of this idea, *see* Silvio Vismara, *Information Cascades Among Investors in Equity Crowdfunding*, 42 ENTREP. THEORY & PRAC. 467, 480–82 (2018) (reporting that every company that reached 80% funded ultimately reached its target).

[46] Silvio Vismara, *Information Cascades Among Investors in Equity Crowdfunding*, 42 ENTREP. THEORY & PRAC. 467, 481 fig.3 (2018) (demonstrating this result in a sample of 132 offerings on UK investment crowdfunding platform Crowdcube in 2014).

88   PRIVATE ORDERING

same thing. By using their technical expertise in this way, angels stand a good chance of investing in promising companies at a fair valuation, avoiding fraudulent ones, and effectively monitoring a company's progress after investing. In other words, angels and VCs use technical expertise to reduce the three fundamental challenges of uncertainty, information asymmetry, and agency costs.

Crowdfunding investors lack this sort of technical expertise. They are regular people, not experts in the field. As Hayek has taught, however, everyone from every background knows certain things that others do not. Their expertise may not be technical or scientific, as with angel investors, but science is "not the sum of all knowledge," wrote Hayek.[47]

Rather, there is another body of "very important but unorganized knowledge": the dispersed bits of information that each person happens to know because of their unique experience, skills, and perspective, what Hayek called "the knowledge of the particular circumstances of time and place."[48] Thanks to this sort of lay expertise, every individual "has some advantage over all others because he possesses unique information of which beneficial use might be made."[49]

Hayek's ideas describe investment crowdfunding well. Each potential investor holds different bits of useful information relating to crowdfunding companies, and each can make beneficial use of that information. For example, an avid video gamer would be familiar with what makes a good game and other aspects of the business in a way that few others could match; such a person could focus all his crowdfunding investments on video games. Other examples can be given: a fitness instructor can spot a promising exercise machine; a home cook knows which small appliances might succeed.

None of these types of knowledge can really be called technical expertise, but the point is that the efforts of each crowdfunding investor to use his own personal knowledge to make wise investments can reduce the trio of problems and increase his likelihood of a good outcome.

d. Crowdsourced Investment Analysis
Beyond the tacit collaboration of the wisdom of the crowd, which relies on investors simply observing one another's decisions, crowdfunding investors can take the more direct route and actually communicate with one another about a given company. As crowdfunding takes place in an online environment, it is easy for investors to communicate their views directly on the hosting platform. Their

---

[47] F.A. Hayek, *The Use of Knowledge in Society*, 35 AM. ECON. REV. 519, 521 (1945).
[48] F.A. Hayek, *The Use of Knowledge in Society*, 35 AM. ECON. REV. 519, 521–22 (1945).
[49] F.A. Hayek, *The Use of Knowledge in Society*, 35 AM. ECON. REV. 519, 521–22 (1945).

collected sentiments can function as a crowdsourced body of investment analysis that reduces uncertainty and information asymmetry.

For public companies, investors can make decisions based on the opinions of professional investment analysts. These highly paid Wall Street analysts are experts in accounting, business, and technology, and they publish their opinions in carefully researched notes and articles. At first blush, it seems doubtful that crowdsourced investment analysis, shared by laypeople—for free—could possibly be anywhere as useful or accurate as that produced on Wall Street.

Crowdsourcing, however, has shown itself to be quite effective in numerous fields, even outshining the efforts of small groups of experts. One famous example is Wikipedia, the crowdsourced encyclopedia that is said to be about as reliable as other leading encyclopedias. As another example, NASA uses crowdsourcing to sort through millions of photographs of Earth taken from space, on the theory that someone familiar with a given locale could easily identify it, whereas few others, nor computers, could readily do so. These sorts of efforts translate well to crowdfunding. Just as thousands of people contribute to Wikipedia and perform other crowdsourced work for free, potential investors can investigate companies and share their findings with the crowd.

As for expertise and credentials, few potential investors will be able to match Wall Street analysts—but some surely will, as discussed previously. If there is a large enough crowd, there is sure to be somebody with expertise in any given field. Moreover, many crowdfunding companies already have a preexisting community of customers or users who are especially knowledgeable about that company. If these sorts of experts share their knowledge on the platform, then the whole crowd can become well informed.

Beyond formal expertise and direct experience, however, is Hayek's idea that practically every member of the crowd knows something that others do not; something particular to their personal experience, skills, and perspective. Each of these distributed bits of information standing alone may not be significant. Gathered together, they constitute a sort of collective wisdom on the prospects of a given company.

Consider again the earlier example of an entrepreneur with a degree from SNU. Only a small portion of the crowd would know that SNU is a highly selective university that produces a lot of CEOs for major companies, thus making the founder's degree from SNU a strongly positive signal. But it would be a simple matter for one of these people who are knowledgeable about SNU to post a note to the platform and share that information with the crowd.

Importantly, the structure of investment crowdfunding creates a financial incentive for crowdfunding investors to share information with one another. This is the result of the interplay between two common components of crowdfunding markets and regulation. First, the United States and most

90 PRIVATE ORDERING

other jurisdictions impose a cap on how much each investor may invest in crowdfunding opportunities, as we will see in the next two chapters. Second, the near-universal practice around the world is to use an all-or-nothing crowdfunding model, meaning that a company must announce a minimum fundraising target in advance, and only receives the money if it raises at least that much.

The combined effect of these two rules is that a crowdfunding investor who spots a great opportunity has an economic incentive to share her views widely. The investor cap effectively prevents any individual investor from funding a company entirely on her own. If an investor keeps her information secret, and the company does not catch the attention of other investors, it will not reach its target and the offer will fail, with the result that she loses the chance to invest. By contrast, if she shares her information with the crowd, the company has a better chance of reaching its target. In this way, those with valuable information about crowdfunding companies have a direct economic incentive to freely share that information with their fellow investors.

There are a few caveats to this line of thinking. For one, it only provides an economic rationale for sharing positive news, as opposed to negative news. If someone has reason to think that a certain crowdfunding company has poor prospects, they may lack an economic incentive to take the time to share their analysis, because they simply don't care whether the company reaches its goal. That being said, experience shows that many people are eager to air negative views online. A disgruntled customer or someone with a negative point of view may need little incentive to prod them to share their opinions.

A second caveat is that it really only applies to retail investors, as "accredited" investors are frequently exempt from the investor cap. The result is that a single accredited investor who spots an attractive investment can simply buy up enough shares herself to ensure that the company reaches its funding target—or could even buy up every share on offer. While this is literally true, it is very unlikely in practice, because accredited investors are able to buy into a company using a method other than crowdfunding. If such an investor actually wanted to invest a huge amount in a crowdfunding company, she could do so through a direct investment, rather than go through the crowdfunding platform—and probably save on fees. Indeed, this is commonly done, as discussed later regarding syndication.

One final concern with crowdsourced investment analysis is that it might give rise to market manipulation. For instance, a promoter could ask a confederate to post false information in order to obtain the initial investment—or could even do so himself using a pseudonym. Simple fraud like this is surely possible, but the gravity of the consequences and the chances of detection are both relatively high, while the potential returns are rather modest, for the reasons explained above regarding the digital trail.

Crowdsourced investment analysis has become a regular feature of investment crowdfunding. This usually takes place directly on the investment crowdfunding platform hosting a given offering. On the web page devoted to a given offering, it will include a "Question-and-Answer" or "Discussion" section, where potential investors post comments and ask questions of the entrepreneur and he responds.

Speaking anecdotally, many of these comments and questions are simplified versions of the types of things that Wall Street analysts ask on quarterly conference calls with public company CEOs: Can you explain this or that assumption that goes into the valuation? Is there a conflict of interest because of this or that? Please provide detail on this or that subsidiary. And the entrepreneur goes on the site and publishes a response for potential to investors to consider. If the entrepreneur refused to respond to questions (I have not seen this in practice), people would probably click away real fast.

Through these questions and comments, crowdfunding investors crowdsource their collective analysis of the company. This happens in the United States, as it is legally required by the JOBS Act and Regulation Crowdfunding provision on "communication channels." But it also happens in the United Kingdom, where it is not legally required, and in New Zealand, where it is only encouraged by the law.

In the United States, Regulation Crowdfunding mandates the communication channels be accessible by the public but that only registered members of a given platform may post comments or questions there. However, in the liberal countries of the United Kingdom and New Zealand, there are no legal rules on these points, so it is interesting to see how they handle it as a matter of private ordering.

In the United Kingdom and New Zealand, the Q&A section is usually restricted to registered users of the platform (as in America) and is hidden from public view (in contrast with America). This is not universally true, but it is the common practice, at least among the leading platforms. The public can neither post nor review the posts of platform members and entrepreneurs, unless they first register with the platform (which is a fairly simple process).

Leading American platforms have added their own tweaks to enhance the utility of crowdsourced investment analysis. StartEngine, for its part, notes how many previous investments each user has made on the platform. The effect is that the questions and comments posted by veterans with many investments under their belts are taken more seriously than those of the rookies. And Wefunder includes on most offering pages a video interview conducted by a knowledgeable investor who quizzes the entrepreneur about the business for the benefit of the crowd.

92   PRIVATE ORDERING

2. Syndication

At the opposite end of the spectrum from the wisdom of the crowd is the idea of "syndication."

This is a method often used by angel investors, whereby they invest in groups or "syndicates." Under this model, one "active" or "lead" investor, often knowledgeable in the relevant industry, researches a company and the proposed terms of investment, and then reports back to the group. If the lead investor likes the company and recommends that the group invest, the other angels contribute cash to the investment but do little, if any, of their own independent research or analysis; they depend and rely on the expertise and diligence of the lead investor.

The members of the group take turns playing the role of lead investor, thus sharing the burden. Sometimes, the lead investor in an angel group will receive "carried interest" or "carry"—meaning a percentage of the profits—off the top of a successful exit as a payment for her efforts. For angel groups, syndication is efficient, as a single angel does most of the work, while all members of the syndicate reap the benefits.

In terms of the three fundamental challenges described in the previous chapter, syndication responds directly to both uncertainty and information asymmetry. The lead investor's knowledge and research gives confidence to the other angels, as does the fact that she is putting her money where her mouth is, by investing alongside the group.

Syndication can be adapted from the angel context to the crowdfunding environment, albeit with a few changes. First, in an investment crowdfunding campaign, the entirety of the crowd creates the syndicate, as crowdfunding is open to the whole public, with investors spread across the country. This stands in stark contrast to angel syndicates, which are members of a formal or informal club based in a certain city or region. While crowdfunding investors may not be able to have in-person meetings like their angel counterparts, online methods of sharing information make it easy for those interested in investment crowdfunding to discuss interesting prospects and share information.

Furthermore, crowdfunding lead investors may not be formally chosen or rotated intentionally, as in angel syndication. In investment crowdfunding, a lead investor is someone who invests a significant sum of money in a campaign, and prior to making the investment, conducts extensive due diligence, to the benefit of the crowd as a whole. They generally are identified, but not always. Notably, someone who takes on this role likely engages in this research and vetting also for their own benefit. That is, while most crowdfunding investments are small, often a few hundred dollars, for a lead investor, it's not worth the time to engage in extensive due diligence unless she plans to invest much more than that—likely

$50,000, $100,000, or more. A lead investor almost always qualifies as an "accredited" investor.

When a lead investor contributes a large amount on the same terms as those offered to the public, this serves as a credible signal to the rest of the crowd of two important points. First, the mere fact that the lead investor can put in such a large slug of cash suggests that she is a relatively wealthy person who has presumably found financial success in the past. This bodes well for her selection of this particular company as a worthwhile investment.

Second, because the lead investor puts in a large amount of her own money, the lead investor demonstrates to the crowd that she really has done her due diligence and believes in the company. Because she has so much "skin in the game," the crowd can trust that the lead investor has done a sufficiently thorough job vetting the company—otherwise, why would she put in so much cash herself? This allows the rest of the investors to follow her lead without having to conduct much due diligence themselves.

Syndication thus serves to reduce information asymmetry and uncertainty. It also helps reduce agency costs because management will not be operating in the dark after the money is disbursed to the company. Rather, because the lead investor is akin to an angel with a substantial stake in the company, he is likely to maintain a relatively close eye on management and try to ensure that they stay on the straight and narrow. The lead investor might even find it worthwhile to seek a seat on the board of directors, or travel to visit the company and talk with management from time to time. After all, she has a lot of money riding on the company—as well as her own reputation as a savvy investor who can pick winners.

Syndication, sometimes informal, has become a notable feature of the investment crowdfunding market around the world. In the United Kingdom, VC funds often serve as lead investors, and they put in large sums, sometimes as much as £1 million (approximately $1.35 million). In New Zealand, the practice has likewise become ubiquitous, as almost every offer that comes to market does so with a lead investor lined up beforehand. These lead investors sometimes put more than NZ$500,000 (approximately $325,000) in a single company, and pretty much every successful company has at least one investor who buys more than NZ$100,000 (approximately $65,000).

Some crowdfunding platforms have adopted the practice of officially identifying a lead investor for at least some of their campaigns. American platform Wefunder, for instance, has started to require that each company designate one person as the "Lead Investor," meaning "an investor who is familiar with the startup and decided to invest on the same terms as those offered" to the public.[50] Wefunder states how much the Lead Investor has invested in the company and

---

[50] *What is a Lead Investor*, WEFUNDER, https://help.wefunder.com/leads/what-is-a-lead-investor (last visited June 18, 2022).

gives her space to explain why she bought in. Other investors can ask the Lead Investor questions, and she can respond on the platform for all to see.

After the deal closes, the Lead Investor "is meant to advocate for investors," and she votes on their behalf, pursuant to a formal power of attorney (although she does not receive carry).[51] This is all roughly analogous to the traditional type of syndication as practiced by angel groups, but in a more inclusive, public forum.

Usually, the lead investor puts money directly into the crowdfunding offering, using the platform just like everybody else. Sometimes, however, companies have the lead investor buy in through an alternative method. (Among other things, this may cut down on fees.) This is typically done though a "Reg. D" offering in the United States, since the lead investor will almost always qualify as accredited. In those cases, the company would simply announce on the platform that "Ms. X [or Fund Y] has invested on the same terms as those offered below."[52]

This sort of "side-by-side" syndication has been especially important in New Zealand, where the law limits companies to raising only NZ$2 million (approximately $1.5 million) per year through investment crowdfunding. A company that wants to, and can, raise more than that will often enlist a VC fund to invest, say, NZ$1 million, on the same terms as the crowdfunding offer, but arranged in a one-on-one deal between the fund and the company. The platform will then tout this lead investment on its website and be in a position to raise a total of NZ$3 million.

Syndication brings together the power of expert investors, on the one hand, and the crowd, on the other, in a synergistic convergence. Syndication on crowdfunding platforms is a way for ordinary people to participate alongside VC funds and for VC funds to bring in additional capital to their portfolio companies.

Finally, for all the benefits that lead investors can provide, there are a few side effects to syndication that may be cause for concern. For one thing, in contrast to the foundational democratizing nature of crowdfunding, it requires a company seeking funding to find and impress one large investor, just as in the case of angel investing. To the extent that finding a lead investor is effectively required to get noticed and funded by the crowd, it shifts crowdfunding away from its egalitarian roots and favors those with connections to wealthy benefactors. Even so, the syndication model is still more inclusive than traditional angel investing, as it invites small investors to participate, while angel investing is the exclusive domain of accredited investors.

---

[51] *Can I Replace My Lead Investor? What If They Quit?*, WEFUNDER, https://help.wefunder.com/lead-investors/can-i-replace-my-lead-investor-what-if-they-quit (last visited Sept. 24, 2022).

[52] *Legal Primer for Founders*, WEFUNDER, https://help.wefunder.com/legal-primer (last visited Aug. 1, 2022) ("If you end up raising more than $5M in your Reg CF raise, we'll spin up a concurrent Regulation D, Rule 506(c) offering so you can raise an unlimited amount from accredited investors.").

Another concern over syndication is that small investors in a crowdfunded company may find themselves in a precarious position with respect to a single large lead investor. The latter could, for instance, use her dominant position to secure special benefits for herself at the expense of the crowd, such as participation in an exit or additional rounds of financing. However, even a lead investor in a crowdfunded company generally receives only a minority stake in the company, leaving ultimate power in the hands of the entrepreneur. In addition, companies that pursue crowdfunding do not want to alienate their small investors by giving preferential treatment to the lead investor. Among other things, these small investors may also be customers and even "brand ambassadors." Nevertheless, this is a real concern that bears notice.

3. Remote Monitoring

Consider again a bartender owner (the principal) who worries that the bartender (her agent) may have his fingers in the till. This is a form of agency cost, and it can be reduced if the principal monitors her agent, such as by installing a camera over the cash register. Even more effective would be for the owner to stand over the cashier's shoulder all day. But as effective as that type of monitoring would be, it would also be very costly, especially in terms of the owner's time. Indeed, at some point the cost of monitoring outweighs its benefits; the owner might be better off just letting the cashier steal a bit here and there. The key question, then, is how to monitor in a cost-effective way.

VCs and angel investors commonly serve on the board of directors of their portfolio companies and pay personal visits to check up on them. This keeps their managers working hard for the good of the company; in other words, it reduces agency costs. And the costs of such monitoring is pretty low, since they invest locally. It just means driving across town from time to time, or attending board meetings once per quarter.

These methods of monitoring make sense in the context of local VC and angel investing, but they do not apply to investment crowdfunding. For one thing, crowdfunding investors are dispersed across the land, so they cannot really have direct physical contact with the entrepreneurs they back. For another, the whole crowd obviously cannot join the board of directors—there aren't enough seats. For a third, crowdfunding investors usually have only a modest stake in any given company, compared to more significant sums invested by VCs and angels. With only a small investment, it hardly makes business sense for a crowdfunding investor to take the time to pay a personal visit to company headquarters.

Yet without any sort of post-investment monitoring, crowdfunding investors are at great risk for agency costs. Once an entrepreneur has the money, it is easy

96 PRIVATE ORDERING

for her to find ways to effectively spend it on herself, rather than advance the corporate venture. High salaries, decadent office perks, and hiring of friends and relatives are all real dangers in the absence of monitoring.

Fortunately, the online world of investment crowdfunding allows crowd-funding investors to employ high-tech, yet inexpensive, methods to monitor their companies from afar. Annual shareholder meetings can easily be conducted over Zoom, Skype, or similar platforms. Key business and financial information can be posted to a website periodically or even in real time. Other examples could be given, and new ones will be developed that are not even conceivable at this time. The key points are that these methods of monitoring can be conducted remotely and that they cost next to nothing to implement. Furthermore, a company could, as part of its effort to woo investors, commit to certain types of remote monitoring, such as posting quarterly reports to its website.

Remote monitoring can be combined with crowdsourcing. Just as potential investors can crowdsource information before buying in, they can also crowdsource information after they have invested. Crowdsourced monitoring responds to the concern that each investor will lack the incentive to monitor because she has only a small amount at stake. By sharing the burden of monitoring among the entire crowd of crowdfund investors, each person can contribute just a bit, but the collective effort can have a powerful effect.

On the flip side, remote monitoring can be centralized and supervised by a single investor. If the company has a lead investor, as discussed earlier under "Syndication," that lead investor can remotely monitor the company and its management for the benefit of the smaller investors. Likewise, if the investors are organized under a "special purpose vehicle" (described in the next chapter), the managers of the SPV can monitor the company on their behalf.

In practice, remote monitoring has been hit-or-miss. Many crowdfunding companies email their investors with electronic annual reports, a simple and inexpensive way for crowdfunding investors to monitor their portfolio companies. In some countries, this is required by law, as in the United States. But even there, compliance is far from perfect, with one estimate suggesting that nearly half of American crowdfunding issuers have never filed an annual report. The same is true elsewhere, namely, that crowdfunding companies, once they have the money, often do not communicate much, if at all, with their investors.

Many investors find this sort of radio silence to be frustrating, and it is likely to discourage them from returning to the platform for other offerings. Crowdfunding platforms recognize this and put pressure on their companies to keep up with their investors "post-raise," but there is only so much that they can reasonably do.

* * *

This chapter focused on private methods, mostly founded in economic analysis, and described a number of powerful nonlegal tools for responding the trio of problems discussed in Chapter Three. But don't fret, my lawyer friends, as the next two chapters are devoted to laws and regulations, as is most of the rest of the book.

Chapter Five
American Law and Practice

Investment crowdfunding was conceived in the United States in the 2000s, although the concept clearly violated American law as it then stood. The Securities Act of 1933—still very much in force today—makes it a federal offense to offer shares of stock, bonds, or other securities to the public without first "registering" them with the SEC. Yet that is just what investment crowdfunding aims to do; recall that I've defined the concept as "the public offering of unregistered securities through an independent online platform."

An amendment to the Securities Act was therefore needed if investment crowdfunding were to be permitted—and this is just what happened in 2012. In that year, a bipartisan Congress passed a new federal statute, the JOBS Act, that created a special new registration exemption for securities sold through SEC-licensed investment crowdfunding platforms.

The JOBS Act established the broad legal framework for investment crowdfunding in the United States, but many of the provisions called for the SEC to draft additional rules and regulations before the market could commence. Congress directed the SEC to promulgate the rules by the end of 2012, but the agency missed that (possibly ambitious) target by several years. The SEC ultimately issued a set of regulations in late 2015, called Regulation Crowdfunding, which allowed the market to open in the United States in 2016; the SEC subsequently amended those regulations in 2020, as will be elaborated in this chapter.

This entire legal framework is designed to address the three fundamental challenges of financial contracting—uncertainty, information asymmetry, and agency costs—that I described in Chapter Three. Yet the theme of this book is that, in crafting a regulatory regime for investment crowdfunding, we should not try to solve the trio of problems solely through legal means. Rather, we should take careful cognizance of the powerful private ordering methods I described in Chapter Four and try to design a synergistic regime that supports and enhances their potency. We should also recognize that there are some things that private ordering cannot handle on its own and focus our regulatory attention in those areas.

In many ways, the current American legal regime follows this ideal and works to support the private ordering methods from Chapter Four. Indeed, the SEC has specifically amended the rules over time in order to better facilitate those private methods.

Investment Crowdfunding. Andrew A. Schwartz, Oxford University Press. © Andrew A. Schwartz 2023.
DOI: 10.1093/oso/9780197688526.003.0006

100 AMERICAN LAW AND PRACTICE

For example, consider the concept of having a "lead investor" who invests a substantial sum based on her deep knowledge of the industry, the company, and its prospects. Such a person often announces her investment and rationale on the crowdfunding platform itself, giving the crowd confidence to follow her lead.

At first, Regulation Crowdfunding thwarted this practice, because it imposed an investor cap on all investors, even wealthy, accredited investors. The effect was to effectively nullify the concept of a lead investor, because the accredited investors who were in a position to serve as a lead investor could not legally invest enough to make it worth their while to research the company carefully. This was a serious problem, and the SEC received complaints from all quarters. Ultimately, the SEC amended the regulations in 2020 to allow accredited investors to contribute an unlimited amount of money to crowdfunding companies.

In other ways, however, American law does not mesh well with private ordering. Certain aspects overregulate, imposing requirements that are not worth their cost, while other aspects underregulate, failing to step in where the law could actually help.

This is most clear in the context of mandatory disclosure, which is the classical legal response to information asymmetry. As I explained in Chapter Four, when it comes to the original solicitation on a crowdfunding platform, mandatory disclosure is generally unnecessary, as entrepreneurs have a private incentive to voluntarily share information with potential investors, and platforms likewise have an incentive to require them to do so.

Once a company raises money from the crowd, however, there is good reason for the law to impose mandatory disclosure, because at that point the company already has the money and no longer needs to impress anybody. Especially if things are going poorly, or if agency costs are high, we should rightly worry that management will not voluntarily disclose these things to the investors. Mandatory "ongoing" disclosure, such as legally required annual reports, can ameliorate this market failure.

As we will see in this chapter, however, American law has this exactly backward. The JOBS Act and Regulation Crowdfunding impose mandatory disclosure at the offering stage, where it is not needed, and yet rely on voluntary disclosure thereafter, just where mandatory disclosure would be most useful. I will explain this problem further in this chapter and describe how it has played out in practice. Peeking ahead, I will eventually recommend in Chapter Seven that the law should generally look to minimize mandatory disclosures for primary offerings and place more emphasis on ongoing disclosures, most notably annual reports.

Before getting to all that, we must lay the groundwork. As such, this chapter will describe the law governing investment crowdfunding in the United States, with a focus on the JOBS Act and Regulation Crowdfunding. Throughout

GOVERNING LAW: THE JOBS ACT AND REGULATION CROWDFUNDING   101

the chapter, I will provide commentary and critiques, with a focus on the key components of the law and the extent to which they complement the web of private ordering I described in Chapter Four.

A. GOVERNING LAW: THE JOBS ACT AND REGULATION CROWDFUNDING

In the United States, investment crowdfunding was illegal until it was authorized by a federal statute called the Jumpstart Our Business Startups (JOBS) Act of 2012.[1] Congress—apparently enamored with acronyms—entitled Title III the "Capital Raising Online While Deterring Fraud and Unethical Non-Disclosure" (CROWDFUND) Act.[2] The JOBS Act—and the CROWDFUND Act it contained in Title III—garnered a large bipartisan majority in Congress and was enthusiastically signed into law by President Barack Obama in April 2012.[3]

Crowdfunding did not immediately commence in 2012, however, since the JOBS Act left many specifics to the SEC to flesh out by regulation. For example, the JOBS Act states that "all investors" must be given the opportunity "to cancel their commitments to invest as the Commission shall, by rule, determine appropriate."[4] (I will cover this under "Cooling Off," later in this chapter.) Thus the investment crowdfunding market could not really go into effect until the SEC decided how to implement this—and many other—portions of the JOBS Act.

In the text of the JOBS Act, Congress gave the SEC until the end of 2012 to promulgate these regulations—which may not have been realistic, especially because Congress directed the SEC to consult with state securities regulators, among others, before issuing its rules.[5] Furthermore, the SEC was very busy with other projects at the time, including drafting regulations pursuant to the 2010 Dodd-Frank Act as well as other aspects of the JOBS Act. It is therefore no surprise that the SEC missed the deadline by nearly two years, and only issued a preliminary proposal for crowdfunding regulations in late 2013.[6]

As a matter of federal law, the SEC, like any administrative agency, is required to publish its proposed regulations, and then take and consider comments from

---

[1] Jumpstart Our Business Startups Act, Pub. L. No. 112-106, §§ 301–05 (2012) (codified in 15 U.S.C.).

[2] JOBS Act § 301 (2012).

[3] Press Release, Office of the White House, President Obama to Sign Jumpstart Our Business Startups (JOBS) Act (Apr. 5, 2012), https://obamawhitehouse.archives.gov/the-press-office/2012/04/05/president-obama-sign-jumpstart-our-business-startups-jobs-act ("Today President Obama will sign the *Jumpstart Our Business Startups (JOBS) Act*, a bipartisan bill that enacts many of the President's proposals to encourage startups and support our nation's small businesses.).

[4] 15 U.S.C. § 77d-1(a)(7).

[5] JOBS Act § 302(c) (providing a deadline of 270 days).

[6] Crowdfunding, 78 Fed. Reg. 66,428 (proposed Nov. 5, 2013) (to be codified at 17 C.F.R. pt. 227).

102 AMERICAN LAW AND PRACTICE

the public, before making its regulations final. I availed myself of this opportunity and submitted a letter to the SEC offering my views, as did many others. The pace was slow, but the SEC eventually revised its proposal and promulgated its final rules, known as Regulation Crowdfunding, in late 2015.[7] Regulation Crowdfunding went into effect six months later, and the American crowdfunding market finally opened for business in 2016.

During the four, long years between the enactment of the JOBS Act in April 2012 and Regulation Crowdfunding going into effect in 2016, a large number of individual states adopted their own "intrastate" regimes to govern investment crowdfunding laws within their borders. This was a diverse group of states, both politically and geographically, including Colorado, Georgia, Massachusetts, and Texas.[8]

The primary impetus for these state-level crowdfunding laws appears to have been the long delay in finalizing regulations for investment crowdfunding under the federal JOBS Act. Indeed, these intrastate investment crowdfunding laws largely mimicked the JOBS Act, except that they were limited to purely intrastate transactions, where the company and all investors are all residents of a single state.

A couple of these intrastate crowdfunding laws made thoughtful changes to the federal scheme, including some that I endorse in this book. Several states, for instance, set the "investor cap" (discussed later in this chapter) in just the way that I would recommend.[9] For the most part, however, these intrastate laws were less an attempt at creating a true parallel scheme for each state, and more a way to express annoyance with the SEC and encourage the agency to hurry up and issue federal regulations—which eventually it did.

As expected, the intrastate crowdfunding laws were rarely used before Regulation Crowdfunding went live—and were rendered largely irrelevant once the federal rules went into effect. Why limit yourself to soliciting investors in your home state once the whole country is available to you? The Colorado legislature, for instance, enacted the Colorado Crowdfunding Act in 2015—but it was two years before the first crowdfunding offering was attempted (and that one apparently failed).[10] Indeed, I am unaware of any money being raised on any Colorado platform, ever.

---

[7] Crowdfunding, 80 Fed. Reg. 71,388 (Nov. 16, 2015) (to be codified at 17 C.F.R. pt. 227).

[8] COLO. REV. STAT. § 11-51-308.5 (2015); 59 GA. COMP. R. & REGS. 590-4-2-.08, et seq. (2012); 950 MASS. CODE REGS. 14.402(B)(13)(o) (2015); 2015 TEX. SESS. LAW SERV. CH. 652 (H.B. 1629).

[9] E.g., MINN. STAT. ANN. § 80A.461(3)(7) ("no single purchaser may purchase more than $10,000 in securities of the [crowdfunding] issuer under this exemption in connection with a single [crowdfunding] offering unless the purchaser is an accredited investor").

[10] Herrick Lidstone, Crowdfunding in Colorado—One Person's Opinion, at 2 (Oct. 13, 2017), https://ssrn.com/abstract=3052254.

GOVERNING LAW: THE JOBS ACT AND REGULATION CROWDFUNDING   103

There may be a few states that have functioning intrastate crowdfunding platforms, but their overall impact is exceedingly small. The upshot is that investment crowdfunding in the United States is, for practical purposes, regulated by the federal JOBS Act and Regulation Crowdfunding, and no further mention will be made of the various intrastate crowdfunding laws just discussed.

Flash forward to 2020. In that year, as part of the government's emergency response to the COVID-19 pandemic, the SEC made a few temporary changes to Regulation Crowdfunding. In order to help small businesses raise money to survive that challenging era, when many of them were shut down by government order, the SEC temporarily relaxed certain regulations, such as reducing the level of mandatory disclosure for small offerings up to $250,000.[11]

Separately, beginning in 2019, the SEC had undertaken a broad reconsideration of all the various exemptions, including investment crowdfunding.[12] After taking public comments, the SEC ultimately approved the final version of these amendments in late 2020, and they went into effect in early 2021.[13] Unlike all other aspects of Regulation Crowdfunding, this set of amendments was adopted by a split vote, with the three Republican commissioners in favor and the two Democratic commissioners opposed.[14] This is not surprising once you realize that the basic effect of the amendments was to liberalize the regulations, such as by raising the issuer limit to $5 million (more on this later in this chapter) and freeing accredited investors from the investor cap.

Stepping back and looking at the JOBS Act and the various iterations of Regulation Crowdfunding, we can see a plain trend. Every change that the SEC has made has been in the liberal, deregulatory direction, in a clear effort to lower costs and encourage entrepreneurs to participate. This makes sense, given the results. As discussed throughout this book, the American crowdfunding market has been pretty smooth, with just one allegation of fraud over the first five years—the exception that seems to prove the rule. (And, as we will see in the next chapter, the liberal regimes in the United Kingdom and New Zealand are doing even better than the more regulatory-focused regimes like the United States.)

To summarize, there are two sources of law that govern investment crowdfunding in the United States. First, the JOBS Act, a federal statute enacted in 2012, which established a broad framework but also empowered the SEC to impose additional regulations. Second, the regulations that the SEC promulgated pursuant to this authority in 2015 and 2020, known collectively as Regulation Crowdfunding.

---

[11] Temporary Amendments to Regulation Crowdfunding; Extension, 85 Fed. Reg. 54,483 (2020).
[12] Concept Release on Harmonization of Securities Offerings, 84 Fed. Reg. 30,460 (2019).
[13] Facilitating Capital Formation and Expanding Investment Opportunities by Improving Access to Capital in Private Markets, 86 Fed. Reg. 3,496 (2021).
[14] Paul Kiernan, *SEC Eases Rules on Funding for Private Firms*, WALL ST. J., Nov. 3, 2020.

B. EXEMPTION FROM REGISTRATION

The most fundamental contribution of the JOBS Act was to add a new "exemption" to the registration requirement of the federal Securities Act of 1933. The general rule of the federal securities laws is that a company must register its securities with the SEC prior to offering them for sale; the registration process essentially requires the company to provide extensive mandatory disclosure about its operation and finances.[15] This is a costly and cumbersome process, but it can be avoided if the transaction is legally "exempt" from the registration requirement. The Securities Act itself specifies several such exemptions, and these are elaborated in SEC regulations.

Two of the best-known exemptions are the "private placement" and "accredited investor" exemptions.[16] Under the former, if you privately solicit investments from your family and friends, and do not publicize the offering, you are exempt from the registration requirement of the Securities Act. This makes good sense, as the primary goal of the federal registration process is to inform and protect public investors with no connection to the company. Close friends and family, by contrast, are likely knowledgeable about the founder and his company and are in a good position to inform and protect themselves. In other words, the close connection between the entrepreneur and the investors gives us confidence that they can handle the trio of uncertainty, information asymmetry, and agency costs on their own.

Similarly, the Securities Act is primarily aimed at protecting ordinary "retail" investors. Thus, if you privately offer securities solely to specially "accredited investors," the transaction is exempt from the registration requirement. The term "accredited investor" is legally defined in the SEC's regulations to include banks, insurance companies, and other institutional investors. Individuals can also qualify as accredited investors if they have sufficient wealth or income. At present, anyone with a net worth (excluding their primary residence) greater than $1 million qualifies as accredited. Similarly, a person who regularly earns more than $200,000 per year also qualifies as accredited.[17] The idea here is that these sorts of institutions or wealthy individuals are presumed to have the resources and sophistication to make investment decisions without the need for a registration statement. In addition, if the investment goes south, they are in a better position to afford the loss than ordinary retail investors.

---

[15] 15 U.S.C. § 77e(c).
[16] 15 U.S.C. § 77d(a)(2) (exempting "transactions . . . not involving any public offering"); *id.* § 77d(a)(5) (exempting "transactions involving offers or sales . . . solely to one or more accredited investors").
[17] 17 C.F.R. §§ 230.215, 230.501(a) (2022).

The SEC has enacted several different regulations pertaining to the accredited-investor exemption. For present purposes, the most important of these is Regulation D, affectionately known as "Reg. D," which itself contains two key rules, Rule 506(b) and Rule 506(c).[18] Rule 506(b) allows a company to raise an unlimited amount of money from accredited investors, but it cannot advertise the offering. VCs and angel investors generally invest under Rule 506(b). Rule 506(c) is similar, except that it allows advertising to the public, as long as the company only actually sells securities to accredited investors.

In the JOBS Act, Congress amended the Securities Act by adding a new, limited, exemption for securities offered through investment crowdfunding.[19] This is a rather different sort of exemption from those involving private placements and accredited investors, because it covers offerings made to the broad public. Crowdfunding investors are strangers to the company that lack the resources to absorb large losses. They are precisely the sort of retail investors that the entire registration process is designed to protect.

For this reason, although investment crowdfunding is exempt from registration, it is governed by an alternative set of legal rules established in the JOBS Act and Regulation Crowdfunding. As a substitute for the registration process, the law imposes a panoply of rules and limitations on investment crowdfunding, including a requirement to file a simplified disclosure statement. This body of rules—working together the methods of private ordering described in Chapter Four—is designed to address the three fundamental challenges of uncertainty, information asymmetry, and agency costs.

The remainder of this chapter will describe the laws and regulations that govern investment crowdfunding in the United States. It is vital to satisfy each and every rule, for a company that fails to comply with all the rules would find that its securities offering was unregistered and not covered by an exemption—and therefore illegal.

C. MANDATORY DISCLOSURE

The signature move of the JOBS Act was to exempt crowdfunding from the ordinary rule that entrepreneurs must register securities with the SEC before offering them to the public, thereby excusing investment crowdfunding companies from the usual mandatory disclosure obligations. The goal was to lower the cost of raising capital for startup companies by minimizing the regulatory burden of crowdfunding.

[18] 17 C.F.R. §§ 230.506(b), (c) (2022).
[19] 15 U.S.C. § 77d(a)(6).

106 AMERICAN LAW AND PRACTICE

This was, nevertheless, a radical change, as mandatory disclosure had always been the touchstone of the federal securities laws. For this reason, the framers of the JOBS Act couldn't quite bring themselves to jettison mandatory disclosure entirely. So, even as the law exempted crowdfunding offerings from the "usual" mandatory disclosure rules for public companies, it imposed an alternative mandatory disclosure regime in its stead. The disclosures required by the JOBS Act are fewer and simpler than those called for in the ordinary registration process, but they are still significant.

Specifically, the JOBS Act requires that crowdfunding companies disclose the following to the SEC, the hosting platform, and the public more generally, eight categories of information about the company:

(A) Name, legal status, physical address, and website address;
(B) Names of directors, officers, and major investors;
(C) Business of the company and its anticipated business plan;
(D) Financial condition;
(E) Purpose and intended use of the proceeds;
(F) Target offering amount and deadline for reaching it;
(G) Price of the securities; and
(H) Ownership and capital structure of the issuer.[20]

In addition to these eight, the JOBS Act authorized the SEC to adopt additional items of mandatory disclosure "for the protection of investors and in the public interest."[21] Against my advice[22]—would you believe?!—the SEC used this authority to add numerous additional items of mandatory disclosure to Regulation Crowdfunding and to read the eight items in the JOBS Act expansively, as we shall see.

It is hard to blame them, given that mandatory disclosure has been the foundation of securities regulation for nearly a century and has, by now, become an article of faith for the SEC.[23] In the end, Regulation Crowdfunding contains more than twenty-five categories of mandatory disclosure, with many of them having subsections of their own.[24]

---

[20] 15 U.S.C. §§ 77d-1(b)(A)–(H).

[21] 15 U.S.C. § 77d-1(b)(I).

[22] Andrew A. Schwartz, *Keep It Light, Chairman White: SEC Rulemaking Under the CROWDFUND Act*, 66 VAND. L. REV. EN BANC 43, 46 (2013) (advising the SEC "to rely primarily on the existing statutory scheme, especially the annual investment cap, and add just a few additional rules and regulations").

[23] The same is true elsewhere. I once gave a talk at the New Zealand Financial Markets Authority, which I playfully dubbed the "House of Disclosure"; the staff there took it as a badge of honor.

[24] 17 C.F.R. §§ 227.201(a)–(bb) (2022).

MANDATORY DISCLOSURE   107

Most of Regulation Crowdfunding's required disclosures are simple and easy to comply with. Companies can easily disclose the number of people they employ and the fees they paid to the platform.

Other mandatory disclosures called for by Regulation Crowdfunding, however, are much more substantial. Crowdfunding companies must describe their business and anticipated business plans;[25] discuss the factors that "make an investment in the issuer speculative or risky";[26] and explain "the risks to purchasers of the securities relating to minority ownership in the issuer"[27]—just to name a few. These are serious disclosures that call for careful drafting.

To put these mandatory disclosure rules into effect, the SEC created a new official form that all crowdfunding companies must complete, designated as "Form C."[28] Form C includes blanks for all of the required disclosures in a question-and-answer format. Form C disclosures are not reviewed or approved by the SEC, but are merely filed with the SEC using its online portal, which makes them available to the public. This process is called a "notice filing" in the trade.

Form C includes a boilerplate risk statement indicating that the securities being offered "have not been recommended or approved by any federal or state securities commission," and warning, ominously, "You should not invest any funds in this offering unless you can afford to lose your entire investment."[29]

The law provides for serious penalties for any mistakes or falsehoods on Form C. The JOBS Act included a special rule providing that even an unintentional misstatement can lead to liability for the company, the entrepreneur, and the directors and officers—unless they can prove that they were sufficiently careful and just made an honest mistake.[30] This encourages due diligence on the part of the company and its principals, but it also hangs like a sword of Damocles over their heads. And as for an intentional misstatement, the consequences are even graver. Beyond traditional fraud, Form C ominously warns entrepreneurs that "intentional misstatements or omissions of material facts constitute federal criminal violations," and cites to a specific federal statute that calls for a prison term of up to five years.[31]

The mandatory disclosures called for on Form C are, I must admit, much simpler and less daunting than the full "Form S-1" required of an IPO. The

---

[25] 17 C.F.R. § 227.201(d) (2022).

[26] 17 C.F.R. § 227.201(f) (2022).

[27] 17 C.F.R. § 227.201(m)(5) (2022).

[28] 17 C.F.R. § 239.900 (2022).

[29] 17 C.F.R. § 239.900 (2022).

[30] 15 U.S.C. § 77d-1(c); Joan MacLeod Heminway, *Crowdfunding and the Public/Private Divide in U.S. Securities Regulation*, 46 TEX. J. BUS. L. 129, 143 (2016) (explaining the liability rule and its origins).

[31] On the other hand, Regulation Crowdfunding also includes a provision that excuses companies for "insignificant deviations from a term, condition or requirement of" the rules it lays down. 17 C.F.R. § 227.502.

108 AMERICAN LAW AND PRACTICE

costs of compliance are thousands of dollars, not millions. According to the government's official estimates, Form C should take just 50 hours to complete, compared to roughly 650 hours for Form S-1.[32] And it makes sense to have a standard form that all companies can use.

Even so, Form C looks more like Form S-1 than it probably should, since the context of crowdfunding is so different than that of a traditional IPO in fundamental ways. The types of companies that use Form S-1 are large, profitable concerns seeking to go public in a traditional IPO and raise hundreds of millions of dollars all at once. They are used to working with auditors, accountants, attorneys, and other independent professionals. They have a substantial operating history, and their (often complex) financial statements are highly relevant to their valuation. They have distinctive "risk factors" that experienced attorneys can describe in careful prose.

Potential investors, collectively and individually, have an incentive to review a company's Form S-1 carefully before investing, since there is so much money at stake. In addition, professional securities analysts read and digest the information in a Form S-1, then convey the gist to institutional investors, who decide whether to buy. In this context, it makes good sense to spend a lot of time and money to comply with these mandatory disclosure rules.

The context of investment crowdfunding is very different. The young startup companies for which it is designed have no, or very little, operating history. Their financial statements are simple and are not very relevant to the value of the company. They have very little contact with accountants or attorneys, and they don't have any special risk factors to share.

Furthermore, the potential investors make very small investments for the most part, so it would be a waste for them to spend too much time researching any given opportunity. There are no professional securities analysts either. For all these reasons, the JOBS Act misses the mark by mandating that crowdfunding companies provide disclosures that are analogous to those called for on Form S-1.

This is not a harmless error, because it costs money to collect and present information about a company. If that information is sufficiently useful to investors that it is worth the cost of generating and disclosing it, then investors will want the company to do so. But if the value is not worth the cost, then disclosing it would be a net loss for all concerned, and the investor would not want the company to do so. Yet if the law requires it to be shared as a matter of mandatory disclosure, the company will have to comply, which harms the company, without good reason.

In a world of voluntary disclosure, the company would disclose a reasonably efficient quantity and type of information. Yet mandatory disclosure can

---

[32] OMB estimates on the face of each form.

easily push beyond that point and require disclosures that are not worth their cost. Crowdfunding companies will nevertheless have to make them, under legal compulsion. This is a loss for all concerned, since the investors, by hypothesis, do not value the information as much as it costs the company to produce.

Alternatively, companies will avoid investment crowdfunding entirely because mandatory disclosure makes the process too expensive—and intrusive. Public disclosure of a company's deepest secrets is a big disincentive to participation, so it is important that we only require as much disclosure as is really necessary. Don't forget that the point of all this was to create an inexpensive way for startup companies to raise a modest amount of money from the public—not to replicate the existing registration process.

Let us look again at the government's estimate of the time it should take a company to complete Form C versus Form S-1. These numbers should be comparable, since it is the same government agency that calculated each one. They state that Form C should take roughly one-tenth of the time it takes to complete Form S-1 (50 hours compared with 650 hours), so let us take that to mean that the cost of complying with the investment crowdfunding regulations is 10 percent the cost of a traditional public offering.

That doesn't sound too bad until you realize that the typical public company raises hundreds of millions of dollars, while the typical investment crowdfunding company raises hundreds of thousands of dollars, as we will see in Chapter Seven. This ratio ($100m:$100k) suggests that to properly scale the compliance costs, Form C should only take one one-thousandth of the time Form S-1 requires. In other words, on a scaled basis, Form C is 100 times more costly to comply with than Form S-1!

These are rough numbers, but the point is clear. The mandatory disclosures called for by Form C are overly expensive for the scale of fundraising. Voluntary disclosure, were it permitted—and it is in the liberal jurisdictions of New Zealand and the United Kingdom, as we'll see in the next chapter—would be more cost-effective.

Beyond the numbers, most of the disclosures mandated by the JOBS Act call for responses drafted by lawyers and accountants. That might be appropriate for traditional public companies, where even the footnotes to financial statements are consequential, and where quarterly earnings-per-share is a key metric. But crowdfunding is meant for startup companies, which generally have very simple finances.

For people considering whether to invest in such ventures, it would be more useful to hear directly from the entrepreneur about her vision and plans. Yet it is really only items (C) and (E) from the JOBS Act list—referring to "business of the company and its anticipated business plan" and "purpose and intended use of the proceeds"—that would provide an investor with insight into those questions.

110   AMERICAN LAW AND PRACTICE

To put a fine point on it: several items of mandatory disclosure are likely not worth their cost. Consider, for example, the required list of "risk factors," which was not in the original JOBS Act, but was added as part of Regulation Crowdfunding (over my strenuous objection).[33] The SEC imported this "risk factor" requirement directly from the usual disclosure demands of a traditional registered offering—changing just a single word.[34]

Under this rule, crowdfunding companies must provide investors with a "discussion of the material factors that make an investment in the issuer speculative or risky."[35] Form C elaborates: "Avoid generalized statements and include only those factors that are unique to the issuer. Discussion should be tailored to the issuer's business and the offering. . . ."[36]

This is an expensive ask that makes sense in a traditional IPO, where there is so much money at stake that it's worthwhile to have every word precisely calibrated by a team of white-shoe lawyers. But those costs are not worth spending in the context of investment crowdfunding, which takes place on a much smaller scale, so it was a mistake, I thought and think, to mandate this specific item of disclosure.

In a bit of poetic justice, the market has found a private ordering response to this risk-factor rule that reduces its cost and burden. One leading investment crowdfunding platform has posted to its website a document listing dozens of sample risk factors that a company can cut and paste into its own Form C, and then edit to make it "unique" and "tailored," as required by law.[37] This "beast of a document"—roughly the length of this chapter—is well-organized, and includes lots of old favorites, such as "no operating history," "no revenue," "highly competitive market," and so on.

For better or worse, this document suggests that the risk-factor disclosure is largely a box-ticking exercise designed to satisfy Regulation Crowdfunding, rather than an effective way "to help investors understand the risks of investing in a specific issuer's offering," as the SEC had hoped.[38] This is further underscored by that same platform's internal policy that every company must disclose "a minimum of six risks."[39]

For all the trouble I give the SEC, I also need to give credit where credit is due. The SEC has taken steps to slim down the mandatory disclosure obligations on

[33] Crowdfunding, 80 Fed. Reg. 71,387, 71,403 (Nov. 16, 2015).
[34] 17 C.F.R. § 229.105 (2022) (requiring a "a discussion of the material factors that make an investment in the registrant or offering speculative or risky").
[35] 17 C.F.R. § 227.201(f) (2022).
[36] 17 C.F.R. § 239.900 (2022).
[37] *How Do I Write Risks?*, WEFUNDER, https://help.wefunder.com/form-c/294942-example-form-c-risks (last visited June 18, 2022).
[38] Crowdfunding, 80 Fed. Reg. 71,387, 71,405 (Nov. 16, 2015).
[39] *How Do I Write Risks?*, WEFUNDER, https://help.wefunder.com/form-c/294942-example-form-c-risks (last visited June 18, 2022).

crowdfunding companies. Most notably, perhaps, was its move to minimize the burden of producing and disclosing audited financial statements.

Recall that item (D) of the JOBS Act list mandates that crowdfunding companies disclose their "financial condition" (income, assets, debt, etc.), which is a sensible rule.[40] The level of financial disclosure required by the JOBS Act is tiered, based on the size of the offering.

For offerings of less than $100,000, the company must merely provide financial statements certified as accurate by the CEO—a relatively simple and inexpensive process. For deals ranging from $100,000 to $500,000, the JOBS Act requires financial statements that have been reviewed by an independent accountant—also a fairly simple and low-cost process. But for offerings over $500,000, the JOBS Act demands audited financial statements—a significant and expensive undertaking.[41]

This last requirement for audited financial statements was a back-breaker, for two reasons. First, the cost of hiring an independent accountant to conduct a formal audit—commonly over $10,000 for a small business—is high in relation to the amount that can be raised, in part because Regulation Crowdfunding requires that the financial statements for every offering, no matter how small, comply with generally accepted accounting principles (GAAP).[42] Plus you have to pay for the audit before you raise the money.

Second, audited financial statements have very limited utility to investors looking at startup companies. The value of these companies is not in their balance sheets, but rather in their potential. To require companies to spend a lot of money on audited financial statements that are not of much use to investors is, to put it politely, inefficient.

The SEC heard these complaints about the JOBS Act's demand for audited financial statements and rode to the rescue with a clever solution, namely, an exception for first-timers. Under Regulation Crowdfunding, a company can raise up to $1 million using unaudited financial statements reviewed by an independent accountant, as long as it's the company's first time raising money via crowdfunding.[43] (Raising over $1 million always requires audited financial statements.)

Veterans that have already conducted a crowdfunding round, and are back again, do have to produce audited financial statements, but it makes sense in this context. The company has, by definition, already raised money, and can use some

[40] 15 U.S.C. § 77d-1(b)(1)(D).

[41] 15 U.S.C. § 77d-1(b)(D). These thresholds ($100,000, $500,000) were stated in the JOBS Act, but the Act also provided that all dollar amounts were to be adjusted for inflation at least once every five years. 15 U.S.C. § 77d-1(b)(1). As such, the SEC raised these figures in 2017 to $107,000 and $535,000, respectively, and they will presumably be raised in the future as well, for the same reason.

[42] 17 C.F.R. § 227.201(t) (2022).

[43] 17 C.F.R. § 227.201(t)(3) (2022).

112 AMERICAN LAW AND PRACTICE

of it on the audit. Also, the company is now more mature, thus making audited financial statements more relevant to investors and thus worth their cost.

This move by the SEC to eliminate a piece of mandatory disclosure to a cost-effective level is just the sort of regulatory response this book advocates. This is not because audited financial statements are worthless, even for startup companies—but because they are not always worth their cost in this context. Importantly, when an audit is worth the cost, say for a company with an inventory that it claims to be quite valuable, the company is perfectly free to call for it—voluntarily.

In the end, the mandatory disclosures imposed by the JOBS Act and Regulation Crowdfunding are, in most ways, not too far from what companies would voluntarily disclose. With or without the law, a company would tell potential investors its name, address, type of business, and basic financial information. To that extent, the mandatory disclosure obligations are harmless, since they don't force any disclosure that would not have otherwise been made. And Form C has the added benefit of providing a standard template for all crowdfunding companies, thereby facilitating comparisons among them.

Yet Regulation Crowdfunding retains at least a couple of onerous disclosure burdens that are likely not worth their cost, including the "risk factor" discussion and the requirement that every financial statement conform to GAAP. These are the exception, not the rule, and the SEC can fix them easily.

But that is a piecemeal solution, and we should also consider the larger question as to whether mandatory disclosure—of any type—is actually necessary or advisable in the context of investment crowdfunding. In Chapter Four, I made the case that crowdfunding entrepreneurs should be expected to provide disclosure voluntarily and thus investors do not need the law to mandate it.

In response to arguments like mine, John Coffee and other scholars developed a sophisticated defense of mandatory disclosure that sounds in law and economics. According to these scholars, mandatory disclosure is an efficient response to two economic issues that market forces would not properly address on their own: (1) agency costs,[44] and (2) information underproduction.[45] This theory largely swept the field in the 1980s and remains the conventional wisdom to this day.

My own contribution to the debate has been to highlight the difference between the "primary market"—where a company seeks to raise capital directly from investors—and the "secondary market"—where investors trade stocks or other securities with one another.[46] Investment crowdfunding is a primary

---

[44] *See* Chapter Three.

[45] Note that "information underproduction" is not the same thing as "information asymmetry," discussed in Chapter Three.

[46] Andrew A. Schwartz, *Mandatory Disclosure in Primary Markets*, 2019 Utah L. Rev. 1069, 1072, 1088–91.

MANDATORY DISCLOSURE 113

market, not a secondary market. It is a way for companies to raise money from investors, not for investors to trade securities among themselves.

If we examine these arguments that agency costs and information underproduction necessitate mandatory disclosure, we can see that they make good sense in the context of secondary markets. But if we shift our gaze to the primary context—the category in which investment crowdfunding squarely lies—these two ideas become largely irrelevant.[47] Even Coffee seems to agree with my idea that mandatory disclosure is only needed for secondary market trading, not primary offerings.[48] This is because agency costs and information underproduction are moot points at the time of a primary offering.

First, agency costs arise only after a company has already sold its securities and investors worry that management will begin to run the company in its own interest, rather than for the benefit of shareholders. The concept of agency costs is irrelevant to the primary market, where promoters are trying to get investors to buy these securities at the outset. In the primary market, the board of directors, CEO, and other managers have not yet become agents, because agency is established by the presence of outside shareholders. Because management has not yet become an agent, there are no agency costs; they are a feature of the secondary market alone.

Second, information underproduction occurs when one company may have relatively easy access to information that would help participants in the secondary market more accurately assess the value of some other company or companies whose securities they trade. Yet it is unlikely that companies will voluntarily collect and disclose information that could be relevant to the value of other publicly traded firms, even if investors would prefer disclosure. Why should Company A go to any trouble to help out Company B, knowing that the latter is unlikely to reciprocate? Mandatory disclosure remedies this collective-action problem by forcing all public companies to share certain types of information, thereby enhancing the accuracy of all securities prices on the public trading market. Information underproduction has almost nothing to do with primary offerings, because new issuers rarely have the same quantity or quality of relevant market information as existing public companies and because a primary offering is merely a one-time event.

To put it all together: the theoretical argument in favor of mandatory disclosure rests primarily on just two justifications—agency costs and information

---

[47] Andrew A. Schwartz, *Mandatory Disclosure in Primary Markets*, 2019 UTAH L. REV. 1069, 1072, 1088–91.

[48] John C. Coffee, Jr., *Market Failure and the Economic Case for a Mandatory Disclosure System*, 70 VA. L. REV. 717, 746 (1984) (saying that while "the theory of voluntary disclosure" was not persuasive with regard to secondary market trading, it "does seem to have some validity as applied to initial public offerings and, to a lesser extent, to all primary distributions").

114 AMERICAN LAW AND PRACTICE

underproduction. And while these two theories apply quite obviously and directly to a secondary market, they don't really pertain to a primary market like investment crowdfunding. And, as discussed in Chapter Four, the incentive to provide voluntary disclosure is strong in the primary context. For this reason, there is good reason to think that mandatory disclosure for crowdfunding offerings, as on Form C, is unnecessary and wasteful.

But that does not mean that mandatory disclosure is entirely useless to investment crowdfunding, as the next section will explain.

D. ONGOING DISCLOSURE

Once a company raises money through investment crowdfunding, it remains subject to legal regulation. The JOBS Act requires crowdfunding companies to produce an annual report on their operations and financial condition and to distribute it to the crowdfunding investors, as well as file it with the SEC.[49] This is another type of mandatory disclosure, but it is required on an ongoing basis, rather than when the company is raising money in the primary market, which we just covered.

Recall that the economic incentives for voluntary disclosure are strongest at the stage of the primary market, because companies have to convince investors to hand over their money. That is why I railed above against mandatory disclosure at that point. Once a company gets the money, however, the private incentives for voluntary disclosure are much weaker. This is just the sort of market failure where the law can step in and address what private methods cannot fully resolve on their own.

To this end, Regulation Crowdfunding mandates that companies who successfully raise money through investment crowdfunding file an annual report on "Form C-AR" (AR stands for Annual Report). Form C-AR is exactly the same as Form C, minus a couple of questions that only made sense at the initial offering, such as the level of transaction fees. It requires financial statements, but they need only be certified as true by the CEO, not audited, nor even reviewed.

As just discussed in connection with John Coffee's work, mandatory disclosure can resolve market failures caused by agency costs and information underproduction. Information underproduction, being a problem for secondary markets, holds very little relevance in investment crowdfunding, as just discussed.

Agency costs, however, are a major concern for investment crowdfunding. Once an entrepreneur has secured enough money to operate the company for a few years, there is good reason to worry that he will use it to benefit himself,

---

[49] 15 U.S.C. § 77d-1(b)(4).

ultimately, rather than advance the corporate interest. Even the information he chooses to share with the investors may be colored by self-interest. In the extreme, a company that raises money from crowdfunding could "go dark" and never say anything to the investors again. If the management is up to no good (meaning high levels of agency costs), the investors would never know it. This is why mandatory disclosure makes good sense in this context, and the annual reports on Form C-AR are a useful and valuable exercise of government power.

There are additional reasons for the law to mandate ongoing disclosure in the form of annual reports. As we will see later in this chapter, the JOBS Act generally prohibits crowdfunded securities from being resold by their original purchasers for one year. And even after that, it is unlikely that a liquid market for such securities will develop, given the very low volume of issuance.

The illiquid nature of crowdfunded securities means that investors might find themselves in a vulnerable position analogous to that of a minority shareholder in a closely held corporation. Crowdfunding corporations will differ from close corporations in that the latter usually have only a handful of shareholders, while the former might end up with thousands of shareholders. But the lack of a liquid secondary market creates the same potential for oppression in the crowdfunding context that is found in the close corporation, a point to which we shall return later in this chapter.

Indeed, the JOBS Act enhances the possibility of such oppression in some ways by permitting investors to resell their crowdfunded securities within the first year back to the company, but not to other ordinary investors. Thanks to the absence of a secondary market for crowdfunded securities, the company (or its controlling group) may be tempted to offer an unfairly low price to cash out the other holders, knowing that they have essentially nowhere else to turn. An annual report does not totally insulate crowdfunding investors from being frozen out, but it could help arm them with information that could be used in a lawsuit against the controlling party.

To some extent, the JOBS Act and Regulation Crowdfunding recognize the importance of ongoing disclosure, as they do require mandatory annual reports from all crowdfunded companies. These annual reports, on Form C-AR, present most of the same disclosures as Form C, as they should. Finally, the obligation to file the Form C-AR annually is enforced by barring a company that fails to file two annual reports from raising money though investment crowdfunding.[50] (The company can come back to the good graces of the SEC and restore its eligibility to participate, if it goes back and files the two most recent annual reports.)

In other ways, American law is a bit lax when it comes to ongoing disclosure. Regulation Crowdfunding only mandates that companies file a single

---

[50] 17 C.F.R. § 227.100(b)(5) (2022).

116 AMERICAN LAW AND PRACTICE

annual report if they have fewer than three hundred "holders of record." Because companies may raise money from the crowd using a special purpose vehicle (SPV) (see later in this chapter), which only counts as a single "holder of record," the effect is that most companies are only bound to file one annual report and then are free to terminate reporting. Even for companies that do not use an SPV, Regulation Crowdfunding mandates only three annual reports, as long as the company has less than $10 million in assets.

The result is that, although ongoing reporting is subject to market failure due to agency costs, Regulation Crowdfunding does not effectively require this sort of mandatory disclosure. Now, if other components of the law mandate ongoing disclosure, it may not be necessary for the crowdfunding regulations to do so as well. And they do—to some extent, at least.

General corporate law, in Delaware and elsewhere, requires an annual meeting of shareholders, so they can elect the board of directors for the coming year and so the shareholders can count on at least some sort of communication once a year. Not every crowdfunding investor is formally a shareholder, however, as any security can be offered in this way, not just shares of common stock (as we will see later in this chapter). Bondholders, for instance, are not invited to annual shareholder meetings, and so they do not fully solve the issue of ongoing disclosure.

In real life, it appears that crowdfunding companies are overwhelmingly compliant with their obligations at the time of the primary offering (as on Form C)—but are much worse when it comes to the required annual reports (on Form C-AR). According to one source, a solid majority of crowdfunding companies have never filed a single annual report.[51] It comes as no surprise that, once the money has been raised, many crowdfunding entrepreneurs find it easy to forget those investors and don't make the effort to share important information with them. This market failure is consistent with the theory I presented earlier in this chapter and in prior work.[52]

Platforms sometimes require, as part of their contract with the companies they list, that the latter provide investors with ongoing disclosure of some sort. SeedInvest, for example, requires that its companies provide investors (and the platform) with quarterly updates on certain, basic information about the business.[53] But such promises are not always fulfilled, and the platform has limited resources to enforce them.

---

[51] *Investment Crowdfunding Issuer, You May Be at Risk!*, CROWDFUND CAPITAL ADVISORS (Apr. 18, 2022), https://crowdfundcapitaladvisors.com/investment-crowdfunding-issuer-you-may-be-at-risk (reporting that 56% of the over 1,000 companies that had closed a successful Regulation Crowdfunding offering by the end of 2020 had not filed a single annual report as of mid-2022).

[52] Andrew A. Schwartz, *Mandatory Disclosure in Primary Markets*, 2019 UTAH L. REV. 1069.

[53] *Issuer Terms and Conditions*, SEEDINVEST, https://www.seedinvest.com/issuer-terms-and-con ditions (last updated Nov. 15, 2021) ("Company shall be responsible for providing quarterly updates directly to SeedInvest and each [investor] who purchased securities in the Offering. . . . Such updates shall include at least the following information: (i) quarterly net sales, (ii) quarterly change in cash

The JOBS Act recognizes this market failure and responds by requiring that all crowdfunding companies provide investors and the SEC with ongoing disclosure of the results of operations and financial statements, at least once a year. Regulation Crowdfunding operationalized this rule by mandating that companies complete Form C-AR on an annual basis and provide it to investors and the SEC (but not the public).

This regulation is not very effective, however, at least not at the present time, as it is being flouted by more than half of American crowdfunding companies.[54] The punishment is that these companies are debarred from using investment crowdfunding in the future. But this is only for the specific company, and the entrepreneur behind it would be able to launch a new offering for a different entity, so this may be a slap on the wrist.

Even for those companies that comply with the annual reporting rule, it has only a very limited effect. As explained earlier in this chapter, the fine print of Regulation Crowdfunding effectively only requires a single annual report from crowdfunding companies. This is insufficient to respond to the market failure that makes ongoing reporting relatively unlikely to come voluntarily.

Ongoing disclosure is one of the few aspects of investment crowdfunding where I find American law to be too liberal and insufficiently regulatory.

E. LICENSED PLATFORMS

Investment crowdfunding, as per my definition, cannot be conducted directly between entrepreneurs and investors. Rather, the form requires that an independent intermediary stand between the two, in the form of an online platform. In Chapter Four, I contended that platforms play a vital "gatekeeping" role in that they curate their offerings and only allow legitimate and promising startup companies to participate. Gatekeeping is a key method of responding to all three of the fundamental problems of startup finance that we cataloged in Chapter Three.

American law puts a great deal of emphasis on platforms, as it should. The JOBS Act and Regulation Crowdfunding impose three rules relating to platforms, all of which synergistically supercharge the private ordering power of gatekeeping. First, American law dictates that all crowdfunding offerings must be conducted

---

and cash on hand, (iii) material updates on the business, (iv) fundraising updates (any plans for next round, current round status, etc.), and (v) notable press and news.").

[54] *Investment Crowdfunding Issuer, You May Be at Risk!*, CROWDFUND CAPITAL ADVISORS (Apr. 18, 2022).

118 AMERICAN LAW AND PRACTICE

through a platform, not directly between entrepreneur and investor. This makes gatekeeping a legal obligation.

Second, US law mandates that investment crowdfunding platforms be formally licensed by the SEC. They can be licensed either as a "broker," which is a longstanding designation, or as a "funding portal," which is a new type of license established by the JOBS Act and Regulation Crowdfunding.[55] Platforms that are licensed as funding portals may only conduct investment crowdfunding offers, while brokers can host other types of offerings as well. This comes in particularly handy when a platform wants to conduct two parallel offerings, one for the public under Regulation Crowdfunding and one for accredited investors under Reg. D. In practice, many platforms have registered both as funding portals and as brokers.[56]

Funding portals and brokers are closely regulated, both by the SEC and FINRA, a self-regulatory organization that they are legally obligated to join.[57] Under Regulation Crowdfunding, these registered platforms cannot hold investor funds themselves but must direct them to a "qualified third party," such as a bank; they cannot list companies owned by their own officers; they must provide new customers with educational materials about investment crowdfunding; and much more.[58] It is not important to list every detail of the licensure regime; the key point is that, if a platform falls short in its legal gatekeeping obligations, the SEC has the power to yank its license and thereby put it out of business. This ever-present threat pushes platforms to guard the gate with even more vigilance than would private pressure alone.

Third, the law places a number of gatekeeping-related duties on platforms, ensuring some minimum level of gatekeeping for the entire industry. Is this necessary, given the private incentives for platforms to act as responsible gatekeepers? It may well be.

As discussed in Chapter Four, there is reason to think that platforms, left to their own private whims, will indeed act as gatekeepers and will conduct some level of due diligence before allowing a company to list. But the level of due diligence, and the strictness with which they curate, may be lower than investors would optimally prefer, because it would take time for investors to realize that the offerings on a given platform are duds. In the absence of a legal obligation, a platform could rationally decide to be a very lax gatekeeper and allow just about any company through. Investors will buy in, and the platform will collect years

---

[55] 17 C.F.R. § 227.300(a) (2022).

[56] StartEngine, for example, does business through two regulated affiliates, one of which (StartEngine Capital, LLC) is a licensed funding portal, while the other (StartEngine Primary, LLC) is a licensed broker.

[57] 17 C.F.R. § 227.300(b) (2022).

[58] 17 C.F.R. §§ 227.300–227.305 (2022). Brokers, unlike funding portals, are allowed to hold investor funds as long as they transmit them promptly. *Id.* § 227.303(e) (2022).

LICENSED PLATFORMS   119

of transaction fees until the jig is up. This is a species of market failure that can be solved through regulation—and that is exactly what American law does.

Regulation Crowdfunding imposes a fair amount of mandatory gatekeeping on platforms. Before listing a company on their site, they are obliged to conduct a "background and securities enforcement history check" on the company, the entrepreneur, company executives, and major shareholders.[59] The rules also require platforms to conduct due diligence on whether the company has complied with its duties under the JOBS Act and Regulation Crowdfunding, and whether the company or offering "presents the potential for fraud or otherwise raises concerns about investor protection."[60] Note that Regulation Crowdfunding does not use the term "due diligence." Rather, it requires that platforms "have a reasonable basis for believing" this or that. And, in order to have a "reasonable basis" for believing something, you generally need to investigate it with due diligence.

All of this is to say that American law effectively forces platforms to act as diligent, if not strict, gatekeepers. This has its upside, in that it addresses two of the three fundamental challenges of startup finance, uncertainty and information asymmetry. The gatekeeping rules encourage investors to participate in the market, thereby advancing the first purpose of investment crowdfunding (see Chapter Two), which is to create a new source of capital for startup companies.

At the same time, however, these gatekeeping rules frustrate the second purpose of investment crowdfunding that I identified in Chapter Two, namely, to create an inclusive system where all entrepreneurs have the chance to pitch their idea to the public, regardless of who they are or where they are from.

This points up a key tension between these two essential purposes of investment crowdfunding. A totally inclusive system would ensure that platforms list any and every company that wants to participate. But platforms need to curate and select the companies they list in order to establish a reputation as a reliable market for investors, as well as to comply with their legal obligations under the JOBS Act and Regulation Crowdfunding. This gatekeeping function aids efficiency, but is exclusive by its nature. Hence, the tension between inclusive and efficient crowdfunding.

The history of Regulation Crowdfunding shows that the SEC wrestled with this tension. At first, in the earliest draft regulations the SEC released for public comment, platforms licensed as funding portals were supposed to simply take all comers. If an entrepreneur sought to solicit investments from the crowd for a nonfraudulent company, a funding portal would be legally obliged to list it, regardless of its view of the entrepreneur or the business. Indeed, Regulation Crowdfunding, as originally proposed, specifically stated that a funding portal

---

[59] 17 C.F.R. § 227.301(c)(1) (2022).
[60] 17 C.F.R. §§ 227.301(a), (c)(2) (2022).

120   AMERICAN LAW AND PRACTICE

"may not deny access to an issuer based on the advisability of investing in the issuer or its offering."[61] This was a radically inclusive rule: every entrepreneur had to be included, and none could be excluded (except for fraudulent operators).

When the SEC put out the draft version of Regulation Crowdfunding for public comment, this rule received a wave of criticism. As I explained in Chapter Four, platforms have a fundamental business need to act as gatekeepers and thereby cultivate and protect a sound reputation among investors, otherwise people may not be willing to invest their money on the site. Under the rule as proposed, funding portals would have been hamstrung in their gatekeeping role—yet that is probably the most important method of private ordering in the entire system.

If curation were prohibited, it would have been impossible for a funding portal to generate and protect its reputation for only listing companies with good prospects. This, in turn, would put platforms licensed as funding portals at a competitive disadvantage versus platforms licensed as brokers.[62] Because of the important of gatekeeping, the draft rule could have effectively destroyed the value of a funding portal license, had it been made final.

A law preventing funding portals from guarding their gate would likewise have led to various inefficiencies for all market participants. First, investors would have had to wade through tons of unsuitable investments in order to find the ones they like. Second, investments would have been spread very thinly among many issuers, leading to many failed campaigns, as the combination of the investor cap and the all-or-nothing rule would make it difficult for any given issuer to reach its target amount. Third, funding portals, who often are compensated through a transaction fee paid by a company that meets its target, would have had to charge higher fees to account for the time and resources they waste on the high number of unsuccessful campaigns. And since the overall success rate would be relatively low in an uncurated marketplace, a large percentage of issuers would have wasted their time and effort trying to get funding. Without going any further, it is clear that the SEC was surely right to back away from the radically inclusive concept it initially put forth.

Due to all these concerns, the SEC received a significant number of complaints that the draft proposal privileged inclusivity over efficiency (although they did not put it in precisely these terms). The SEC, for its part, was persuaded that the system would only work, or would at least work much better, if funding portals had the legal authority to select which companies to include, and which to exclude, from their sites.

---

[61]   78 Fed. Reg. 66,428, 66,486.
[62]   This rule would have applied only to platforms holding a funding portal license from the SEC.

So, in response to the broad public opposition it received, the SEC made a 180-degree turn and changed the rule to expressly allow all platforms to exercise their discretion to limit the companies that they allow on their platforms.[63] This is synergistic with the private incentive for gatekeeping described in Chapter Four.

This change between the proposed and final version of Regulation Crowdfunding might suggest that efficiency is more important than inclusivity, but that is not really the lesson to be learned. Rather, it was more a question of balancing, or optimizing, the multiple purposes of investment crowdfunding. On this score, the SEC was probably right to raise efficiency over inclusivity, as some level of gatekeeping and exclusivity is needed for crowdfunding to function; total inclusivity is simply too inefficient to work in practice. More broadly, this regulatory history shows the vitally important role that gatekeeping plays in the investment crowdfunding market.

To conclude this point, the legal approach to platforms in the JOBS Act and Regulation Crowdfunding is strongly synergistic with the powerful private ordering method of gatekeeping.

F. ISSUER LIMIT

Under American law, a company is legally limited to raising a certain maximum amount of money each year via investment crowdfunding. This rule is known as the "issuer limit," because it places a limit on the company issuing the securities. Regulation Crowdfunding provides for a $5 million annual issuer limit; how we got there is an interesting tale, to which I will return in a few paragraphs.

The issuer limit is a distinctive feature of investment crowdfunding and is one element of the definition I offered in Chapter One. There is no similar issuer limit for private placements; if your friends or family can afford it, and you can convince them, you are perfectly free to sell them $10 million worth of securities. So too with VCs and angels; a VC-backed company might raise $50 million or $100 million in a single fundraising "round." And the same can be said for traditional public IPOs, which can even run to the billions of dollars.

The issuer limit represents the maximum loss that crowdfunding investors, as a group, can suffer from the failure of any single company. The issuer limit also ensures that no one company can raise so much money via crowdfunding that its failure could cause significant social harm. Even if an offering "goes viral" and investors engage in herding behavior due to the "madness of the crowd," the

---

[63] 17 C.F.R. § 227.402 (2022) (empowering crowdfunding portals to "[d]etermine whether and under what terms to allow an issuer to offer and sell securities . . . through its platform").

122 AMERICAN LAW AND PRACTICE

company can only raise funds up to the issuer limit. The result is that the madness ends before it can really get going.

Contrast this with initial coin offerings (ICOs) of cryptocurrencies, like bitcoin or ether, which lack an issuer limit. This allows herding investors to pour billions, or even trillions, of dollars into a single asset—with the result that a failure could cause significant harm to many people.

For example, one cryptocurrency platform called Bitconnect tricked investors around the world to invest billions of dollars in 2017 by promising them returns as high as 40 percent per month using a "volatility software trading bot"—but it was just an old-fashioned Ponzi scheme.[64] In the end, the founder was criminally indicted (and then vanished), and the "investors" collectively lost more than $2 billion.[65] For another example, a stablecoin known as Terra collapsed in 2022, causing $40 billion of dollars in losses for investors—orders of magnitude worse than the worst-case scenario in any crowdfunding company.[66] I could go on—unfortunately—but the point is that unlimited fundraising can lead to enormous and widespread harm.

In investment crowdfunding, the issuer limit is a powerful prophylactic against this type of grand explosion. It does not entirely solve the problem of herding, but it does sharply limit its potential harm.

Okay, an issuer limit is a good idea. But does it need to be mandated by law? Or could it come about through private ordering? Couldn't a platform just impose its own issuer limit, as it saw fit?

Although a platform could, in theory, try to set its own issuer limit, I think it would be an unstable situation and would likely to lead to market failure. In a competitive environment, I think each platform would want to offer a higher limit, as a way of attracting companies with high hopes of raising a lot of money. Thus if one platform has a $100,000 issuer limit, a rival could attract business away from it by offering a higher limit of, say, $500,000. The first platform could respond by raising its own limit to $1 million, and a third platform might come on the scene offering a $2 million limit. Pretty soon, the whole thing would unravel and we would not have any issuer limit anywhere, just as we see in the unregulated world of ICOs, NFTs, and the like.

The law can solve this market failure by imposing a uniform issuer limit that all platforms and companies must adhere to, and that is exactly what Congress

---

[64] Complaint, SEC v. BitConnect, No. 21 Civ. 7349 (S.D.N.Y. Sept. 1, 2021).

[65] Press Release, U.S. Dep't of Justice, BitConnect Founder Indicted in Global $2.4 Billion Cryptocurrency Scheme (Feb. 25, 2022), https://www.justice.gov/opa/pr/bitconnect-founder-indic ted-global-24-billion-cryptocurrency-scheme.

[66] David Yaffe-Bellany & Erin Griffith, *How a Trash-Talking Crypto Founder Caused a $40 Billion Crash*, N.Y. TIMES, May 18, 2022.

did in the JOBS Act.[67] This was a fine and sensible decision, and one that all other jurisdictions have followed, as we shall see in Chapter Six.

The text of the JOBS Act provides for a $1 million issuer limit but, after a while, the $1 million limit turned out to be too confining. It was just too low to accommodate the realistic needs of many promising startup companies, which were more in the range of several million dollars. In addition, the costs of legal compliance are effectively higher when you can raise only a small amount of money. If it costs, say, $50,000 to raise money via crowdfunding, that amount does not change much if you are raising $1 million or $5 million, but the $50,000 represents 5 percent of the former and only 1 percent of the latter.

The low $1 million issuer limit was, in my view, a major reason why the American investment crowdfunding market got off to a slow start, a subject to which we will return in Chapter Seven. Every time the SEC took public input, this concern was raised, and many commenters, myself included, advocated for a higher issuer limit. Ultimately, the SEC was persuaded to act. As part of the 2020 amendments to Regulation Crowdfunding, it raised the issuer limit to $5 million per year.

An alert reader might ask, how could the SEC do that, given that the text of the JOBS Act sets the issuer limit at $1 million (which it does)? It is one thing for the SEC to issue a regulation that interprets an unclear statute, or announces rules pursuant to its statutory authority—but the SEC cannot flatly override the law laid down by Congress, can it? It turns out that Congress had previously granted the SEC authority to create special exemptions to the Securities Act when "necessary or appropriate[,] in the public interest, and is consistent with the protection of investors."[68] The SEC rarely uses this authority, but it did in this case, demonstrating just how confident it was that the $1 million issuer limit set by Congress should be raised to $5 million.[69]

As a final point on the issuer limit for investment crowdfunding, it bears noting that money raised pursuant to other exemptions—such as from accredited investors—does not count toward the $5 million issuer limit. The technical term for this is "non-integration," in the sense that money raised through those other methods will not be integrated with capital raised through crowdfunding when enforcing the $5 million limit. This means that an entrepreneur is perfectly free, under the law, to raise $5 million through investment crowdfunding as well as additional sums from friends, family, angel investors, VCs, or anybody else.

As discussed in regard to syndication in Chapter Four, this non-integration rule allows for crowdfunding campaigns to sometimes appear to exceed the

---

[67] 15 U.S.C. § 77d(6)(A).
[68] 15 U.S.C. § 77z-3.
[69] Two commissioners dissented from this decision, however.

124   AMERICAN LAW AND PRACTICE

$5 million issuer limit. The way it works is this: if an offering is so popular that it is bumping up against the $5 million limit, the crowdfunding platform can move any accredited investors into a concurrent offering under Reg. D, thereby freeing up more room under the limit for non-accredited investors to participate.[70]

G. INVESTOR CAP

As a sort of parallel to the issuer limit just discussed, the JOBS Act also imposed an annual cap on the amount an individual may legally invest in crowdfunding companies. The purpose of this investor cap is to limit the potential harm to retail investors by preventing them from putting too much money into the unregistered securities of speculative startup companies.

The investor cap is an innovative form of investor protection, one not found in other areas of securities law. Its goal, and effect, is to make retail investors into "mini" accredited investors. Recall from Chapter One that accredited investors are allowed to invest in unregistered securities because they have the financial cushion to absorb the loss of most, or even all, of the money they put in. In the same way, the investor cap in the JOBS Act limits the amount of money a person can invest (and potentially lose) to a small, defined percentage of her assets or income. It's like an airbag in an automobile: only relevant in a total crash, but vital in that instance.

Under American law, the investor cap is structured as a limit on the total amount that a person may cumulatively invest in all crowdfunded securities purchased over a twelve-month period. A person could invest up to the cap in one offering, or she could spread her investments over multiple companies, as long as the total stays below the legal limit. The cap also applies to all investments made on various intermediary platforms. So if an investor has hit her annual limit after investing in one or more offerings on Platform A, she may not legally move over to Platform B and start making investments.

Note that the JOBS Act's investor cap does nothing to encourage diversification, since a person could put her entire annual allocation into a single company. In other countries, like Australia and Canada, the investor cap is not cumulative but offering-by-offering, which does have the beneficial effect of preventing an investor from putting all her eggs in one basket.

The investor cap is not a simple dollar amount. Rather, it varies from person to person, based on her income and net worth. Under the JOBS Act, a person

---

[70] *Legal Primer for Founders*, WEFUNDER, https://help.wefunder.com/legal-primer (last visited Aug. 1, 2022) ("If you end up raising more than $5M in your Reg CF raise, we'll spin up a concurrent Regulation D, Rule 506(c) offering so you can raise an unlimited amount from accredited investors.").

may invest a maximum of 5 percent of her annual income or net worth in crowd-funding issuers per year.[71] If her annual income or net worth exceeds $100,000, she can invest 10 percent, instead of 5 percent, up to an absolute limit of $100,000 per year. And if her annual income or net worth is very low—or even zero—she may invest up to $2,000 per year.

This is an overly complex rule that often leads platforms to ask investors to state their annual income and net worth. After all, the platform is required by Regulation Crowdfunding to have a reasonable basis for believing that the investor is under her legal limit for the year.[72] Yet this is very personal information that most people would prefer not to share, and the fact that the law requires such disclosure probably deters at least some of them from participating.[73]

What about accredited investors? The investor cap in the JOBS Act, as well as the original version of Regulation Crowdfunding, applied with full force to accredited investors. This was a strange, if not entirely nonsensical, decision since accredited investors are presumed to be able to handle losses of any size. Furthermore, accredited investors are very useful to investment crowdfunding as they are precisely the type that serve as lead investors and put a large amount of their own money into a company. But by capping their investments in crowd-funding, the JOBS Act had the unfortunate effect of discouraging them from participating. It's just not worth their time.

For all these reasons, there was broad agreement that the law should be changed in order to excuse accredited investors from the investor cap. To its credit, the SEC took heed of the criticism, and one of the amendments it made in 2020 to Regulation Crowdfunding was to eliminate the investor cap for accredited investors, which was clearly the right choice. For all other investors, however, the same overly complex and intrusive sliding-scale rule is still in place.

---

[71] 15 U.S.C. § 77d(6)(b).

[72] 17 C.F.R. § 227.303(b)(1) (2022).

[73] There are even further ambiguities and complexities in the JOBS Act's investor cap, but they are so silly as to only merit attention in the footnotes. Most notably, the statutory text ("5 percent of the annual income or net worth of such investor") is ambiguous as to whether the 5 (and 10) percent rule applies to the "greater of" or the "lesser of" annual income or net worth. Consider, for example, a retired person with an annual income of $60,000 and a net worth of $300,000. Should the 5 percent rule apply because his annual income is under $100,000, or should the 10 percent rule apply because his net worth is over $100,000? And, either way, should the percentage be calculated on the greater of the two figures ($300,000) or the lesser of the two figures ($60,000)? Under the "lesser of" reading of the statute, this investor would be subject to the 5 percent rule calculated on the basis of his income, yielding an annual cap of $3,000. Under the "greater of" reading, the limit would be calculated using the 10 percent rule calculated on the basis of his net worth, yielding an annual cap of $30,000. The SEC—those poor souls!—has gone back and forth over the restrictive "lesser of" rule and the liberal "greater of" rule. In its original proposal for Regulation Crowdfunding, the SEC adopted the "greater of" rule, only to switch to the "lesser of" rule in the final version. More recently, however, the SEC changed course once again and reverted to the "greater of" rule in the revised regulations issued in 2020. The takeaway from this footnote—for those who have stayed awake to this point—is that this is no way to run a railroad, and a much simpler rule—like that of Australia or Canada—would be preferable.

126   AMERICAN LAW AND PRACTICE

Overall, the investor cap is a good idea, imperfectly executed in American law. By capping the maximum losses any individual can suffer, it cabins the harm that anyone can suffer from a bad investment. Given the risks of startup companies, and the likelihood that many will fail, it is sensible to rein in enthusiastic investors ready to drain their entire bank account to invest in "the next big thing."

Although paternalistic, the investor cap seems like a reasonable price to pay for all the liberal features of investment crowdfunding. This investor cap allows the entire investment crowdfunding project go forward without fear that retail investors will suffer unaffordable investment losses.

H. ALL OR NOTHING

Thinking back to the old world of reward crowdfunding, there are two leaders in the field, Kickstarter and Indiegogo, and each follows a different basic model of fundraising. First, there is the "all-or-nothing" model, whereby the fundraiser announces a target level of funds at the outset of the campaign. Potential backers peruse the various projects available on the site, and then pledge their money to one(s) they like; these pledges are tallied on an ongoing basis on the site. If a given project reaches its target amount within a set time frame, the money is collected from those who pledged; if a project fails to meet its target, then the deal is off and no money changes hands. Hence, you either get all—meaning at least the target amount—or nothing.

The alternative model, which doesn't really have a name, asks for a funding target, but allows the fundraiser to keep whatever amounts are pledged by the end of the set time period, even if they fall short of the target. Indiegogo follows this model, or at least allows it, under the moniker "flexible funding." Kickstarter, by contrast, follows the all-or-nothing method.

The JOBS Act, for its part, came down on Kickstarter's side and imposed a mandatory all-or-nothing model for investment crowdfunding in the United States. Crowdfunding companies are required to set a target funding amount and a time frame to reach it.[74] If enough investors contribute within the relevant time, the deal succeeds and the company gets the money. If the amount falls short of the target by the deadline, then the investors get their money back.[75] Companies must also announce a maximum amount they are willing to take.[76]

This all-or-nothing model is a key component of American law, and it works synergistically with the wisdom-of-the-crowd phenomenon I described in

[74] 15 U.S.C. § 77d-1(b)(1)(F).
[75] 15 U.S.C. § 77d-1(a)(7)
[76] 17 C.F.R. § 227.201(h) (2022).

Chapter Four. The effect of the all-or-nothing rule is that any individual investor who selects a "bad"—meaning unpopular—investment will be saved from his poor choice by the wisdom of the crowd. This is because an unpopular investment will not reach its target funding amount, and the deal will be called off. Rather than walk off the cliff alone, such an investor will be pulled back to safety by the crowd.

Note that the alternative (Indiegogo) model would not have this salutary effect. If an individual investor selects a dud of an investment (and doesn't cancel it (see later in this chapter)), the company will get that money at the end of the relevant time period. This could easily be a disaster. Consider, for example, a company that wants to raise money to develop a new type of battery for an electric car and sets a target of $2 million. If it only can get $20,000 worth of investments, it is much better for the deal to be canceled than for it to go through. The poor investors would have all their money eaten up by the costs of raising it, and the company has no chance of developing the battery with only $20,000.

Another benefit of the all-or-nothing rule is that it creates an economic incentive for investors to crowdsource their investment analysis, an aspect of private ordering that I described in Chapter Four. Thanks to the investor cap described earlier, a single investor cannot usually push the company all the way to the target, and even if he likes the company, his investment will be canceled if it falls short. In order to help the company reach the target funding, the investor has an incentive to share his information and opinions with other investors.

All this shows the value of the all-or-nothing model. Importantly, VCs and angel investors follow a similar sort of model, albeit informally. They invest in so-called "rounds," and a round only comes to fruition once there is a critical mass of capital pledged, at least informally. The JOBS Act and Regulation Crowdfunding wisely followed these exemplars by adopting the all-or-nothing model.

The idea was a good one, but the execution was not, for the simple all-or-nothing model enacted in the JOBS Act and Regulation Crowdfunding can be easily gamed by companies and platforms. There is no "minimum" target in the law, and no relation between the minimum and the maximum. Thus, there is nothing to stop a company from setting its funding target at some absurdly low level, say $100, and the maximum at, say, $1 million. Once that low bar is cleared, the company is home free and will get the money regardless of how little or how much is ultimately raised—and the platform will receive its commission for hosting a "successful" offer. Unfortunately, this is not at all merely hypothetical but appears to happen every day.

Rather than setting the funding target on an individual basis, the leading American platforms appear to impose uniform funding targets on all, or nearly all, of the companies they list. Wefunder sets the funding target at $50,000, Republic and SeedInvest set it at $25,000, and StartEngine requires that every company on its site set a funding target of just $10,000.[77] This last one in particular defeats the purpose of the all-or-nothing rule, as it effectively ensures that the company will meet the target and thereby "succeed" in its crowdfunding campaign.

But it is a bit silly for a company that really needed $200,000 to call it a success to have raised $12,000. In fact, it's worse than silly, since the whole $12,000 will go toward the costs of raising the funds, harming the company and the investors at the same time. The platform, by contrast, might not mind, since it receives its commission (which it would not get if the offer were to fail).

Furthermore, because the rule allows for any minimum and maximum, companies routinely select a minimum of $10,000 and a maximum of $1 million. This is bonkers. A company that seeks to raise anywhere between $10,000 and $1 million clearly has no idea what amount of funding it actually needs.

This gaming of the all-or-nothing rule is not a universal practice, but appears to be distinctive to the American market. In New Zealand, for instance, companies announce very reasonable funding targets, as well as maximums that make sense. At the leading Kiwi platforms (PledgeMe and Snowball Effect), the lowest funding targets are around NZ$100,000, and many offers have funding targets of NZ$1 million or more. To take just one example, chocolate company OCHO announced a crowdfunding offering in 2021 with a funding target of NZ$300,000 and a maximum limit of NZ$500,000. Now there's a company that knows how much money it wants to raise.

Another problem with the rule in Regulation Crowdfunding is that there is no legal limit on the deadline, so companies routinely give themselves many months, or even a year or more, to reach their funding target. This is a common occurrence on all platforms. Crowdfunding companies often choose a deadline a full year ahead, knowing that they can close the offering "early" as long as they give the investors forty-eight hours to cancel (we will cover this later in this chapter under "Cooling Off").

The effect of such a long time frame is to undermine the whole point of having a deadline in the first place, which is to test the crowd's appetite for what the company has to offer. In addition, it may also harm the company by keeping its attention on the crowdfunding campaign for many months, rather than getting on with business.[78]

---

[77] *Company FAQ*, STARTENGINE, https://www.startengine.com/company-faqs (last visited May 20, 2022) ("*What if I raise less than my funding goal?* We require that companies set a minimum funding goal of $10,000 for their campaign. This way if you raise less than your maximum funding goal, you can still collect the investments you raised as long as your campaign has raised more than $10,000.").

[78] Further, depending on the cooling-off rule in place, a very long deadline can effectively "trap" the funds of the people who commit to the offering.

ALL OR NOTHING   129

Again, this is a distinctively American issue. In the United Kingdom, for instance, the leading platforms keep offers open for much shorter timespans, such as thirty or sixty days. Canada and Australia, for their part, have addressed this issue by adopting a legal limit of ninety days—a move that I would support.

All in all, the all-or-nothing model is a useful structure, but it is not presently working well in the United States. Why Americans seem intent on finding loopholes in the regulations when others do not is a question for another time. But the fact remains that Regulation Crowdfunding's laissez-faire approach to the funding target and maximum is insufficient.

I accordingly would recommend that this regulation be revised and tightened up to prevent the sort of gaming and abuse we have seen to date. I generally support a light-handed approach to regulation, but this is a market failure that the law can and should try to resolve.

One way to address the low target problem is to create a new rule that links the maximum to the funding target, such that a company is only legally allowed to raise a certain multiple (perhaps four times) of the funding target. For example, if a company announces a funding target of $20,000, it would only be legally allowed to raise up to a maximum of $80,000 (assuming a four-times multiple); if it announces a target of $250,000, it can raise up to $1 million.

A rule like this would effectively force a company to think carefully about how much funding it really needs and would rehabilitate the power of the all-or-nothing model in the United States. Were such a rule in effect, platforms would not have their listing companies all use a standard funding target like $10,000 or $25,000, as they commonly do now. This would be a big change from the current practice, but a good one, I think.

If my proposed rule were enacted, a crowdfunding company would have to analyze its individual circumstances and set its funding target at an amount that it actually needs to raise. Typical funding targets would likely be in the range of $100,000, $250,000, or even $1 million (as we see in other jurisdictions). Having to reach those lofty targets in order to get a penny would present a real test of the investors' view of the company—which is exactly the point of the all-or-nothing regime.

Finally, there should be some regulatory guardrails on the deadline as well. Regulation Crowdfunding should be amended to include a legal limit on the length of time that a crowdfunding offer can remain open. Canada has done just that, imposing a legal limit of ninety days, which seems like a reasonable choice. This concentrates the discussion among the crowd and allows the company to raise money and then get back to its primary business, whatever it may be.

That discussion among the crowd does not happen "in real life"; it takes place on the online platform's "communication channels."

130   AMERICAN LAW AND PRACTICE

I. COMMUNICATION CHANNELS

Certain aspects of Regulation Crowdfunding are specifically intended to enhance the effectiveness of the private ordering methods I described in Chapter Four. One good example is the legal requirement that platforms provide "communication channels by which persons can communicate with one another and with representatives of the issuer about offerings made available on the intermediary's platform."[79]

Online message boards or the like can be a useful way for investors to share information with one another. They also can serve as a forum where potential investors can ask questions of the entrepreneur that can be answered right there on the forum, for all to see. In Chapter Four, I called this process "crowdsourced investment analysis" and argued that it responds well to uncertainty and information asymmetry. By mandating that all platforms provide "communication channels," the SEC consciously sought to facilitate this valuable method of private ordering: "We anticipate that communication channels provided by the intermediary will provide a forum through which investors could share information to help the members of the crowd decide whether or not to fund the issuer."[80]

This all makes sense, but was this legal rule necessary? Or should we expect platforms to provide "communication channels" on their own, as a matter of private ordering? On the one hand, it seems quite likely that, left to their own devices, platforms would establish message boards, Q&A functions, and the like, so maybe the rule was not needed.

On the other hand, Regulation Crowdfunding's rules on communication channels do add value, in that they mandate certain beneficial features that might not otherwise be forthcoming. Most importantly, Regulation Crowdfunding requires that company founders or employees, as well as paid promoters, clearly identify themselves as such when they post something to the communication channel. It is useful for investors to know that a given statement came from a self-interested person—and such a person might obscure his self-interest, or at least not highlight it, if there were no legal obligation to do so.

Regulation Crowdfunding also requires that communication channels be accessible to the public, and only permits people formally registered as users on the platform to post to them. These rules make good sense. As for the former, sunlight is the best disinfectant, and the public nature of the communication channels should chasten anyone thinking of manipulating the market, as every utterance will be both public and indelibly marked on a digital trail. The SEC,

---

[79] 17 C.F.R. § 227.303 (2022).
[80] 80 Fed. Reg. 71,388, 71,426; *id.* at 71,425 ("We believe that one of the central tenets of the concept of crowdfunding is that the members of the crowd decide whether or not to fund an idea or business after sharing information with each other.").

independent "watchdogs," and concerned citizens can easily track who said what when, and wrongdoers can be held to account. And as for the latter rule, this would likely have been the free choice of platforms anyway, since allowing anyone to post is an invitation to anarchy. So the rule was probably not needed, but is probably not harmful either.

J. ANY SECURITY

American law allows companies to offer any type of "security" via investment crowdfunding. The term "security" is defined in the Securities Act to include all types of financial contracts.[81] Hence companies can sell anything from plain vanilla stocks and bonds to more exotic types.

The most familiar type of security is a share of "common stock," which is what people trade on traditional public stock markets, like the New York Stock Exchange. Common stockholders are usually thought of as the "owners" of a corporation, and they hold the power to elect the board of directors to manage the company on their behalf. And if the directors fail to work diligently and loyally for the company, a common stockholder can bring a lawsuit against the offenders for breach of fiduciary duty. Finally, if a corporation ceases to do business and liquidates or declares bankruptcy, the common stockholders are entitled to the "residual"—whatever is left over after employees, bondholders, and all other claimants are paid.

Common stock is just one of the many types of securities that a company can legally crowdfund. Another familiar type is a bond, which represents a loan from the investor to the company. The terms of the bond specify the interest rate and the term, meaning the date when the principal is to be repaid. Bondholders do not own the company in the way that common stockholders do, and the board of directors does not owe them any fiduciary duties. Rather, a bond is a matter of contract between the company and the bondholders.

Beyond stocks and bonds, many other types of instruments qualify as securities. "Preferred stock" lies somewhere in between common stock and a bond. Like a bond, the rights are spelled out in contractual terms, and they commonly include a certain level of dividends and a "liquidation preference" (meaning that preferred stockholders must be paid before the common stockholders in the event of a liquidation). Often, preferred stock is also "convertible" to common stock, at a ratio laid out in the terms of the contract—such a security is dubbed

---

[81] 15 U.S.C. § 77b(a)(1) ("The term 'security' means any note, stock, treasury stock, security future, security-based swap, bond, debenture, . . . investment contract, . . . or, in general, any interest or instrument commonly known as a 'security'. . . . ").

132 AMERICAN LAW AND PRACTICE

"convertible preferred stock." The precise terms of a share of preferred stock varies from one to the next, however; there is no standard set of terms.

Still other types of securities can be sold via crowdfunding, including options (contracts to buy or sell stock (or another security) at a given price), profit-sharing agreements, and much more. Indeed, any kind of "investment contract"—meaning an investment of money in a common enterprise with the expectation of profits to be derived from the efforts of others—qualifies as a security that can be crowd-funded.[82] Imagination is the only limit.

One particular type of security that merits discussion is the Simple Agreement for Future Equity (SAFE). The SAFE is a recent innovation, dating only to 2013, and was developed to facilitate seed-stage investments in startup technology companies, primarily in Silicon Valley.[83] Although the SAFE is new and fairly obscure, the SEC has considered banning it from crowdfunding, even as the crowdfunding market-place has embraced the form.

A SAFE is not a form of equity, like common stock, and SAFE holders do not have the right to vote for directors or sue for breaches of fiduciary duty. Nor is a SAFE a debt instrument that pays interest or matures on a certain date. Rather, it is a contractual instrument that converts to equity upon the occurrence of a certain event defined in the SAFE itself. The usual triggering events are if the company goes public, is sold, or raises another round of financing, but they vary from SAFE to SAFE.

One key advantage of a SAFE is that it defers the need to value the company until later investors come in. Because the company is more mature at that point, and because the later investors are usually more sophisticated and experienced, it is easier to establish a fair valuation at that time. The SAFE holders then receive common stock at the same valuation as the later investors. Depending on the terms of the SAFE, the holders may receive a valuation that is even more attractive than the later investors receive; this can be accomplished in several ways, most simply by promising SAFE holders a specified percentage discount on the ultimate price of the common stock.

The SAFE became rather popular in the American crowdfunding marketplace during the first few years of crowdfunding.[84] Despite its popularity, however, some commentators and market participants expressed concern that SAFEs are

---

[82] SEC v. W.J. Howey Co., 328 U.S. 293 (1946) (classic definition of "investment contract" as used in the Securities Act).

[83] Joseph M. Green & John F. Coyle, *Crowdfunding and the Not-So-Safe SAFE*, 102 VA. L. REV. ONLINE 168, 171 (2016).

[84] Usha R. Rodrigues, *Financial Contracting with the Crowd*, 69 EMORY L.J. 397, 458 n.323 (2019) (noting that 26% of crowdfunding offerings involve SAFEs).

not appropriate for crowdfunding companies or investors.[85] These critics raise numerous concerns over the propriety of crowdfunding SAFEs.

First, SAFEs are not familiar like stock or bonds, and they are not really as simple as their name suggests. There is no single form of SAFE that is universally utilized; important terms vary from one to another. Second, crowdfunded companies may never trigger a conversion event listed in their SAFEs, leaving their investors in limbo. A company that raises money through crowdfunding is unlikely to go public, and it may never be sold or even raise a further qualifying round of funding. SAFE holders could find that their securities are zombies that do not pay dividends, do not confer voting rights, and, as such, are effectively worthless.

Due to these concerns, the SEC published an investor bulletin in 2017 to warn crowdfunding investors of the risks posed by SAFEs.[86] Not long thereafter, the SEC considered restricting the sorts of securities that could be offered via investment crowdfunding to traditional varieties of equity (common stock) and debt (bonds). In proposed amendments to Regulation Crowdfunding published in 2020, the SEC announced that it planned to bar companies from selling exotic types of securities, singling out SAFEs in particular.[87] The SEC received public comments both in support of and in opposition to its proposal to ban SAFEs and, in the end, decided to maintain the status quo whereby companies can issue any and all securities—including SAFEs—through crowdfunding.[88] In light of the risks posed by SAFEs, however, the SEC took care to remind companies of their obligation to "clearly describ[e] the terms of the offered securities, especially in the case of non-traditional securities, such as SAFEs."[89]

In practice, several of the leading crowdfunding platforms in the United States have embraced SAFEs and use them for all or nearly all of the companies they list. On the other hand, at least one leading platform, StartEngine, has banned them from its site entirely.[90] In other words, the market appears to have resolved

---

[85] *E.g.*, Joseph M. Green & John F. Coyle, *Crowdfunding and the Not-So-Safe SAFE*, 102 VA. L. REV. ONLINE 168, 182 (2016) ("we believe that SAFEs are not well suited to being used in crowdfunding transactions"); Howard Marks, *Are SAFE Notes Not Safe for the General Public?*, STARTENGINE (Mar. 13, 2020), https://www.startengine.com/blog/are-safe-notes-not-safe-for-the-general-public (CEO of crowdfunding platform explaining that his platform does not allow companies to offer SAFEs because "they are not well-structured" for investment crowdfunding).

[86] Investor Bulletin, U.S. Sec. & Exch. Comm'n, Be Cautious of SAFEs in Crowdfunding (May 9, 2017), https://www.sec.gov/oiea/investor-alerts-and-bulletins/ib_safes.

[87] Facilitating Capital Formation and Expanding Investment Opportunities by Improving Access to Capital in Private Markets, 85 Fed. Reg. 17,956, 18,001 (proposed Mar. 31, 2020).

[88] Facilitating Capital Formation and Expanding Investment Opportunities by Improving Access to Capital in Private Markets, 86 Fed. Reg. 3,496, 3,547–48 (Jan. 14, 2021).

[89] Facilitating Capital Formation and Expanding Investment Opportunities by Improving Access to Capital in Private Markets, 86 Fed. Reg. 3,496, 3,548 (Jan. 14, 2021) (citing 17 C.F.R. § 227.201(m)).

[90] Howard Marks, *Are SAFE Notes Not Safe for the General Public?*, STARTENGINE (Mar. 13, 2020), https://www.startengine.com/blog/are-safe-notes-not-safe-for-the-general-public.

134   AMERICAN LAW AND PRACTICE

this issue; those who want to invest in SAFEs may do so, and those who want to avoid them can do that too.

More generally, different crowdfunding platforms have endorsed different types of securities. Most companies on StartEngine seem to offer common stock, of various types. Other platforms, led by Mainvest and Honeycomb, specialize in bonds and other type of debt offerings. These debt-focused platforms generally do smaller deals and are more focused on existing small businesses that need a loan, rather than brand-new startup companies seeking equity.

K. SPECIAL PURPOSE VEHICLE

From the outset, one problem with raising money via crowdfunding was that the result would be hundreds or thousands of new investors. Before a crowdfunding round, a startup company might have had a simple and clean "cap table" with, say, three people, each owning a third of the shares. Afterward, it might have 1,003 shareholders; this is known as a "messy" cap table, and it is anathema to the world of startup finance.

At best, this is an inconvenience, since the company now has to keep track of all of these investors on the capitalization table that lists everyone with a claim on the company. All else being equal, most startup companies would prefer to avoid having such large numbers of investors, as it creates administrative complexity. The company has to keep track of the name and address of every investor and has to contact them from time to time for votes or approvals. It is obviously much simpler to communicate with three shareholders than three hundred.

Beyond administrative issues, basic principles of corporate law give shareholders, in particular, a panoply of rights. Shareholders can demand to review the company's books and records; they can propose shareholder resolutions; they can even bring a so-called derivative lawsuit against the company executives and directors. These rights are useful, but they can also be abused, and among hundreds of shareholders there may well be one or two gadflies with the time and inclination to distract management using these tools of corporate governance.

But the worst part of having hundreds or thousands of investors is that it can jeopardize the company's ability to raise capital in the future. Angel investors, and especially VCs, are understandably wary of buying into a company with so many fellow investors. They know that any one of them can gum up the works, and so they generally refuse to invest in startup companies with messy cap tables.

This is a big problem, as the near-universal hope of crowdfunding companies and their investors is that the company will attract additional funding rounds, especially from VCs, in the future. This is most obvious in the case of SAFE investors, as their investment depends on a future round coming to fruition, but is also true more generally. If the very act of raising money through crowd-funding renders the company toxic for future fundraising rounds, rational entrepreneurs will steer clear of the market. This relates to the adverse selection issue described in Chapter Three and is another culprit for the slow start in the United States.

The SEC, through public comments and otherwise, was made aware of this problem and addressed it directly in the 2020 amendments to Regulation Crowdfunding. The solution came in the form of a new rule that authorized crowdfunding companies to employ a "crowdfunding vehicle" (more popularly known as a special purpose vehicle (SPV)).[91] A crowdfunding vehicle is defined as a company whose sole ("special") purpose is to invest in a company that it-self would be eligible to raise money through investment crowdfunding. In other words, people invest in the SPV, and the SPV then invests in the company. The result is that company only adds a single investor—the SPV—to its cap table.

This simple solution solved the messy cap table problem in one fell swoop. Huzzah!

L. ELIGIBLE COMPANIES

Pursuant to the JOBS Act, almost any type of company is eligible to raise money through crowdfunding, regardless of the type of business it pursues, its age, or its location. Although the focus of the law is on startup companies, crowdfunding is not legally limited to them; any type of private company may participate. That said, there are certain limits and exclusions on the types of companies that are eligible to raise money through crowdfunding.

First, all participating companies must be incorporated or organized in the United States.[92] Any sort of legal entity will do, whether a corporation, limited partnership, public benefit corporation, limited liability company (LLC), or any-thing else, and it may operate anywhere, so long as the company is incorporated in an American state. For this reason, many seemingly "foreign" companies are eligible to participate. For example, a Delaware corporation founded by a Korean, with a headquarters in Mexico City, and conducting business throughout Africa would be eligible.

Second, because the intent of the law is to advance startups and small businesses, the JOBS Act bars publicly traded companies (such as those listed on the New York Stock Exchange) from the crowdfunding market.[93] This is hardly a

---

[91] 17 C.F.R. § 270.3a-9 (2022).
[92] 15 U.S.C. § 77d-1(f)(1).
[93] 15 U.S.C. § 77d-1(f)(2).

136 AMERICAN LAW AND PRACTICE

problem for them, though, since they are large businesses that can readily access capital in other ways.

Third, the JOBS Act prohibits "investment companies" from raising money via investment crowdfunding.[94] An investment company is defined, for these purposes, as one whose primary business is to invest in securities of other companies. Under this rule, mutual funds, hedge funds, and VC funds, among others, cannot raise money through crowdfunding. An operating company that incidentally invests in other companies is not barred from crowdfunding, however, as that is not its primary business.

Fourth, American investment crowdfunding law includes a "bad actor" exclusion for companies (and platforms) run by, or affiliated with, someone convicted of a crime related to the financial markets in the recent past.[95] Platforms are required to enforce this rule, by conducting a background and securities enforcement check of the directors, officers, promoters, and so forth.[96] The "bad actor" definition goes beyond criminal convictions and encompasses anyone subject to civil orders excluding them from the securities industry, for instance, but the SEC has the power to waive this disqualification rule in appropriate circumstances.[97]

Fifth, a company that has previously raised money via crowdfunding but failed to file its annual report to shareholders as required (see the earlier "Ongoing Disclosure" section) may not conduct another crowdfunding offering.[98] A company barred by the rule can be forgiven by filing annual reports for the most recent two years; once those two reports are filed, the company is once again eligible to crowdfund.

Sixth and finally, only companies with an actual business plan are allowed to solicit money through investment crowdfunding. The business plan can be simple and early-stage, but some sort of "specific business plan" is required.[99] This is a low bar.

Collectively, these six rules serve as a very modest limits on the types of companies that can legally raise money through investment crowdfunding. Just about any private company would qualify, which is consistent with the inclusive nature of the concept, and as it should be. Some other countries have placed additional limits. Italy, for instance, limits investment crowdfunding to "innovative" companies, meaning those that own a patent, employ a large number of PhD holders, or engage in other specific activities—and this limitation has hindered the Italian crowdfunding market.

---

[94] 15 U.S.C. § 77d-1(f)(3).
[95] 17 C.F.R. §§ 227.100(b)(4), 227.503 (2022).
[96] 17 C.F.R. §§ 227.301(c)(1) (2022).
[97] 17 C.F.R. § 227.503(b)(2) (2022).
[98] 17 C.F.R. § 227.503(b)(5) (2022).
[99] 17 C.F.R. § 227.100(b)(6) (2022).

The American rules, by contrast, are light-handed and serve to include just about any company that would want to participate.

M. ADVERTISING AND PROMOTION

Entrepreneurs seeking to raise money via crowdfunding have a strong need to get the word out. In order to hit the funding target, they need to sign up a large number of individuals, since each one is constrained by the investor cap. Furthermore, the online nature of investment crowdfunding means that the key to reaching enough people is through emails that can be forwarded and social media posts that can be "liked" and "shared," as well as advertising of every kind.

At the same time, Congress wanted people to consider the full set of mandatory disclosures provided on Form C before investing. They reasonably feared that people would decide to buy in based on an advertisement or a social media post that touts the company's bright possibilities but omits important information that would be found on Form C, like financial statements and risk warnings.

For this reason, the JOBS Act tightly constrained the ability of crowdfunding companies to advertise their offering to potential investors, nearly to the point of prohibition.[100] The original version of Regulation Crowdfunding put this into practice by allowing issuers to promote their offering by publishing simple, textual advertisements that direct investors to the online funding platform, such as through a web link, where they would find the full set of mandated disclosures on Form C. Other types of advertising or promotion were off-limits.

Once again, this proved to be overly restrictive, and, once again, the SEC was willing to reconsider. The 2020 amendments to Regulation Crowdfunding liberalized the advertising rules, to some degree. The revised rules allow entrepreneurs or promoters to mention the purpose of the money being raised and the company's progress toward meeting the target. The revised rules also authorize oral solicitation, so long as the speaker directs the listener to the official Form C.[101]

Finally, the 2020 amendments allow companies to gauge whether there might be sufficient interest among investors—informally known as "testing the waters"—without first having to file a Form C.[102] Under this new rule, an entrepreneur could invite people to sign up on social media and thereby generate a list of potential investors. If a lot of people are interested, she can go forward and spend the money to file a Form C (which must include any documents shared as part of

---

[100] 15 U.S.C. § 77d-1(b)(2) (providing that a crowdfunding company "shall not advertise the terms of the offering, except for notices which direct investors to the funding portal or broker").

[101] 17 C.F.R. §§ 227.204(a)–(b) (2022).

[102] 17 C.F.R. § 227.206 (2022) ("Solicitations of interest").

138 AMERICAN LAW AND PRACTICE

the testing-the-waters process[103]). If only a few seem to notice, she can abandon the idea and not waste a lot of money on compliance costs. These were all useful changes to Regulation Crowdfunding.

N. COOLING OFF

Under basic rules of contract law, once you agree to a deal, you are legally bound to it, even if you later change your mind. That is what makes a contract a contract and not merely an idle promise. Of course, you could draft a contract that gives you the right to walk away, but that will cost you more, because you are getting more from the other side. Refundable airline tickets are always more expensive than nonrefundable ones.

In the JOBS Act, however, Congress decreed that crowdfunding investors must be given the right to cancel their commitments and instructed the SEC to flesh out the details.[104] Thus in Regulation Crowdfunding, the SEC granted crowdfunding investors the legal right to cancel a commitment any time until the final forty-eight hours before the offer closes.[105] This right to cancel is sometimes called a "cooling-off period," as it is meant to give the investor time to calm down and reconsider his choice.

In one sense, this mandatory cooling-off period is friendly and helpful to investors, and synergistic with both the wisdom of the crowd and crowdsourced investment analysis discussed in Chapter Four. If a person commits, say $500, to a crowdfunding company, but then learns disconcerting news on the platform's communication channel, he can cancel the pledge and move on.

In another sense, however, this right to cancel might not ultimately benefit crowdfunding investors. Recall that a contract with a right to cancel always costs more than one without, since it gives the holder more rights. Hence by mandating that every crowdfunding investment contract include a right to cancel, the JOBS Act effectively raised the price of every security for every investor. Maybe it was worth it, but maybe not.

At the extreme, this right to cancel could discourage high-quality companies (i.e., those that could raise money from angels or VCs, if they wanted) from raising money via investment crowdfunding. From the perspective of the company, which needs to meet its target by the deadline in order to get funded, it is terribly nerve racking to know that all the promised investment can blow away, like dust in the wind, at any moment until the final forty-eight hours.

---

[103] 17 C.F.R. § 227.201(z) (2022).
[104] 15 U.S.C. § 77d-1(a)(7).
[105] 17 C.F.R. § 227.304(a) (2022).

A right to cancel may be a good idea but the rule provided by Regulation Crowdfunding is suboptimal. Peeking ahead to the next chapter, we will see that other jurisdictions have adopted cooling-off periods that give an investor the right to cancel within a few days of making the commitment, but then the window closes and he is bound. This is a superior model because it protects investors and at the same time provides certainty to a crowdfunding company that its funding commitments will come through, allowing it to meet its target.

O. RESALE RESTRICTIONS

Investment crowdfunding is, as I emphasized in Chapter Four, a "primary" market, meaning one where companies sell securities directly to the subscribing investors, rather than a "secondary" market, where investors trade those securities among themselves. For this reason, the JOBS Act and Regulation Crowdfunding are almost entirely comprised of rules governing the primary offering.

There is one part of the law, however, that does relate to secondary trading: under the JOBS Act and Regulation Crowdfunding, crowdfunded securities cannot be resold after purchase for one full year.[106] There are a few exceptions to this one-year holding period. The buyer is allowed to transfer crowdfunded securities in that first year to the company that issued them, to an accredited investor, to a family member, or as part of a formal registered offering.[107]

This is very different from how we approach the secondary market for ordinary publicly traded securities that trade on recognized national exchanges, like NASDAQ. Holders of those sorts of securities are free, under the law, to resell their securities to anyone and at any time—and federal law specifically preempts the states from applying their own securities laws to such transactions.[108] But this sort of federal preemption does not apply to crowdfunded securities.

The effect of the one-year holding period, combined with the lack of preemption of state law, is that a liquid secondary market for crowdfunded securities is practically impossible under current law. But even if the law allowed it, secondary trading would never be as simple and liquid as on a traditional stock exchange.

This is simply because the number of shares in the marketplace is orders of magnitude smaller for a crowdfunded company than a traditional public

---

[106] 15 U.S.C. § 77d-1(e).
[107] 15 U.S.C. § 77d-1(e)(1).
[108] 18 U.S.C. § 77(r).

140 AMERICAN LAW AND PRACTICE

company. Publicly traded companies issue millions of shares, making it easy to find someone who wants to buy or sell a few. Crowdfunded companies, by contrast, have only hundreds or thousands of securities outstanding, making it difficult and expensive to transact in them. For this reason, no liquid secondary market (of any note[109]) has developed in the United States—and we should not expect one to develop anytime soon.

This lack of a secondary market for crowdfunded securities has key implications for corporate governance. In effect, it means that crowdfunding investors are in a position analogous to minority investors in a so-called close (or closely held) corporation. Close corporations are usually small and generally do not pay dividends, but the defining feature of a close corporation is that there is no liquid market for their securities. The result is that the investors are stuck and cannot "exit" their investment, even if they want to. And this, in turn, means that they are at special risk of abuse and oppression by the company and the other shareholders.

There are lots of ways for this abuse to play out, and they are often given colorful names, like "squeeze-out" and "freeze-out." One classic move is for the minority investor to be offered a low price for her shares. Since there is no liquid market, it's effectively "an offer he can't refuse." Another is to merge the company into an empty shell in order to "cash out" the minority shareholders at a low price. Corporate law understands the plight of the minority investor in a close corporation well and has developed both specific doctrines and special statutes to address it.[110]

Even though they may end up with a large number of shareholders, crowdfunded companies are very much like close corporations with respect to this opportunity for oppression. Recall from Chapter Two the example of Meow Wolf, an immersive art company that crowdfunded more than $1 million from hundreds of investors in 2017 and then "forced" these investors to sell their shares back to the company two years later at a much higher price.[111] Thus the shareholders were squeezed out, just as they might be in a traditional close

---

[109] StartEngine, for instance, has established a platform called "Secondary," which is an online trading system that matches buyers and sellers of crowdfunded securities, but it has apparently seen only very limited trading in just a handful of companies. *Secondary*, STARTENGINE, https://www.star tengine.com/trade (last visited Aug. 1, 2022).

[110] *E.g.*, Wilkes v. Springside Nursing Home, Inc., 353 N.E.2d 657, 662 (Mass. 1976) ("one peculiar aspect of close corporations [is] the opportunity afforded to majority stockholders to oppress, disadvantage or 'freeze out' minority stockholders"); 8 DEL. C. §§ 341–56 (establishing a set of optional "Special Provisions" for "Close Corporations").

[111] Judith Kohler, *Meow Wolf Putting the Bite on Investors Who Anted Up When It Needed Help, Critics Say*, DENVER POST, Aug. 7, 2019.

corporation. Even if these shareholders received a fair price, many were still upset about being squeezed out.[112]

Close corporations have been around a long time, and both legal rules and contractual terms have been developed to address the problem of opportunism that is inherent in their nature. These doctrines and contracts may be usefully transplanted to the context of crowdfunding. As a doctrinal matter, courts should be receptive to the idea that crowdfunded companies should be treated as akin to close corporations, with the result that the controlling shareholder in such an enterprise (often the entrepreneur) owes the crowd-shareholders a fiduciary duty of "utmost good faith and loyalty."[113]

In addition, crowdfunding companies should employ the well-known contractual tools to address this risk of abuse. For example, a crowdfunded company can enter into a "buy/sell agreement" with the investors that dictates when the company can buy them out and at what price. (This is exactly what Meow Wolf did, by the way.[114]) A buy/sell agreement can be drafted to give the investors substantial leverage, and it can be altered in any way that the parties would like. It could, for instance, require an independent valuation. Or it could include a term giving the investors the right to either buy or sell at the price offered by the company. Such a term would encourage the company (and likely the entrepreneur) to only offer to buy out the investors at a price it would take itself.

I need not continue with other potential deal terms, as the imagination of lawyers knows no bounds. The platforms, as well as the lead investors, are well placed to request or require one or more of these sorts of contractual resolutions to the problem of close corporations. This has begun to happen in practice. Wefunder, for instance, requires that each company have a lead investor who represents all the crowdfunding participants and advocates on their behalf. This concentration of power should help avoid abuse and encourage fair treatment of the investor body.

* * *

To conclude, the American legal regime established by the JOBS Act and Regulation Crowdfunding does a decent job of working synergistically with the private ordering methods discussed in Chapter Four to respond to the three fundamental challenges of startup finance in a low-cost manner. The most valuable

---

[112] Teya Vitu, *Meow Wolf's Buyback Dismays Crowdfunders*, SANTA FE NEW MEXICAN, Aug. 7, 2019 ("I'm making money, but it would have been nice if I had an option to leave my original investment in.") (quoting investor).

[113] Wilkes v. Springside Nursing Home, Inc., 353 N.E.2d 657, 661 (Mass. 1976).

[114] The securities included the following term: "[T]he company may, at any time . . ., by notice to the [investor], redeem all or any portion of the Shares at a price per share equal to the fair market value thereof as reasonably determined . . . by the Company's board of directors." Teya Vitu, *Meow Wolf's Buyback Dismays Crowdfunders*, SANTA FE NEW MEXICAN, Aug. 7, 2019.

142   AMERICAN LAW AND PRACTICE

components are probably the issuer limit and the requirement that platforms be licensed by the SEC. Other aspects are not worth their cost, and this would include some, if not all, of the mandatory disclosure rules relating to offerings. Still others could stand to be improved, such as the all-or-nothing rule, which is useful but easy to game.

The American system may not be perfect but, because it was the first, it became the model for the world. In the next chapter, we will see that this legal regime established in the United States has been highly influential across the globe. Many countries copied it essentially wholesale, and others made conscious changes. In short, the JOBS Act and Regulation Crowdfunding set the standard on which other investment crowdfunding regimes are modeled. We will take a comparative look at several jurisdictions in the next chapter.

Chapter Six
Comparative Law and Practice

Like blue jeans or Coca-Cola, investment crowdfunding is an American original that has been embraced worldwide. From the time the United States enacted the JOBS Act in 2012, dozens of other countries have followed suit and amended their securities laws to authorize this new form of securities market. Investment crowdfunding is truly a global phenomenon, touching every continent, and it continues to expand as I write these words.

In this chapter, we will look at the law governing investment crowdfunding in five jurisdictions—Australia, Canada, the European Union, New Zealand, and the United Kingdom—to see how they compare to the American standard. With the exception of the United Kingdom, all of these systems hew closely to the model established by the JOBS Act and Regulation Crowdfunding—but they are not exact copies of American law, and different countries changed different things.

This chapter will lead directly into the next and final one, where I'll offer my recommendations on how to design an optimal regulatory regime for investment crowdfunding. To that end, my goal in this chapter is not to catalog every rule in every jurisdiction, but rather to highlight what we can learn from a comparative review. What can we learn from the choices made in these jurisdictions?

Before getting to the substance, permit me to defend my choice of just these five jurisdictions. Admittedly, this discussion overlooks many jurisdictions, as scores of nations around the world have enacted investment crowdfunding laws over the past decade. But I limit the discussion to these five for a few reasons.

Firstly, since so many countries have adopted investment crowdfunding legislation by now, it would be overwhelming to try to describe every law in every country. Secondly, a global catalog would also be repetitive, since most jurisdictions have modeled their crowdfunding regimes on the JOBS Act and Regulation Crowdfunding. Thirdly, a detailed and exhaustive review could grow stale, as investment crowdfunding is a very young field, and the legal landscape is still developing and changing.

Okay, so we cannot examine every country, but why choose this particular group of five? For one thing, this set of countries represents a good sample of the variety of regimes in place around the world, including those organized on a national level, like Australia, on a subnational level, as with the Canadian provinces, and on a supranational level, as in the European Union. For another, this

Investment Crowdfunding. Andrew A. Schwartz, Oxford University Press. © Andrew A. Schwartz 2023.
DOI: 10.1093/oso/9780197688526.003.0007

144 COMPARATIVE LAW AND PRACTICE

list includes the oldest and largest crowdfunding markets in the world, both in an absolute sense and on a per capita basis. They also have a fairly stable set of crowdfunding regulations. While they may be subject to some change in the coming years, they are unlikely to be totally overhauled, so it is not necessarily futile to describe their current state.

In addition, these countries are all developed economies that are broadly comparable to the United States, facilitating the comparative project of this book. Because these other jurisdictions are a lot like the United States, we can focus on the distinctions in their legal regimes, knowing that most other variables are being held roughly constant. The history, traditions, and laws in these jurisdictions are all similar to the United States, thus providing a fair comparison. They all have democratically elected legislatures, and they all enforce contracts and provide legal protection for private property in a manner similar to the United States (although the European Union may be a bit different from the others).

More important than these general commonalities, however, is the fact that all these countries share the same basic approach to securities regulation. They all have analogs to the Securities Act of 1933 that require securities to be registered with a government regulator akin to the SEC (e.g., Australian Securities and Investment Commission, New Zealand Financial Markets Authority). This registration process calls for copious mandatory disclosure in all of these countries, as in the United States. Finally, like the United States, all of these jurisdictions have exemptions to the registration requirement for sales to accredited investors (known as "wholesale," "high net worth," or "sophisticated' investors) or to friends and family.

For all these reasons, this chapter will focus on the investment crowdfunding laws enacted in Australia, Canada, the European Union, New Zealand, and the United Kingdom. In crafting their own crowdfunding laws, each of these five jurisdictions has made different choices and altered the formula in various ways.

Geography plays a role, with some following the lead of their close neighbors and adopting comparable legal rules for investment crowdfunding. Canada, for instance, has largely duplicated the American JOBS Act and its related regulations. Similarly, the European Union enacted a unified approach for the entire bloc. Other countries have veered away from their neighbors in their approach to regulating investment crowdfunding. The United Kingdom, as might be expected, has taken a dramatically different tack than the European Union. More surprisingly, New Zealand and Australia have enacted rather different systems, even though those two countries often seek to harmonize their securities laws. All that said, this chapter is not organized by geography.

Rather, I think the best way to think about the various legal regimes around the world is to split them into two broad types, which I call the "standard model" and the "liberal model." The defining difference between the two models is their approach to the three fundamental challenges of uncertainty, information asymmetry, and agency costs. The standard model relies primarily on legal regulation to address these three challenges. The liberal model, by contrast, depends primarily on private ordering to address this trio of problems. There is not a bright line between the two models, as all legal systems rely on both private and legal methods. It is a question of emphasis.

The American legal regime I described in Chapter Five established the world's first regulatory system of investment crowdfunding; indeed, that is one reason why I call it "standard." The other reason I call it "standard" is that this model regulates investment crowdfunding using the traditional tool for regulating public securities markets—namely, mandatory disclosure. It requires companies to provide investors and the government with certain specified information in a precise format, often via an official form. Beyond mandatory disclosure, the standard model also includes numerous other hard-and-fast legal rules designed to protect investors, including issuer limits, investor caps, advertising restrictions, cancellation rights, and more.

The standard model imposes the highest costs on companies seeking financing, because it depends so much on legal regulation, as opposed to private ordering. For the same reason, it also arguably provides the greatest protection to investors, although it may protect them too much. Regardless, it is quite popular internationally, and this chapter will use Australia, Canada, and the European Union as examples of the standard model, apart from the United States.

The liberal model of investment crowdfunding regulation is simply a liberalized, deregulated version of the standard model. Rather than imposing a great deal of law and regulation, the liberal model relies primarily on the methods of private ordering I described in Chapter Four. Most importantly, the liberal model abandons mandatory disclosure and official forms, instead relying on platforms and companies to decide what information to share and how to present it. In addition, countries following the liberal model have relaxed or eliminated many other rules imposed by the standard model, including investor caps and advertising limits, although they retain some features of the standard model, most notably issuer limits and a licensure requirement for platforms.

Without mandatory disclosure, and with fewer rules overall, the liberal model is friendlier to companies seeking financing, and thus may be expected to lead to more companies getting more funding. On the other hand, investors receive arguably less protection than they do under the standard model, with the result that only a brave politician would endorse the liberal model, even if he thought it socially beneficial, on balance. For this reason (known formally as "public choice" economics), the liberal model is rarely found in practice. New Zealand

146 COMPARATIVE LAW AND PRACTICE

and the United Kingdom are the leading jurisdictions to have adopted the liberal model, and so I describe their unusual legal regimes below.

To situate the reader: the JOBS Act and Regulation Crowdfunding, which were the subjects of Chapter Five, established the template for the standard model. This chapter provides examples of other jurisdictions that followed the standard model—namely, Australia, Canada, and the European Union. After that, this chapter will describe the two leading examples of the liberal model: New Zealand and the United Kingdom. By focusing our comparison on just a few jurisdictions, we can get a good sense of the two different models of investment-crowdfunding regulation—the standard model and the liberal model. For the reader's convenience, the chapter concludes with a chart (Table 6.1) listing the key components of investment-crowdfunding regulation in all six of the jurisdictions covered in this book.

A. STANDARD MODEL

The standard model of investment crowdfunding regulation depends mainly on formal legal regulation to address the three fundamental challenges of uncertainty, information asymmetry, and agency costs. The United States follows the standard model, as do dozens of other countries around the world. In this section, we will take a close look at Australia, Canada, and the European Union as exemplars of the standard model.

1. Australia

Australia rarely finds itself behind its smaller neighbor, New Zealand (rugby aside[1]). Yet that is just what happened with investment crowdfunding in the two Oceanic countries in the 2010s. New Zealand, as we will discuss later in this chapter, followed swiftly behind the United States and enacted its own investment crowdfunding law in 2013, which went into effect the following year. Australia took notice of the JOBS Act and the New Zealand law as early as 2013 and began considering whether and how to regulate investment crowdfunding, a process that stretched over five full years.[2]

---

[1] In the Bledisloe Cup, the annual rugby competition between Australia and New Zealand, the All Blacks have won the last twenty in a row. In banking, finance, and other commercial arenas, however, Australia holds the upper hand.

[2] *See, e.g.*, AUSTRALIAN GOVERNMENT, ADVANCING AUSTRALIA AS A DIGITAL ECONOMY: AN UPDATE TO THE NATIONAL DIGITAL ECONOMY STRATEGY (2013), https://apo.org.au/node/34523; AUSTRALIAN GOVERNMENT, CORPORATIONS AND MARKETS ADVISORY COMMITTEE, CROWD SOURCED EQUITY FUNDING (2014).

An initial draft bill was introduced in the Australian Parliament in 2015.[3] Following two years of discussion and refinement, Australia adopted the Corporations Amendment (Crowd-Sourced Funding) Act in 2017. This new law—the CSF Act—added special new amendments to the Corporations Act 2001, the primary source of securities regulation in Australia, to allow for investment crowdfunding (which they call "crowd-sourced funding," or CSF).[4] The CSF Act, supplemented by related regulations from the Department of the Treasury,[5] went into effect in late 2017. But it had a fatal flaw.

Australian corporate law defines multiple categories of companies, with different public reporting obligations. Almost all companies in Australia (roughly 99.7 percent) are organized as "proprietary" companies,[6] akin to a private company in the United States—and yet the original 2017 legislation only allowed "public companies" to raise money through crowdfunding![7] The effect was to exclude nearly every company from participation, including practically every startup company and small business that investment crowdfunding is meant to serve. For this reason, the original CSF Act was essentially useless.

The Australian Parliament, to its credit, admitted its mistake and amended the CSF Act the following year specifically to allow proprietary companies to raise funds through investment crowdfunding.[8] The result is that investment crowdfunding is governed by the Corporations Act 2001, as amended by both the 2017 and 2018 CSF Acts, as well as the CSF Regulations, which were drafted by the Department of the Treasury.[9] Australia's legal framework only went into effect in late 2018, four years behind New Zealand.

The Australian legal regime squarely aligns with the standard model and largely tracks the JOBS Act and Regulation Crowdfunding from the United States. It has all the usual features of the standard model, including mandatory disclosure and caps on both participating companies and investors. It is also comprehensive and complex, just like the American original. In addition to the CSF Act, the Australian Securities and Investments Commission (ASIC) has put out well over one hundred pages' worth of regulatory guidance in order to explain all the rules.[10]

---

[3] Corporations Amendment (Crowd-sourced Funding) Bill 2015 (Cth) (Austl.).

[4] Corporations Amendment (Crowd-sourced Funding) Act 2017 (Cth) (Austl.).

[5] Corporations Amendment (Crowd-sourced Funding) Regulations 2017 (Cth) (Austl.).

[6] Akshaya Kamalnath & Nuannuan Lin, *Crowd-Sourced Equity Funding in Australia—A Critical Appraisal*, 47 FED. L. REV. 288, 290 (2019).

[7] Corporations Amendment (Crowd-sourced Funding) Act 2017 (Cth) s 738H(1)(a) (Austl.).

[8] Corporations Amendment (Crowd-sourced Funding for Proprietary Companies) Act 2018 (Cth) s 41 (Austl.).

[9] Corporations Act 2001 (Cth) pt 6D.3A (Austl.).

[10] *See* Australian Securities and Investments Commission, *Regulatory Guide 261: Crowd-sourced funding: Guide for companies* (2020) (120 pages); Australian Securities and Investments Commission, *Regulatory Guide 262: Crowd-sourced funding: Guide for intermediaries* (2018) (53 pages).

148   COMPARATIVE LAW AND PRACTICE

Investment crowdfunding in Australia is, like elsewhere, focused on domestic startups and small businesses. Companies must have their principal place of business in Australia, and a majority of directors must reside within the country.[11] Publicly listed companies are excluded, as are investment companies, and only companies with assets and revenue under A\$25 million (roughly \$20 million) may participate.[12]

Australia imposes an issuer limit of A\$5 million per year,[13] and crowdfunding companies are required to provide certain mandated disclosures via an "offer document"—although there is no official form to use, as in Canada and the United States.[14] A crowdfunding offer can remain open only for a maximum of three months—a point to which I shall return when discussing the Canadian regime later in this chapter.[15]

Under the law, the offer document must include specific information about the company, the offer, and the rights of investors, as well as a boilerplate warning about the risks of investment crowdfunding.[16] The offer document must be drafted in a manner that is "clear, concise and effective" and cannot be misleading or deceptive.[17] Financial disclosures are mandated, and a company that raises more than A\$3 million must provide a formally audited financial statement.[18] There is no required form to use, although ASIC has provided an optional template for companies to use if they wish.[19]

Under the Australian legislation, people may invest up to A\$10,000 (approximately \$8,000) per offer and participate in as many offers as they wish.[20] The hosting platform is obliged to enforce this investor cap, which is easy enough to do.[21] Wealthy investors, known as "sophisticated" investors in Australia (and roughly equivalent to "accredited" investors in the United States), are exempt from this limit.[22] This facilitates the practice of syndication, which we discussed

---

[11] Corporations Amendment (Crowd-sourced Funding) Act 2017 (Cth) ss 738H(1)(b)-(c) (Austl.).

[12] Corporations Amendment (Crowd-sourced Funding) Act 2017 (Cth) ss 738H(1)(e)-(f), (2) (Austl.).

[13] Corporations Amendment (Crowd-sourced Funding) Act 2017 (Cth) s 738G(2) (Austl.).

[14] Corporations Amendment (Crowd-sourced Funding) Act 2017 (Cth) s 738J (Austl.).

[15] Corporations Amendment (Crowd-sourced Funding) Act 2017 (Cth) s 738N(4)(a) (Austl.).

[16] Corporations Regulations 2001 (Cth) regs 6D.3A.02-06 (Austl.).

[17] Corporations Amendment (Crowd-sourced Funding) Act 2017 (Cth) ss 738K, 738U(1)(a) (Austl.).

[18] Corporations Act 2001 (Cth) s 328D(1) (Austl.).

[19] Australia Securities Investment Commission, *Regulatory Guide 261: Crowd-sourced funding: Guide for public companies* ss 261.140–.141 (2020).

[20] Corporations Amendment (Crowd-sourced Funding) Act 2017 (Cth) s 738ZC(1)(b)(i) (Austl.).

[21] Corporations Amendment (Crowd-sourced Funding) Act 2017 (Cth) s 738ZC(1)(b)(i) (Austl.).

[22] The relevant statutory section refers to "Caps on investment by *retail* clients," implying that sophisticated investors are exempt. Corporations Amendment (Crowd-sourced Funding) Act 2017 (Cth) s 738ZC(1)(b)(i) (Austl.).

in Chapter Four, by allowing wealthy investors to make large cornerstone investments and act as a lead investor for the crowd.

Australia's investor cap is much more liberal than the American version, and it differs in two key ways. First, Australia's cap is based on a flat dollar amount rather than a sliding scale based on a percentage of net worth or income. Second, the cap applies to each investment, rather than a cumulative cap that applies to all investments made in a given year.

Australia's distinctive approach to the investor cap has multiple benefits. It requires no calculations, making it simple to understand and easy for platforms to enforce, as they need not consider any other investments made on their own or other platforms. It also eliminates the need for platforms to ask investors to provide personal financial information about their income or net worth.

One notable weakness of the Australian investor cap is that it does not really protect investors from losing more than they can afford. Because they can invest up to A\$10,000 in as many companies as they wish, an enthusiastic investor could quickly invest her entire life savings, split among a number of crowdfunding companies. An American-style cumulative annual cap, by contrast, would prevent such an outcome.

In this way, the Australian investor cap is much more liberal and permissive than the American one. The main goal of the Australian cap is to encourage investors to diversify their investments among a number of companies and not put all their eggs in one basket. The main goal of the American investor cap, by contrast, is to protect investors from taking large risks that could lead to ruinous losses. Australia puts more responsibility on each investor to decide how much she can realistically stand to invest, and possibly lose, in investment crowdfunding. Given that people are generally free to buy or invest as much as they want in whatever they want, I think that Australia's approach is the superior choice.

On the other hand, Australian investment crowdfunding law is less liberal than its American counterpart in at least one important way—although the Aussies seem to be of two minds about it. Let me explain. In the United States, companies are allowed to sell any type of security, from stock to preferred shares to SAFEs (see Chapter Five). The Australian statute on investment crowdfunding, at first, follows this lead and allows for any type of security.[23] In the same section, however, it allows this broad scope to be narrowed by regulation to only certain types of securities.[24] And this is just what happened: Australia's

---

[23] Corporations Amendment (Crowd-sourced Funding) Act 2017 (Cth) s 738G(1)(a) (Austl.) ("An offer is eligible to be made under this Part if . . . it is an offer by a company for the issue of securities of the company . . . .").

[24] Corporations Amendment (Crowd-sourced Funding) Act 2017 (Cth) s 738G(1)(a)(c) (Austl.) ("An offer is eligible to be made under this Part if . . . the securities are of a class specified in the regulations.").

150 COMPARATIVE LAW AND PRACTICE

regulations provide that crowdfunding companies may only offer "fully-paid ordinary shares" (common stock).[25] No other type of security may be sold via investment crowdfunding.

Another difference between Australia and America relates to way the two jurisdictions handle cancellations by investors who change their mind after making an investment. In the United States, investors may freely cancel their investments, and get their money back, at any time until the final forty-eight hours before an offer closes. Australia is stricter, as investors are given a "cooling-off" period that allows them to withdraw their investment within five business days of making it—but, after that, they are bound.[26]

In this way, Australia provides more certainty to crowdfunding companies that the offer is going to succeed; five days after someone makes an investment, it is "money in the bank." In America, by contrast, it is possible that some or all of your investors will abandon you as late as three days before your deadline, leaving companies unsure whether they will actually get funded until the last moment.

Most other aspects of Australia's investment crowdfunding regime essentially mimic the United States: platforms must provide a "communication facility" to allow potential investors to make posts regarding the offer and ask questions of the company; advertising is limited to direction to the official offer on the platform; and platforms must be licensed by ASIC and are obliged to do some specified types of due diligence on the companies and offers they host (this is appropriately referred to in the statute as their "gatekeeper obligations").[27]

The investment crowdfunding market in Australia is very young, with only a couple of years of experience. It only really opened for business in late 2018, when the amendments to allow proprietary companies went into effect. Right out of the gate, the Australian investment crowdfunding market jumped ahead of the United States, on a per capita basis. In 2019, the first full year under the current system, Australian crowdfunding companies raised A$31 million, or roughly A$1 per person—and those numbers doubled by 2021.[28]

One reason for Australia's relative success is that it has leveraged its close ties with the United Kingdom and New Zealand, the two most mature investment crowdfunding markets in the world, to quickly gain the benefit of all the lessons that those countries have learned over the past decade or so. Indeed, one of the leading Australian platforms, Equitise, is based in Sydney, but it initially set up

---

[25] Corporations Regulations 2001 (Cth) reg 6D.3A.01 (Austl.).

[26] Corporations Amendment (Crowd-sourced Funding) Act 2017 (Cth) s 738ZD(1) (Austl.) (this cooling-off period is "for retail clients," implying that sophisticated investors do not have this right under the law (although platforms might provide it anyway)).

[27] Corporations Amendment (Crowd-sourced Funding) Act 2017 (Cth) ss 738ZA(5), 738ZG, 738C, 738Q (Austl.).

[28] See Chapter Two, tbls. 2.2, 2.3.

STANDARD MODEL   151

shop in New Zealand in 2014, explicitly to gain experience that it could then bring home to Australia, once the legal regime was fully in place.[29]

One key lesson from the United Kingdom and New Zealand was the importance of syndication. From the outset, then, Australian companies and platforms sought out established angels and VCs to play the role of lead investor. For example, Zero Co., a sustainable packaging company, raised the maximum A$5 million in a single investment crowdfunding offer on Birchal, one of the leading Australian platforms, in 2021. More than 3,000 people piled into the deal, which sold out in a record seven hours. One reason for its wild popularity was that this offer had a well-known lead investor in the form of Square Peg, one of Australia's largest VC firms, which invested A$6 million in Zero Co. on substantially the same terms as the crowd.[30] This is syndication in action.

Zero Co. also demonstrates the importance of brand ambassadors. The company's business model is for customers to refill and reuse bottles for detergent, shampoo, and the like in an effort to reduce the use of single-use plastic containers. This is a network-type business where the more people that participate, the more efficient and effective it will be for all concerned. By raising money through investment crowdfunding, Zero Co. energized and incentivized its most loyal customers, many of whom surely bought into the offering. It looks like the company could have raised all the money it needed from angels and VCs, but it makes sense that the company specifically sought to include its customers as part of its "journey."

There have been very few "exits" for crowdfunding investors, simply because the Australian market is so new. One notable exception is Activated Nutrients which, in 2021, became the first crowdfunded company to be publicly listed on the Australian Stock Exchange (ASX). The company had previously raised A$330,000 from 150 investors on Birchal in 2019, and two years later the company launched an oversubscribed IPO on the ASX, where it raised A$8 million. This was not only a successful "exit" for these investors, it was also a significant milestone for the entire market.

All in all, Australia's approach to investment crowdfunding is a clear example of the standard model pioneered in the United States. It features a couple of improvements over the American original, like the improved cooling-off period and the flat A$10,000 investor cap that applies on a per-offer basis. The market is small but growing fast, and has a bright future.

---

[29] Equitise, *Who Are We?*, https://equitise.com/about-us (last visited Sept. 24, 2022) ("The Equitise founders . . . quit their jobs to start an equity crowdfunding platform—a concept which had taken off in several other markets including the UK. But there was one hurdle—retail equity crowdfunding was not yet legal in Australia. So whilst lobbying the government [in Australia], they headed to New Zealand to gain first-hand experience in retail equity crowdfunding. After proving the model and a lot of lessons later, they headed home in time for the 2017 change in legislation.").

[30] BIRCHAL, FUNDED! CROWD-SOURCED FUNDING (CSF) IN AUSTRALIA FY2022, at 2 (2022).

152   COMPARATIVE LAW AND PRACTICE

2. Canada

Most countries regulate investment crowdfunding at the national level, but not in Canada, where securities regulation is regulated by each province (and territory), from Nova Scotia to the Yukon. Canada does not have a national securities regulator akin to the SEC; rather, each province has its own agency or commission that regulates the offering of securities within the jurisdiction. Hence it was impossible for the Parliament of Canada to enact a single national legal regime for investment crowdfunding akin to the JOBS Act in the United States. Nevertheless, once the JOBS Act was passed in 2012, several provinces went to work, each enacting a different set of laws to govern investment crowdfunding within its provincial borders.

It all began—as things rarely do—in Saskatchewan, which enacted Canada's first crowdfunding law in Canada in 2013.[31] Two years later, in 2015, Saskatchewan and a large group of other provinces, including Quebec, British Columbia, and Manitoba, all adopted similar—though not identical—investment crowdfunding regulations, which they called "Start-Up Crowdfunding Exemptions."[32] They also agreed to allow interprovincial transactions among the group.

Unfortunately, these harmonized rules had two fundamental flaws. First, Ontario, home to nearly half of the Canadian population, did not join the group, nor did Alberta, undermining this cooperative attempt to create a nationwide crowdfunding market. Second, these 2015 rules were overly restrictive, making the process too costly for the amount of money one could raise. The issuer limit was C$250,000 per offering, up to a maximum C$500,000 per year, and the rules required mandatory disclosure on an official form very much like Form C. This overregulation, combined with Ontario's absence, rendered the 2015 regime ineffective.

In 2016, Ontario stepped up to the plate and adopted its own investment crowdfunding law, called "Crowdfunding," and another group of provinces, including Quebec, agreed to enact the same rules in their jurisdictions.[33] Ontario's regime turned out to be just another instance of an overly regulatory version of the standard model. Because of the high regulatory burden, compared to the low issuer limit of C$1.5 million, the "Crowdfunding" regulations were effectively unusable. Indeed, as of 2020, not a single company had used that regime to raise funds.[34]

---

[31] General Order 45-925, *Saskatchewan Start-up Crowdfunding Prospectus and Registration Exemption* (Dec. 5, 2013) (Sask.).

[32] Multilateral CSA Notice 45-316, *Start-up Crowdfunding Registration and Prospectus Exemptions* (May 14, 2015) (Can.).

[33] Multilateral Instrument 45-108, *Crowdfunding* (Nov. 5, 2018) (Can.).

[34] *CSA Notice and Request for Comment: Proposed National Instrument 45-110 Start-up Crowdfunding Registration and Prospectus Exemptions* 2 (Feb. 27, 2020).

STANDARD MODEL   153

Eventually, the Ontario Securities Commission threw in the towel and abandoned the regulations it had passed. In 2020, it joined up with the other group of provinces by issuing a temporary order to allow companies and investors in Ontario to follow the rules of the Start-Up Crowdfunding Exemptions.[35] But because that rule imposed a C$250,000 issuer limit, with a lot of standard-model regulation, this was not much of an improvement.

Meanwhile, Alberta was living up to its maverick reputation, adopting in 2016 a set of rules that incorporated some aspects of the liberal model and some aspects of the standard model too. In some ways, Alberta's rules were highly deregulatory, such as by not even requiring the use of a crowdfunding platform and allowing companies to raise money directly from investors.[36] This is so radical that it falls out of the definition of investment crowdfunding that I provided in Chapter One ("via online platforms"). In other ways, Alberta's rules were highly regulatory, most notably in that they did not exempt offerings from the usual registration requirement. This too falls out of my definition ("unregistered"). For all its wildness, Alberta's system was also effectively unusable—and unused.[37]

With different rules in place in each province and separate but overlapping groups of provinces that endorse one set of regulations or another, the result was severe disharmony. It was a challenge even to figure out the relevant rules that apply to a given company or investor. In a word, it was a disaster.

After more than five years of effort, Canada was pretty much back where it started. After multiple attempts, it still lacked a functioning national legal regime for investment crowdfunding. Even worse, it could not even point to a province with a model that worked and could be adopted by others. Fortunately, the Canadian securities regulators were well aware of the problems, and they did not give up.

This problem of fragmentation and disharmony in securities markets is longstanding in Canada, and the various provincial regulators have even formed an organization, the Canadian Securities Administrators (CSA), to come together and create uniform rules, called National Instruments, that they can adopt in parallel. Thus in 2020, the CSA announced a proposal for a new National Instrument that would govern investment crowdfunding and could be adopted nationwide.[38] After considering public comment, this new National Instrument

---

[35] O. Instrument 45–506, *Start-Up Crowdfunding Registration and Prospectus Exemptions (Interim Class Order)* (July 30, 2020) (Can.).

[36] Alta. Sec. Comm'n, Rule 45-517, *Prospectus Exemption for Start-up Businesses* (Oct. 31, 2016) (Can.).

[37] CSA Notice and Request for Comment, *Proposed National Instrument 45-110 Start-up Crowdfunding Registration and Prospectus Exemptions* (Feb. 27, 2020) (Can.) (reporting that, as of the end of 2019, six companies raised a total of roughly C$130,000 in Alberta).

[38] *CSA Notice and Request for Comment: Proposed National Instrument 45-110 Start-up Crowdfunding Registration and Prospectus Exemptions* (Feb. 27, 2020).

154 COMPARATIVE LAW AND PRACTICE

45-110 was approved and adopted by every provincial securities regulator, and it went into effect in 2021.[39]

Finally, Canada had a uniform regulatory framework for investment crowd-funding. Canada's early efforts had failed, putting the country years behind its southern neighbor. But, in at least one way, the delay ended up working to their benefit: by 2020, investment crowdfunding had been up and running for four years in the United States, and even longer elsewhere. Canada was able to look out over the world (as well as reflect on its own experience) and consider whose crowdfunding regulations it wanted to emulate and whose it wanted to avoid. This is, more or less, the same approach as I am taking in this book.

National Instrument 45-110 represents a significant improvement over all the earlier attempts by the provinces. Rejecting the radicalism out of Alberta, as well as Ontario's onerous regime, the National Instrument falls squarely in the standard model, relying primarily on regulation, but not overly so. Moreover, National Instrument 45-110 has several features that are superior to its American counterpart, as I will highlight. Maybe slow and steady really does win the race.

National Instrument 45-110 requires that companies provide mandatory disclosure on an official government form (Form 45-110F1)[40] and imposes an annual issuer limit of C$1.5 million, a low but not unreasonable number.[41] The law includes an investor cap, set at a flat C$2,500 per offering, with no cumulative annual limit.[42] This investor cap, which is flat and noncumulative, is similar to the Australian one discussed earlier and is superior, in my view, to the sliding-scale and cumulative investor cap we have in the United States. Reasonable people can differ over what is the appropriate level for a per-offering cap—Australia uses A$10,000, compared to C$2,500 in Canada—and I come down somewhere in between, as we shall see in Chapter Seven.

Under National Instrument 45-110, an investor has the right to cancel his commitment within two business days after it is made.[43] This is similar to the Australian rule, which provides for five days, and is very different from the American rule, which is based on when the offer is due to close, not when the commitment is made. For the same reasons discussed earlier relating to Australia, I think that Canada has the better of the Americans on this one. As

---

[39] Nat'l Instrument 45-110, *Start-up Crowdfunding Registration and Prospectus Exemptions* (June 24, 2021) (Can.).

[40] Nat'l Instrument 45-110, *Start-up Crowdfunding Registration and Prospectus Exemptions* § 5(1)(h) (June 24, 2021) (Can.).

[41] Nat'l Instrument 45-110, *Start-up Crowdfunding Registration and Prospectus Exemptions* § 5(1)(g) (June 24, 2021) (Can.).

[42] Nat'l Instrument 45-110, *Start-up Crowdfunding Registration and Prospectus Exemptions* § 5(1)(p)(i) (June 24, 2021) (Can.). If the investor "has obtained advice from a registered dealer that the investment is suitable for the purchaser," then the investor cap is C$10,000 per offering. *Id.* § 5(1)(p)(ii).

[43] Nat'l Instrument 45-110, *Start-up Crowdfunding Registration and Prospectus Exemptions* § 5(1)(j)(1) (June 24, 2021) (Can.).

between the five-day cooling-off period in Australia, and the two-day cooling-off period in Canada, either one is reasonable.

Like Australia, the Canadian legal regime provides that crowdfunding offers can only remain open for a maximum of ninety days.[44] Under American law, by contrast, there is no analogous limit. Although Canada limits the parties' freedom, which should be avoided if possible, it may make sense to impose a legal constraint on the deadline in order to protect companies from being pressured by platforms to keep their offers open longer than they want.

Consider that platforms generally charge a transaction fee based on the amount of capital raised, with the result that the more money a company can collect, the greater the fees for the platform. Furthermore, because of the wisdom-of-the-crowd/herding effect, it is hard to raise the first bit of money, but, once an offering gains popularity and reaches a certain level of funding, it can really take off. The platform has to put time and effort into every offering, but it likely earns the bulk of its fees from the group of companies that blow the house down and raise millions of dollars in a single go.

Putting these points together, we can imagine a company that has hit its minimum target, and raised, say, C$150,000. That may be all the company really needs or wants, and it would like to close the offer and collect the money, especially since time is of the essence for startup companies. But from the platform's perspective, things are just getting started, and it has a keen interest in holding the offer open and raising more and more money. If the platform can get this company to raise the maximum C$1.5 million, it will make ten times the fee it would collect at this point—and the additional effort will be minimal.

The total effect is that platforms have an economic incentive to keep an offer open longer than is optimal for the company. Moreover, platforms will often hold overwhelming bargaining power over the brand-new startup companies that list on their site. Among other things, if the company stands up for itself, the platform might refuse to do business with it in the future. The upshot is that we may not want to give platforms and companies unfettered freedom to set the deadline for their offerings. In light of all this, Canada's ninety-day maximum deadline is a good idea and should be emulated elsewhere.

To sum up, investment crowdfunding in Canada is built on the standard model, with a couple of improvements. The market is in its infancy as I write, since National Instrument 45-110 was only adopted in 2021. Yet there are enthusiastic platforms that have been working and waiting for this moment, and the market stands a good chance of growing quickly now that a decent set of national rules is in place.

---

[44] Nat'l Instrument 45-110, *Start-up Crowdfunding Registration and Prospectus Exemptions* § 5(1)(i) (June 24, 2021) (Can.).

156 COMPARATIVE LAW AND PRACTICE

3. European Union

Beginning in the early 2010s, many European countries enacted investment crowdfunding legislation, including France, Spain, and Germany. Italy, for its part, enacted its own statute, the Decreto Crescita Bis, in 2012, the same year as the JOBS Act. These European regimes tended to emulate the standard model that had been adopted in the United States, often including issuer limits, investor caps, mandatory disclosure, and the use of a licensed platform.

Although at least some European countries moved relatively quickly to authorize investment crowdfunding, the market was very small and growing slowly. In first-mover Italy, the total amount raised was a minuscule €3 million per year during 2014–2017, across all platforms and for all companies combined. Other countries had better results, but they were still quite modest as of the mid-2010s. In Germany, the total amount raised was about €30 million per year; in France, the market was about €55 million per year; and in Spain, roughly €15 million per year.[45]

One reason for the sluggish volume—though not the only one—was that each European country had adopted its own legal regime for investment crowdfunding. The result was that residents of one EU country often could not lawfully invest in companies located in another, sharply limiting the number of participants and the amount of capital available. The fragmented regulatory landscape made it tough to raise money across borders—a particular problem for Europe.

The European Union studied the issue for several years, publishing various reports, studies, and impact assessments from as early as 2013.[46] Ultimately, in 2018, the EU Commission proposed a unified legal regime that would govern all crowdfunding platforms, investors, and companies within the European Union. After two years of consideration and revisions, the EU Parliament and Council ultimately adopted a revised, and more tightly regulated, version of those rules in 2020, and they gave it the whimsical name Regulation (EU) 2020/1503.[47]

Regulation (EU) 2020/1503 authorizes and governs investment crowdfunding platforms, companies, and investors across all European countries. By its terms, this new regime was set to replace and supersede national regulation of

[45] CAMBRIDGE CENTRE FOR ALTERNATIVE FINANCE, SHIFTING PARADIGMS: THE 4TH EUROPEAN ALTERNATIVE FINANCE BENCHMARKING REPORT (2019).

[46] E.g., EUROPEAN COMMISSION, COMMUNICATION: UNLEASHING THE POTENTIAL OF CROWDFUNDING IN THE EUROPEAN UNION (2014); EUROPEAN COMMISSION, CONSULTATION DOCUMENT: CROWDFUNDING IN THE EU—EXPLORING THE ADDED VALUE OF POTENTIAL EU ACTION (2013).

[47] To be fair, the full title is "Regulation (EU) 2020/1503, of the European Parliament and of the Council of 7 October 2020 on European crowdfunding service providers for business, and amending Regulation (EU) 2017/1129 and Directive (EU) 2019/1937, 2020 O.J. (L 347)"—which does roll off the tongue.

investment crowdfunding in November 2022, although the uptake has been slow and the European Union was forced to extend that date until November 2023.[48] The reasons for this extension are worth noting, and we will return to them in a moment.

Regulation (EU) 2020/1503 is long and complex; it has fifty-one articles, two annexes, and nearly eighty prefatory paragraphs.[49] This alone suggests that the European Union has followed the standard model of relatively heavy regulation, rather than the light-handed liberal model. A look at the essential provisions of Regulation 2020/1503 confirms the suspicion that it is another example of the standard model of crowdfunding regulation and broadly similar to the JOBS Act and Regulation Crowdfunding.

Perhaps most notably, the EU regulation requires that crowdfunding companies provide a set of mandatory disclosures, known as a "key investment information sheet" (KIIS) to prospective investors. The KIIS is analogous to the Form C required by the SEC, as it requires crowdfunding companies to disclose more than thirty specific pieces of information.[50] The European Union leaves it to individual countries whether the KIIS must be filed with their national securities regulators, but the rules make clear that this is merely a notice filing and that the regulators shall not review or pass on their quality.[51] Rather, Regulation (EU) 2020/1503 puts the onus on the crowdfunding platform and requires that it "have in place and apply adequate procedures to verify the completeness, correctness and clarity" of the KIIS.[52]

Regulation (EU) 2020/1503 follows the standard model in many other ways. Companies are bound to an issuer limit of €5 million (approximately $5.5 million) per year. All offerings are to be conducted through an online platform ("crowdfunding service provider"). And these platforms, in turn, must be formally licensed by their home securities regulator, such as the Autorité des Marchés Financiers in France.

---

[48] European Commission, Delegated Regulation extending the transitional period for continuing to provide crowdfunding services in accordance with national law as referred to in Article 48 of the EU Crowdfunding Regulation (July 12, 2022).

[49] *See generally* REGULATION ON EUROPEAN CROWDFUNDING SERVICE PROVIDERS (Eugenia Macchiavello ed., 2022); THE EU CROWDFUNDING REGULATION (Pietro Ortolani and Marije Louisse eds., 2021).

[50] Regulation (EU) 2020/1503, of the European Parliament and of the Council of 7 October 2020 on European crowdfunding service providers for business, and amending Regulation (EU) 2017/1129 and Directive (EU) 2019/1937, 2020 O.J. (L 347) annex I.

[51] Regulation (EU) 2020/1503, of the European Parliament and of the Council of 7 October 2020 on European crowdfunding service providers for business, and amending Regulation (EU) 2017/1129 and Directive (EU) 2019/1937, 2020 O.J. (L 347) art. 23(14).

[52] Regulation (EU) 2020/1503, of the European Parliament and of the Council of 7 October 2020 on European crowdfunding service providers for business, and amending Regulation (EU) 2017/1129 and Directive (EU) 2019/1937, 2020 O.J. (L 347) art. 23(11).

158 COMPARATIVE LAW AND PRACTICE

Similarly consistent with the standard model, platforms are required to act as gatekeepers and conduct certain minimal types of due diligence on the companies they list, such as a criminal background check and anti-money-laundering review. Investors must receive a boilerplate explanatory statement and risk warning, a test of their knowledge, and a four-day cooling-off period ("reflection period"), during which they may revoke their investment. ("Sophisticated" investors are exempt from most of these rules.)

While mostly emulating the standard American model, the European Union has diverged in at least two ways, one in a liberal direction, the other in a regulatory direction. The liberal change is that the EU rules do not impose an investor cap. Platforms are required to advise investors to invest no more than 10 percent of their net worth, to simulate for investors the impact of losing that amount, and even to provide a special risk warning for any single investment over €1,000 or 5 percent of their net worth. Yet if, after receiving all those warnings, an investor still wants to invest a much larger amount, she may legally do so. This is a liberal change from the more paternalistic investor cap imposed by the JOBS Act and Regulation Crowdfunding.

The European Union also imposes one regulatory obligation not present in the US or other typical standard models: platforms in the European Union are legally obliged to conduct an online quiz of each investor's knowledge and experience relating to startup finance. This simple assessment, which must be repeated every other year, is an additional safeguard not in place in the United States. But it is a very modest mandate and likely only requires an investor to "click through" a couple of boilerplate questions every couple of years.

Those exceptions aside, the EU approach is overwhelmingly consistent with the standard model as adopted in the United States. The very fact that the legislation took several years to be drafted, then two years to be adopted, and then three years (and counting) to be put in practice, suggests that Regulation (EU) 2020/1503 imposes a significant—perhaps burdensome—level of regulation on investment crowdfunding.

Regulation (EU) 2020/1503 has not proved immediately popular among existing European platforms and national securities regulators. As of mid-2022, just months before the original deadline, just one European investment crowdfunding platform had been authorized under Regulation (EU) 2020/1503,[53] and only a handful of European platforms had even applied for such authorization.

Instead of applying, at least some European investment crowdfunding platforms lobbied for an extension of the deadline, on the ground that "the extensive set of requirements" established by Regulation (EU) 2020/1503 are overly

---

[53] This pioneer was the Spanish arm of Crowdcube, a UK-based platform. Mark Tyler, *Investing without Borders: Crowdcube Receives European Authorisation*, CROWDCUBE, Apr. 20, 2022.

"burdensome," compared to the national laws in effect.[54] The European Union ultimately granted a one-year extension until late 2023,[55] so we must wait and see what, if any, bloc-wide regulatory regime Europe might adopt. Perhaps the European Union will consider the merits of the liberal model, to which we now turn.

B. LIBERAL MODEL

The liberal model of investment crowdfunding regulation depends mainly on private ordering to address the three fundamental challenges of uncertainty, information asymmetry, and agency costs. New Zealand and the United Kingdom are the two leading examples of the liberal model.

1. New Zealand

Once the United States passed the JOBS Act in 2012, other countries sought to enact investment crowdfunding laws of their own. Among the very first movers was the South Pacific island nation of New Zealand, which happened to be crafting a once-in-a-generation overhaul of its system of securities regulation at exactly that moment.

Securities law in New Zealand previously had been governed by the Securities Act (1978) and Securities Markets Act 1988. In response to the financial crisis of roughly 2008–2009, however, that country embarked on a comprehensive reform effort that ultimately resulted in the passage of the Financial Markets Conduct Act (FMCA) in 2013.[56] This new foundational statute made countless changes to New Zealand securities law, and among them was an express authorization for the then brand-new idea of investment crowdfunding.[57]

Regulations were promptly issued the next year, and the New Zealand market opened for business in 2014, two years ahead of its model, the United States.

---

[54] Eur. Sec. and Markets Auth., Final Report: ESMA's Technical Advice to the Commission on the possibility to extend the transitional period pursuant to Article 48(3) of Regulation (EU) 2020/1503, May 19, 2022.

[55] European Commission, Delegated Regulation extending the transitional period for continuing to provide crowdfunding services in accordance with national law as referred to in Article 48 of the EU Crowdfunding Regulation (July 12, 2022).

[56] *See generally* VICTORIA STACE ET AL., FINANCIAL MARKETS CONDUCT REGULATION: A PRACTITIONER'S GUIDE (2014) (describing and analyzing the FMCA).

[57] Financial Markets Conduct Act 2013, s 390(a) (NZ) (providing that "a person may hold a market services licence to act as a provider of prescribed intermediary services (for example, . . . a crowd funding intermediary if prescribed by regulations)").

160 COMPARATIVE LAW AND PRACTICE

Almost immediately, the Kiwi investment crowdfunding market was humming with activity and among the leaders in the world (on a per capita basis).[58]

New Zealand was keenly interested in facilitating investment crowdfunding, primarily as a way to ameliorate the longstanding lack of startup capital in the country. Unlike in the United States, where talented entrepreneurs can obtain millions of dollars from any of a number of well-established VCs, New Zealand has long had a much shallower pool for early-stage capital financing—a problem that was exacerbated by the financial crisis of 2008–2009.

When the FMCA passed in 2013, angel investors were investing just NZ$30 million (approximately $20 million) per year in all New Zealand companies combined, and VCs not much more.[59] By comparison, at that same time, American angels were investing roughly $10 billion per year—and American VCs invested several multiples of that figure. In New Zealand, VC funding was so meager that the government had even established a state-run VC fund in 2002, called the New Zealand Venture Investment Fund (NZVIF). Despite the addition of this government funding, VC funding remained scarce in New Zealand, especially in the years following the financial crisis, to the point that even highly promising startup companies had trouble finding capital in New Zealand.[60]

It was in this context that New Zealand authorized investment crowdfunding in the FMCA. Looking back to the three purposes of investment crowdfunding from Chapter Two, New Zealand was not as explicitly interested in inclusive entrepreneurship or inclusive investing. Although it was certainly not opposed to such things, the main focus in New Zealand was on creating a new source of early-stage business capital—the kind that might have come from angels and VCs, had they been present in sufficient numbers.[61]

New Zealand's legal regime for investment crowdfunding was expressly modeled on the JOBS Act.[62] However, in an conscious effort to make investment crowdfunding as usable and efficient as possible, New Zealand enacted a much more liberal regime—"light-handed," as they would say. The Kiwis' goal was to hold compliance costs down by keeping the regulations to a minimum.[63] Thus

---

[58] *See* Chapter Two, tbl. 2.3.

[59] Andrew A. Schwartz, *The Gatekeepers of Crowdfunding*, 75 WASH. & LEE. L. REV. 885, 922–24 (2018).

[60] NZVIF, DISCUSSION PAPER: INSTITUTIONAL INVESTMENT IN VENTURE CAPITAL AND PRIVATE EQUITY IN NEW ZEALAND 1 (2012) ("A major issue for New Zealand's capital markets is the lack of sufficient capital to meet the needs of young high growth companies. . . . $200 million of investment capital is needed each year to meet the existing demand, over double what is currently available.").

[61] NEW ZEALAND GOVERNMENT, BUILDING CAPITAL MARKETS 23 (2013).

[62] N.Z. MINISTRY OF BUS., INNOVATION & EMP'T, FINANCIAL MARKETS CONDUCT REGULATIONS: DISCUSSION PAPER 237 (2012).

[63] Press Release, Commerce Minister Simon Power, Govt responds to capital market recommendations (Feb. 19, 2010) ("For companies, capital markets need to be more accessible

LIBERAL MODEL 161

the FMCA, in its liberal fashion, relies primarily on the types of private ordering I discussed in Chapter Four, rather than government regulation, to govern the investment crowdfunding market in New Zealand.[64]

For example, the New Zealand government knew that the JOBS Act includes an annual investor cap, designed to protect investors from losing more than they can afford.[65] But it decided not to include one in the FMCA in an effort to liberalize the regime and thereby facilitate its use.[66] The Kiwis viewed the American sliding-scale approach as being a good idea in theory but too costly and inconvenient to put into practice.[67] Thus they took the liberal approach and rejected the whole idea of an investor cap.

More broadly, there are only a few legal rules in New Zealand crowdfunding—the rest is left to private ordering. For one, all listings must be hosted by an online platform licensed by the Financial Markets Authority (FMA), the New Zealand equivalent of the SEC.[68] For another, the law imposes an issuer limit of NZ$2 million (approximately $1.5 million) per year.[69] For a third, companies may only sell common stock as opposed to any type of security, as in the United States.[70] (For this reason, Kiwis generally call this practice "equity crowdfunding" rather than "investment crowdfunding.") Finally, platforms must also prominently display a specific boilerplate warning about the risks of crowdfunding on their websites.[71]

---

and more effective at providing funding at least cost, and tailored to their growth aspirations. This requires the Government to . . . reduce compliance costs as far as possible.").

[64] N.Z. MINISTRY OF BUS., INNOVATION & EMP'T, FINANCIAL MARKETS CONDUCT REGULATIONS: DISCUSSION PAPER 239 (2012) ("[Because] crowd-funding platforms are internet based, they create new ways to achieve the[] purposes [of securities regulation]. Instead of individual investors making investment decisions based on [a traditional prospectus], crowd-funding allows open, transparent, two-way communication between the issuer and investors. Instead of due diligence processes and adviser recommendations it draws on the 'wisdom of the crowd' to ascertain the quality of investment opportunities and uncover risks.").

[65] OFFICE OF THE MINISTER OF COMMERCE, FINANCIAL MARKETS CONDUCT REGULATIONS PAPER 4—LICENSING REGIMES 18 (Cabinet Bus. Comm. June 2013).

[66] OFFICE OF THE MINISTER OF COMMERCE, FINANCIAL MARKETS CONDUCT REGULATIONS PAPER 4—LICENSING REGIMES 18–19 (Cabinet Bus. Comm. June 2013).

[67] OFFICE OF THE MINISTER OF COMMERCE, FINANCIAL MARKETS CONDUCT REGULATIONS PAPER 4—LICENSING REGIMES 18–19 (Cabinet Bus. Comm. June 2013) ("A cap that varies according to income or net worth would add more complexity to the regime and may be even more difficult to enforce without imposing significant costs and inconvenience on investors and providers.").

[68] Financial Markets Conduct Act 2013, sch 1, cl 6 (NZ).

[69] Financial Markets Conduct Regulations 2014, reg 186(g) (NZ).

[70] Financial Markets Conduct Regulations 2014, reg 185(1)(a)(i) (NZ) (defining "crowd funding services" as a "facility by means of which offers of *shares* in a company are made" (emphasis supplied). "Shares," in turn, is defined by New Zealand law as what Americans would call "common stock," but note that they can be designated as non-voting. Companies Act 1993, ss 36–37 (NZ).

[71] Financial Markets Conduct Regulations 2014, reg 196 (NZ) ("The warning statement must be in the following form: 'Warning statement about crowd funding[:] Equity crowd funding is risky. *Issuers using this facility include new or rapidly growing ventures. *Investment in these types of businesses is very speculative and carries high risks. You may lose your entire investment, and must be in a position to bear this risk without undue hardship. New Zealand law normally requires people who offer financial products to give information to investors before they invest. This requires those

162 COMPARATIVE LAW AND PRACTICE

Beyond those few rules, New Zealand's law is spare and light-handed. Most radically, there is no mandatory disclosure, no official government form, and the FMA does not review or approve of individual offerings. Rather, it is up to each private platform to decide what disclosure to demand from the companies they list, without direct input from the FMA.

In this way, New Zealand broke with a century of tradition and completely exempted crowdfunding companies from mandatory disclosure obligations. In the United States and other standard-model jurisdictions, crowdfunded companies are legally required to provide specified financial and business disclosures, but New Zealand consciously departed from this model. Rather than mandating certain disclosures on a certain form (as in the standard model), the content, manner, and style of disclosure is left up to the company's business judgment and guided by the hosting platform. This is at the heart of the liberal model.

Another key liberal aspect of New Zealand investment crowdfunding law relates to the investor cap, discussed earlier, which is a standard feature of most legal regimes. Australia, for instance, imposes an investor cap of AU$10,000 per company. New Zealand, in its liberal way, has no investor cap at all. Kiwis are free to invest as much as they desire, and in as many companies as they wish.

The essence of the New Zealand investment crowdfunding regime is that the FMA licenses and monitors the platforms, and the platforms, in turn, are empowered to operate and govern the market, largely unfettered by rules or regulations. Because of the immense responsibility this system places on the platforms, the FMA conducts a rigorous review prior to issuing a platform a license, akin to the process conducted by the SEC. The FMA also supervises and monitors the platform on an ongoing basis.

To obtain a license, a platform must demonstrate that it has proper systems and procedures to operate a crowdfunding site, such as an effective method to enforce the NZ$2 million issuer limit.[72] As for gatekeeping, platforms must have adequate policies for identifying and managing the risk of fraud; this includes a requirement that the platform confirm the identity of an issuer's directors and officers using publicly available information.[73]

In addition, New Zealand companies are bound by the general "fair dealing" obligation that governs all securities offerings in that country, and platforms are

---

offering financial products to have disclosed information that is important for investors to make an informed decision. The usual rules do not apply to offers by issuers using this facility. As a result, you may not be given all the information usually required. You will also have fewer other legal protections for this investment. Ask questions, read all information given carefully, and seek independent financial advice before committing yourself."). Other jurisdictions have similar boilerplate warnings.

[72] Financial Markets Conduct Regulations 2014, regs 186(a), (g) (NZ).
[73] Financial Markets Conduct Regulations 2014, reg 186(c) (NZ).

charged with enforcing it.[74] "Fair dealing" has a specific meaning in New Zealand law, as it refers to the statutory prohibition on "misleading or deceptive conduct, the making of false or misleading representations, and the making of unsubstantiated representations."[75] But even here, New Zealand depends heavily on private ordering, as it counts on the platforms to make sure that the listing companies' representations are honest and true. It is up to the platforms to police the fair dealing rules, not the FMA, at least in the first instance.

While there is no mandatory disclosure or government forms, Kiwi platforms are legally required to have adequate internal disclosure standards and processes such that investors are able to readily obtain "timely and understandable information to assist [them] to decide whether to acquire the shares."[76] One way to comply with this obligation is for the platform to provide a space on its website where potential investors can pose questions to the issuer to answer online (just like the communication channels described in Chapter Five).

Another liberalization in New Zealand's crowdfunding law is that it permits companies to advertise their offerings in any manner they wish. This is in stark contrast to the United States, which places strict restrictions on such advertising. Any advertisements must comply with New Zealand's fair dealing rules, but, beyond that, companies are free to spread the word in any way they wish. That said, the New Zealand advertising and media industry has a voluntary industry code that places (voluntary) limits on financial advertising of all types, including investment crowdfunding.[77]

Yet another liberal aspect of New Zealand's crowdfunding regime is that any type of company—private or public, small or large, and in any industry—can participate. This represents a clear distinction with most other jurisdictions, which place various limits on the type of company eligible to raise funds via crowdfunding.

There are other liberalizations in New Zealand's crowdfunding laws. For one thing, platforms are not required to set a minimum target or follow the all-or-nothing rule, both of which are mandatory under US law. For another, there are no legal limits on the secondary market for crowdfunded shares in New Zealand, unlike in the United States, where a secondary market is expressly prohibited for one year after issuance. That is, a crowdfunding investor in New Zealand is free to trade his shares with others from the moment he gets them.[78] For a third, New

---

[74] Financial Markets Conduct Regulations 2014, reg 186(e) (NZ).
[75] Financial Markets Conduct Act 2013, s 17(1)(a) (NZ).
[76] Financial Markets Conduct Regulations 2014, reg 186(1)(d) (NZ).
[77] Advertising Standards Authority, Financial Advertising Code (2022).
[78] This is more theoretical than practical, however, given that there is no organized secondary market.

164 COMPARATIVE LAW AND PRACTICE

Zealand has no rescission, cancellation, or cooling-off period. Once an investor pledges to invest, he is bound.

To summarize: New Zealand's investment crowdfunding regime is light-handed and much less heavily regulated than that of the United States and other countries that follow the standard model. It is a clear example of the liberal model—indeed, it is the archetype for the concept. Given that it is among the oldest systems in the world, and among the most liberal, how has New Zealand's legal regime for investment crowdfunding fared in practice? The question is key, and not just for the Kiwis.

The United States and most other countries have followed the standard model because they believed that intense legal regulation is vital to an honest and successful investment crowdfunding marketplace. They feared that a deregulated legal regime would lead to a market crawling with fraudsters and tenuous companies, and that overly optimistic investors would lose more than they could afford.

New Zealand, conveniently for our purposes, has put this theory to the test. Does fraud and failure run rampant there, since the market is overseen by private parties, not the government? Do companies refuse to provide information to potential investors, since there is no mandatory disclosure required? New Zealand has had a functioning investment crowdfunding market for nearly ten years. What are the results?

The results are good. The minimal regulation imposed in New Zealand keeps costs very low and encourages capital formation, and the structure of the market empowers private ordering to protect investors.

In economic terms, New Zealand's investment crowdfunding market immediately became a significant source of early stage capital in that country. Scaled for the size of its population, New Zealand has consistently outshone the United States and most other jurisdictions.[79] In the first four years of investment crowdfunding in the United States (2016–2019), New Zealand companies raised seven times more money than did their American counterparts, on a per capita basis. This gap has shrunk as the American market has grown but, even in 2021, the biggest year to date for investment crowdfunding in the United States, Kiwi companies still raised much more money, scaled by population.[80]

Investment crowdfunding has become integrated into New Zealand's financial ecosystem, working synergistically with angel investors, VCs, and the traditional public market.

---

[79] Chapter Two, tbl. 2.3.

[80] These numbers actually understate the impressive Kiwi performance. The low issuer limit of NZ$2 million means that a great deal of fundraising via Kiwi crowdfunding platforms is not counted in the official statistics, since it is conducted through a side-by-side wholesale offering.

Take, for instance, Greenfern Industries, a medicinal cannabis and hemp food company. Greenfern first raised roughly NZ$1.8 million on one crowdfunding platform in 2019, then raised the legal maximum of NZ$2 million on another platform in 2020. Because that latter fundraising reached the legal limit, the platform conducted a side-by-side offering for wholesale investors; these angels and VCs contributed nearly NZ$1 million more. Then, in 2021, the company raised an additional NZ$2 million from wholesale investors (likely VCs) and then was listed on the New Zealand Stock Exchange (NZX)—the Kiwi version of the New York Stock Exchange—later that year.[81]

New Zealand has also seen its share of failures. Renaissance Brewery, the very first Kiwi company to raise money through investment crowdfunding, went into "voluntary administration" (akin to bankruptcy) three years later.[82] An established clothing chain in the country, Andrea Moore, raised NZ$750,000 in 2016, but was out of business eighteen months later.[83] Outcomes like this are unfortunate, but they are the nature of the beast when it comes to investing in speculative ventures. Some are going to fail.

Importantly, these companies failed honestly, due to business reversals, rather than fraud or other misbehavior. In fact, New Zealand has seen just one violation of the fair dealing rules—the equivalent of securities fraud in the United States—after nearly a full decade of investment crowdfunding in the country.[84] This is a clean record.

How has New Zealand achieved such impressive results? In brief, it kept costs very low by eliminating mandatory disclosure and minimizing other regulatory burdens, thereby encouraging companies and investors to participate. As for investor protection, New Zealand depends primarily on private ordering, rather than comprehensive legal regulation, supplemented by regulatory oversight by the FMA as needed.

2. United Kingdom

The legal status of investment crowdfunding in the United Kingdom is very different from all the other countries we have seen. In the United States, Australia, Canada, the European Union, and New Zealand, the government first established

---

[81] GREENFERN INDUS. LTD., NZX LISTING PROFILE (2021), https://www.nzx.com/companies/GFI/documents.

[82] Tom Pullar-Strecker, *Renaissance Brewing, First NZ Company to Get Equity Crowdfunding, Goes into Administration*, STUFF, Oct. 10, 2017.

[83] Tamsyn Parker, *Andrea Moore Investor Complains to Market Watchdog*, N.Z. HERALD, Aug. 4, 2018.

[84] *See* Chapter Four (discussing Medical Kiwi, which admitted to making false and misleading statements).

166 COMPARATIVE LAW AND PRACTICE

a legal regime for investment crowdfunding and then, subsequently, the market opened for business. In the United Kingdom, by contrast, the market opened for business first, without the benefit of a special regulatory regime like the JOBS Act—and the government has never bothered to build one. Rather, the UK government, as well as its securities regulator, the Financial Conduct Authority (FCA), has largely left the industry to govern itself via private ordering.[85]

The fact that investment crowdfunding in the United Kingdom was born of private actions, rather than legal directives, has greatly shaped the market from its inception until today. The FCA allowed it to develop on its own for a few years and, even then, refrained from adopting a special regulatory regime to govern investment crowdfunding. The upshot is that investment crowdfunding in the United Kingdom has always been organized and governed almost entirely by private ordering, rather than a dedicated regulatory regime, as in all the other countries discussed earlier.

In other words, the United Kingdom has adopted the most liberal version of the "liberal model" I described previously. In this way, the approach taken in the United Kingdom is the polar opposite of the United States and other standard-model jurisdictions, making it very useful to our comparative analysis.[86] Indeed, the United Kingdom is even more liberal than New Zealand in that the Brits have not adopted any rules or regulations that apply exclusively to investment crowdfunding, while the Kiwis do have a dedicated regulatory regime, namely, the FMCA.

UK investment crowdfunding commenced in the early 2010s, when Crowdcube and Seedrs launched the first investment crowdfunding platforms in the country. This was just after the global financial crisis of 2007–2009, at a time when startup companies were having a particularly hard time finding capital, and the founders of these platforms were motivated by the very same purposes described in Chapter Two. Without waiting for regulatory changes that might never come, these two platforms brought investment crowdfunding to the United Kingdom by making clever use of several features of existing law.

First, Seedrs and Crowdcube, along with a handful of others, obtained one-off licenses from the FCA as "authorized persons," which is analogous to a broker-dealer license in the United States. Under UK law, only authorized persons may

---

[85] As of the early 2010s, the United Kingdom's securities regulator was known as the Financial Services Authority (FSA), but it was reorganized in 2013 and renamed the Financial Conduct Authority (FCA). For the sake of clarity, I refer only to the FCA throughout the text, even though it may technically have been the FSA at the time.

[86] John Armour & Luca Enriques, *The Promise and Perils of Crowdfunding: Between Corporate Finance and Consumer Contracts*, 81 MODERN L. REV. 51, 64 (2018) ("These two countries have taken very different approaches to the regulation of CF [crowdfunding]. The UK . . . imposes no detailed disclosure obligations on equity CF. On the other hand, the US applies burdensome disclosure regulations to equity CF . . . .").

carry out financial promotions and arrange investment deals, and the license can be tailored to permit this or that specific type of operation. Hence these nascent UK platforms requested specific authority to carry on an investment crowdfunding platform open to the public, and the FCA granted them each an individualized authorization to conduct crowdfunding offerings.

Second, UK securities law generally mandates that public offerings include a "prospectus," which is a mandatory disclosure document akin to a registration statement for an IPO in the United States. The compliance costs are also similar, running well over €1 million.[87] But the United Kingdom has long had an exemption to the prospectus requirement for "small" securities offerings, defined as those seeking to raise less than €8 million (roughly £7.5 million or $8 million).[88] The nascent UK platforms took this small offering exemption and ran with it. They converted this small offering exemption into a crowdfunding exemption by only permitting companies to raise up to €8 million on their sites. The result is that investment crowdfunding in the United Kingdom is effectively subject to an issuer limit of €8 million, not too far from the $5 million issuer limit in the United States. (Note that this is not actually a legal limit for crowdfunding in the United Kingdom; it just means that a company needs to issue a prospectus if it wants to raise more than €8 million. Although rare, this has happened in practice, such as when Monzo raised £20 million in a single offering in 2018.)

Third, UK law generally prohibits "private" companies from offering securities to the public.[89] If you want to sell stock to the public, you need to go through the formal IPO process, issue a prospectus, and become a so-called public limited company—yet the point of crowdfunding is to avoid this costly process. Investment crowdfunding platforms in the United Kingdom satisfy—or get around—this rule by positioning themselves as a sort of private club rather than a public forum. Before a person can access the details of the offerings or make an investment, she must register with the platform, choose a user name and password, and so forth. In this way, the investment opportunity is only being offered to the members of the platform, not the public at large, and so it does not qualify as a public offering.[90] And this, in turn, makes it okay for the platforms to offer their users the chance to buy securities in private companies.

---

[87] John Armour & Luca Enriques, *The Promise and Perils of Crowdfunding: Between Corporate Finance and Consumer Contracts*, 81 MODERN L. REV. 51, 55 (2018).

[88] These figures are in euros, rather than pounds, because the UK rules implemented EU law many years before departing the European Union in what has become known as Brexit, and they have been carried forward. This €8 million figure, by the way, has been in effect since 2018; previously it had been set at €5 million.

[89] Companies Act 2006, pt. 20, c. 1 § 755 (UK).

[90] Gareth Malna & Celine O'Connor, *Crowdfunding: Restriction on "Offers to the Public,"* BURGES SALMON, May 11, 2017, https://www.burges-salmon.com/news-and-insight/legal-updates/crowd funding-restriction-on-offers-to-the-public (last visited Aug. 31, 2022); Companies Act 2006, pt. 20, c. 1 § 756(3)(a) (UK).

168 COMPARATIVE LAW AND PRACTICE

Thanks to these maneuvers, investment crowdfunding platforms launched in the United Kingdom as early as 2011, giving that country a significant head start on the rest of the world. For the first year or two, investment crowdfunding in the United Kingdom was a bit out of the mainstream, given its novelty and uncertain regulatory status. In addition, other countries had begun to enact specialized crowdfunding laws. The United States passed the JOBS Act in 2012, and New Zealand enacted the FMCA the next year. Moreover, as investment crowdfunding grew, it was starting to become unwieldy for the FCA to authorize each platform on an ad hoc basis.

Hence, in 2013, the FCA announced that it planned to clarify and generalize its approach to investment crowdfunding.[91] After consulting crowdfunding platforms, other market participants, and the public, the FCA published a document in 2014 called "Policy Statement PS14/4," in which it stated its general regulatory approach to investment crowdfunding—which was to be hands-off and rely primarily on private ordering, especially gatekeeping, to govern the market.

This was a key moment in the development of investment crowdfunding in the United Kingdom. Prior to this time, investment crowdfunding represented a small, obscure corner of the startup investing market. Part of the problem was that crowdfunding was thought to be suspect in the VC community, based on the "lemons problem" described in Chapter Three. On the theory that only the weakest prospects would deign to participate, it was thought at the time that a VC fund wouldn't touch a crowdfunded company with a ten-foot pole. But when the FCA published PS14/4, it gave its imprimatur to the market, and thereby emboldened entrepreneurs and investors—including VCs and angels—to participate in investment crowdfunding. No longer was investment crowdfunding an edgy alternative; it had joined the establishment.

PS14/4 is not a fully fleshed-out legal regime for regulating of investment crowdfunding, as in the case of the JOBS Act in the United States or the FMCA in New Zealand. Instead, PS14/4 explains how investment crowdfunding fits into the existing rules for securities offerings in the United Kingdom and makes just a couple of minor amendments relevant to this new type of securities market. At its core, PS14/4 simply confirmed that investment crowdfunding was to be governed by general principles of UK securities law, and not a specialized legal framework. Indeed, the FCA went out of its way to clarify that PS14/4 is "media-neutral" and applies to all firms marketing and selling private company securities in the United Kingdom, whether over the internet or any other medium.[92]

---

[91] FIN. CONDUCT AUTH., CONSULTATION PAPER CP13/13: THE FCA's REGULATORY APPROACH TO CROWDFUNDING (AND SIMILAR ACTIVITIES) (2013).

[92] FIN. CONDUCT AUTH., POLICY STATEMENT PS14/4: THE FCA's REGULATORY APPROACH TO CROWDFUNDING OVER THE INTERNET, AND THE PROMOTION OF NON-READILY REALISABLE SECURITIES BY OTHER MEDIA 40 (2014).

LIBERAL MODEL   169

PS14/4 is extremely light-handed, and it places near-total responsibility on the platforms to govern and police the market through private ordering. PS14/4 instructs investment crowdfunding platforms that they have the same two basic responsibilities imposed on every authorized person.

First, platforms must ensure that every listing on their site is "fair, clear and not misleading."[93] These listings are not submitted to, nor reviewed by, the FCA—it is up to the platform to check that they are accurate and fairly presented. This standard prohibits not only full-on misrepresentations, it also bars misleading half-truths. For instance, if you say that you "ate a sandwich for lunch"—but it was actually an ice-cream sandwich—that would be misleading, and the platform would be responsible for the violation.

Furthermore, in fulfilling this duty, the FCA expects "sufficient detail to be provided" so that an investor receives "a balanced indication of the benefits and the risk involved, including whether or not any due diligence has been carried out on an investee company, the extent of the due diligence, and the outcome of any analysis."[94]

Second, platforms need to confirm that investment crowdfunding is an "appropriate" type of investment for any given investor. This means that the platform must confirm that each investor has the knowledge and/or experience to appreciate the risks involved.[95] This can be—and is—accomplished via generic questionnaires that can be completed with just a few clicks of the mouse.

In this way, the United Kingdom adopted an ultra-liberal version of the liberal model I described earlier. Rather than drafting a thick rulebook like the Americans did in Regulation Crowdfunding, the Brits left it almost entirely to the platforms to organize and govern the market through private ordering. The United Kingdom has practically none of the rules or regulations in place in the United States and elsewhere. Most notably, the United Kingdom has entirely abandoned mandatory disclosure for investment crowdfunding offers.

Whereas American law specifies each type of information that must be disclosed, the United Kingdom imposes no specified mandatory disclosures.[96] The United Kingdom depends on crowdfunding platforms to ensure that

---

[93] Fin. Conduct Auth., Policy Statement PS14/4: The FCA's Regulatory Approach to Crowdfunding over the Internet, and the Promotion of Non-Readily Realisable Securities by Other Media 42 (2014).

[94] Fin. Conduct Auth., Policy Statement PS14/4: The FCA's Regulatory Approach to Crowdfunding over the Internet, and the Promotion of Non-Readily Realisable Securities by Other Media 42 (2014).

[95] Fin. Conduct Auth., Policy Statement PS14/4: The FCA's Regulatory Approach to Crowdfunding over the Internet, and the Promotion of Non-Readily Realisable Securities by Other Media 36 (2014).

[96] Fin. Conduct Auth., Policy Statement PS14/4: The FCA's Regulatory Approach To Crowdfunding over the Internet, and the Promotion of Non-Readily Realisable Securities by Other Media 13 (2014) ("we do not prescribe minimum standards of . . . disclosure").

170   COMPARATIVE LAW AND PRACTICE

companies provide sufficient disclosures to comply with the standard of "fair, clear and not misleading." The format, style, and content of the disclosures are not specified, in stark contrast to the United States and its required Form C, or the European Union and its required KIIS.

In addition, the United Kingdom does not require platforms to conduct any specific due diligence on the companies they list.[97] In the United States, New Zealand, and elsewhere, crowdfunding laws usually impose certain specified gatekeeping and due diligence obligations on platforms, such as a mandate to conduct a criminal background check on the entrepreneurs behind the companies they list. In the UK, platforms are required to tell investors what type of due diligence they do, and don't do—but there is no minimum standard or checklist.[98]

Yet, as already discussed previously in Chapter Four, UK crowdfunding platforms nevertheless do act as private gatekeepers that pick and choose among the companies that seek to list on their sites. A primary part of this gate-keeping function is to investigate (with as much diligence as is due) the various companies that want to participate. To that end, UK platforms have developed and implemented their own due diligence procedures, despite the fact that due diligence is not a legal requirement. In Chapter Four, we saw the examples of Crowdcube's "Due Diligence Charter" and a similar document at Seedrs, which they drafted and published. This is consistent with the discussion in that chapter about the economic incentive for platforms to act as diligent gatekeepers.

There is one way in which PS14/4 follows the standard model—but even there it does so in a very liberal way. PS14/4 imposes an investor cap limiting the amount of money that individuals may invest in crowdfunded offerings. At first blush, this investor cap looks similar to the one adopted in the United States and elsewhere, but a close look at the details shows that it is actually a very modest limitation.

Recall that in the United States, non-accredited investors are subject to an annual investor cap of either 5 or 10 percent of their net worth or annual income. The United Kingdom has a similar rule, in that non-accredited investors may invest up to 10 percent of their net assets per year. "Net assets" is defined to exclude the value of one's primary residence, as well as insurance and pensions, so

---

[97] FIN. CONDUCT AUTH., POLICY STATEMENT PS14/4: THE FCA'S REGULATORY APPROACH TO CROWDFUNDING OVER THE INTERNET, AND THE PROMOTION OF NON-READILY REALISABLE SECURITIES BY OTHER MEDIA 13 (2014) ("we do not prescribe minimum standards of due diligence").

[98] FIN. CONDUCT AUTH., POLICY STATEMENT PS14/4: THE FCA'S REGULATORY APPROACH TO CROWDFUNDING OVER THE INTERNET, AND THE PROMOTION OF NON-READILY REALISABLE SECURITIES BY OTHER MEDIA 13 (2014) (noting that the FCA "expect[s] sufficient detail to be provided [by the platform,] including whether or not any due diligence has been carried out on an investee company, the extent of the due diligence, and the outcome of any analysis").

the effect is that it covers a person's investible assets. Also, the 10 percent limit covers not only crowdfunded investments (as in the United States) but all illiquid investments, such as buying stock in a small family business.

Each investor must self-certify that they have not exceeded this 10 percent cap in order to participate in a UK crowdfunded offering. The platforms are not obliged to check to see whether the investors are telling the truth, and so it is simply based on the honor system. In this way, it is not so far from the European Union's rule that investors must be advised not to invest more than 10 percent, but that they are ultimately free to invest as much as they wish.

Furthermore, institutional, high net worth, and "sophisticated" investors are not limited by this 10 percent cap, nor are retail investors that receive professional investment advice or management. Most notably for our purposes, a non-accredited investor can qualify as a "sophisticated" investor simply by making two investments on a crowdfunding platform.[99] The result is that the 10 percent investor cap only really applies to retail investors making their first couple of investments on a UK crowdfunding platform. Once they have done that, they are free (though not obligated) to self-certify as a sophisticated investor, and thereby escape the investor cap. The effect of this rule is that the investor cap is a minor constraint on crowdfunding in the United Kingdom, consistent with the liberal philosophy.

Another exception to the liberal nature of UK investment crowdfunding is its cooling-off rule, which is actually highly restrictive. UK consumer-protection law provides investors with a right to cancel their commitments for two weeks after making them. This is not specific to investment crowdfunding, but is a general feature of UK law that applies to any investment agreement made "at a distance," which includes online transactions.[100] The idea that investors should have the chance to "cool off" and reconsider such decisions, which may have been made in haste or even by mistake, is sensible. But two weeks is probably too long for the context of crowdfunding, as it creates a long period of uncertainty for the issuer. Fortunately, the FCA has recently floated the idea of a twenty-four-hour cooling off period for investment crowdfunding participants, which would be an improvement.[101]

On the whole, the United Kingdom's legal approach to investment crowdfunding is extremely liberal and depends almost entirely on private ordering. This was a conscious choice, as the FCA was sympathetic to the country's need

---

[99] FIN. CONDUCT AUTH., CONDUCT OF BUSINESS SOURCEBOOK § 4.12.8 (2022) (allowing a person to "self-certify" as a "sophisticated investor" if she has "made more than one investment in an unlisted company in the [past] two years").

[100] The Financial Services (Distance Marketing) Regulations 2004, § 10 (UK).

[101] FIN. CONDUCT AUTH., CONSULTATION PAPER CP 22/2: STRENGTHENING OUR FINANCIAL PROMOTION RULES FOR HIGH RISK INVESTMENTS, INCLUDING CRYPTOASSETS 28 (2022).

172 COMPARATIVE LAW AND PRACTICE

for additional sources of startup capital and understood that a regulatory-heavy legal regime would have snuffed out this emerging market.

The centrality of private ordering to the UK investment crowdfunding market can be seen quite vividly in one notable episode that happened six years after the release of PS14/4. In 2020, the United Kingdom's two leading investment crowdfunding platforms—Seedrs and Crowdcube—announced that they planned to merge to create an investment crowdfunding powerhouse. Less than six months later, however, the United Kingdom's antitrust regulator, the Competition and Markets Authority (CMA) disapproved of the deal, and it was terminated.[102] Because these two platforms controlled more than 90 percent of the investment crowdfunding market in the United Kingdom, the CMA was concerned that a merger could have lessened the competitive pressure they face, potentially leading to higher fees and less innovation. This is consistent with the liberal model, which relies heavily on the incentives provided by market competition.

Over the course of a decade, these UK platforms had grown into a significant source of startup capital in the United Kingdom. In the CMA's decision, it observed that investment crowdfunding had "become an important part of the overall financial ecosystem" in the United Kingdom.[103] This is high praise, even if it frustrated the merger. In fact, investment crowdfunding recently outpaced traditional angel investing in the United Kingdom, as many of the people who would have invested as local angels seem to have switched to online platforms—especially during the COVID-19 pandemic era of 2020–2021.[104] The result is a democratic convergence, where angels and VCs invest alongside the crowd, shoulder to shoulder.

The United Kingdom has the most investment crowdfunding experience of all jurisdictions. The UK market has raised the most money and funded the most companies, many of which have funny names. Some have been big successes, like Monzo, while others have crashed, like Rebus (both of which are discussed in Chapter Four). More broadly, many of the companies funded on Seedrs and Crowdcube have gone on to bigger and better things.

At the very least, the vast majority of UK companies remain in operation, years after raising money from the crowd. One report on UK crowdfunding looked at the roughly 700 companies that had raised money via investment crowdfunding from 2013 to 2015, and found that almost 150 of them had failed by mid-2018, equivalent to 21 percent.[105] This number, however, is much better than for the

---

[102] COMPETITION AND MKTS. AUTH., ANTICIPATED ACQUISITION BY CROWDCUBE LIMITED OF SEEDRS LIMITED: PROVISIONAL FINDINGS REPORT (2021).

[103] COMPETITION AND MKTS. AUTH., ANTICIPATED ACQUISITION BY CROWDCUBE LIMITED OF SEEDRS LIMITED: PROVISIONAL FINDINGS REPORT (2021) 5.

[104] BRITISH BUSINESS BANK, SMALL BUSINESS FINANCE MARKETS 2020/21, at 91–92 (2021).

[105] James Titcomb, *One in Five Firms Raising Cash Via Crowdfunding Sites Has Gone Bust*, SUNDAY TELEGRAPH, July 8, 2018.

average startup—about half of all new UK businesses fail within three years—suggesting that the crowd is being presented with a reasonably high caliber (or calibre) of company. In addition, the quality of the companies listed on investment crowdfunding platforms has greatly improved over time, at least anecdotally, with the result that this 21 percent figure is likely outdated.

Importantly, crowdfunding investors in the United Kingdom have started to see some successful "exits," meaning transactions that allow them to cash out of the company. As expected, this has taken some time but has recently started to flow. Consider that, prior to 2020, only ten companies that raised money on Seedrs reported an exit—but then, in 2020, Seedrs marked seven exits.[106]

For example, Mindful Chef, a meal-kit startup company founded in 2015, first raised £1 million on Seedrs in 2016 at a valuation of £3 million, and then followed it up the next year by raising another £2 million on Crowdcube at a valuation of £7 million.[107] Two years after that, in 2020, global food giant Nestle acquired Mindful Chef, providing an exit for the crowdfunding investors. The purchase price was not disclosed, but Crowdcube reports that its investors got a 350 percent return on their investment,[108] suggesting that Nestle bought Mindful Chef at a valuation of over £30 million and that the earliest crowdfunding investors (who had invested at a £3 million valuation) made a "ten bagger."

Other crowdfunding companies have reported nice multiple returns for the crowdfunding investors. Igloo Energy, a smart-home clean energy provider, crowdfunded £600,000 from 500 investors in 2019.[109] Just one year later, those investors were offered more than triple the price they paid by Osaka Gas, an international energy infrastructure firm.[110] Other examples include Camden Town Brewery (200 percent return upon acquisition by AB InBev), New Galexy (3,000 percent return upon private equity sale), and Cell Therapy (270 percent upon management buyout).[111] More broadly, Crowdcube reports that more than 50,000 of its investors have had the chance to realize more than £60 million in returns from investments made on its platform.[112]

---

[106] *Mindful Chef to Be Acquired by Nestlé, Marking Seedrs' 7th Exit in 2020*, SEEDRS, https://www.seedrs.com/insights/blog/investing/mindful-chef-is-acquired-by-nestle-marking-seedrs-7th-exit-in-2020 (last visited Aug. 1, 2022).

[107] *Mindful Chef*, SEEDRS, https://www.seedrs.com/mindful-chef (last visited June 18, 2022).

[108] *How Many Exits Have There Been from Businesses That Have Funded on Crowdcube?*, CROWDCUBE, https://help.crowdcube.com/hc/en-us/articles/115000038984 (last visited Sept. 24, 2022).

[109] *Igloo Energy*, SEEDRS, https://www.seedrs.com/iglooenergy (last visited Sept. 24, 2022).

[110] *Seedrs Portfolio Sees 5 Primary Exits Since the Start of 2020*, STARTACUS, https://startacus.net/culture/seedrs-portfolio-sees-5-primary-exits-since-the-start-of-2020 (June 10, 2020).

[111] *Investor Returns*, CROWDCUBE, https://www.crowdcube.com/explore/investing/investor-returns (last visited June 18, 2022). New Galexy subsequently changed its name to ContractPodAI.

[112] *How Many Exits Have There Been from Businesses That Have Funded on Crowdcube?*, CROWDCUBE, https://help.crowdcube.com/hc/en-us/articles/115000038984 (last visited Sept. 24, 2022).

174   COMPARATIVE LAW AND PRACTICE

Table 6.1 Key Investment Crowdfunding Regulations in Selected Jurisdictions

	US	Australia	Canada	EU	NZ	UK
Licensed Platforms	Yes	Yes	Yes	Yes	Yes	Yes
Mandatory Disclosure	Yes	Yes	Yes	Yes	No	No
Issuer Limit	US$5m	A$5m	C$1.5m	€5m	NZ$2m	€8m
Investor Cap	5% of income/net worth per year	A$10,000 per offer	C$2,500 per offer	None	None	10% of investible assets per year
Securities Allowed	Any	Equity	Any	Any	Equity	Any
Cooling-Off Period	Prior to 2 days until closing	5 days	2 days	4 days	None	14 days

It's not all sunshine and roses, though. Just as in the United States and New Zealand, there has been one reported case in the United Kingdom where a crowdfunding platform fell short of its obligation to ensure that the company's disclosures were "fair, clear and not misleading."[113] Given that there have been thousands of successful crowdfunding rounds in the United Kingdom, this is an impressive record, and one consistent with the idea that a liberal approach to investment crowdfunding can yield a clean—and vibrant— marketplace.

All in all, the United Kingdom has an ultra-liberal approach to investment crowdfunding, with few rules and ample room for discretion by platforms and companies—and it has served it well.

* * *

With that, we are in position to move to the next. Before getting there, however, Table 6.1 summarizes the key legal aspects of investment crowdfunding regulation in the countries considered in this chapter and the previous one.

---

[113] *In re Mr. S*, UK Fin. Ombus. Serv., Ref. DRN7590473, at 10 (2021) (ordering Crowdcube to repay £18,000).

Chapter Seven
Lessons Learned

We are now up to speed on investment crowdfunding—what it is, how it works, and how it is regulated—in theory and practice, around the world. We understand that investment crowdfunding is driven by three purposes: to create a new online channel for entrepreneurs to raise capital; to create an inclusive market open to all entrepreneurs; and to democratize the startup capital market by inviting everyone to invest (Chapter Two).

We also know that investment crowdfunding, like any system of entrepreneurial finance, must respond to the three fundamental challenges of uncertainty, information asymmetry, and agency costs (Chapter Three). As we have seen, investment crowdfunding depends both on private ordering (Chapter Four) and on legal regulation (Chapters Five and Six) to respond to those three fundamental challenges.

We compared the regulatory regimes in the United States, Australia, Canada, the European Union, New Zealand, and the United Kingdom and saw that different jurisdictions have taken different approaches to regulating investment crowdfunding. The United Kingdom and New Zealand are the leading "liberal" jurisdictions, meaning that they rely primarily on private ordering, rather than regulation, to govern the investment crowdfunding marketplace. The United States, the European Union, Australia, and Canada, by contrast, all follow the "standard model," in that they depend primarily on law and regulation to serve this purpose.

We looked at the performance in these various jurisdictions and saw that the investment crowdfunding market is small but growing quickly in the United States and in other countries following the standard model. In the liberal jurisdictions of the United Kingdom and New Zealand, where investment crowdfunding has had longer to develop, the market has become an important part of the financial ecosystem.

After all of this, what have we learned? How can investment crowdfunding best be regulated?

There are so many issues—investor caps, issuer limits, all-or-nothing, special purpose vehicles—that I cannot summarize it all here. I have offered plenty of commentary and recommendations throughout the book, which I hope will be helpful to a jurisdiction deciding on a new legal regime for investment crowdfunding or one that is reforming an existing set of rules. My goal in this chapter

Investment Crowdfunding. Andrew A. Schwartz, Oxford University Press. © Andrew A. Schwartz 2023.
DOI: 10.1093/oso/9780197688526.003.0008

176 LESSONS LEARNED

is to step back and summarize the large points I've made over the preceding chapters, as well as to clean up a few loose ends.

For investment crowdfunding to fully flower, it requires a carefully calibrated regulatory regime. While it cannot be fully laissez-faire, the regulatory burden must nevertheless be as light as possible—simply because investment crowdfunding is conducted on a very small scale. Recall that every jurisdiction imposes an issuer limit, meaning that companies may only legally crowdfund up to a certain dollar amount, presently $5 million in the United States, C$1.5 million in Canada, and similar amounts elsewhere.

Thus, the whole concept of investment crowdfunding depends on a very simple and inexpensive process for offering securities. For crowdfunding to be a realistic financing option, compliance costs must be kept to an absolute minimum. This means that the regulatory framework needs to be exceptionally liberal—the exact opposite of our usual tendency in securities regulation (both in the United States and abroad). Accordingly, I would call on policymakers to accept the challenge of embracing a simple, low-cost regime that lacks all the usual bells and whistles of "investor protection," like mandatory disclosures, direct regulatory oversight, and so forth.

Policymakers should also be daring and be willing to try out new, even untested, methods of regulation. As long as the law imposes an issuer limit on companies and an investor cap on the crowd, the potential harm from fraud or failure is contained. Nobody is going to lose their life's savings, and no company's failure is going to cause "systemic" harm or anything of the sort.

Thanks to these limits and caps, governments should feel emboldened to liberalize other aspects of investment crowdfunding regulation. It's like making policy with a net underneath. Policymakers should view investment crowdfunding as a sort of "regulatory sandbox" where they can attempt things that might work but they were too afraid to try in the past—such as abandoning mandatory disclosure (a point to which we shall return in a moment).

The best way to keep compliance costs down is to reject the standard model and enact a liberal regime that minimizes the number and complexity of regulations. If it is a close case, make the liberal choice and deregulate. But then how will we respond to concerns over fraud, business failure, and the three fundamental challenges of entrepreneurial finance? The answer is to follow the lead of New Zealand and the United Kingdom and depend on the private ordering methods described in Chapter Four.

We saw there that private ordering can be a powerful means of organizing and policing the investment crowdfunding market. Key methods mentioned in Chapter Four include gatekeeping, voluntary disclosure, wisdom of the crowd, and syndication. These techniques have sound theoretical bases, and they seem to work reasonably well in practice too. When designing a legal regime for investment crowdfunding, policymakers should familiarize themselves with these private ordering methods (may I recommend Chapter Four?) and craft a set of regulations that work synergistically to enhance them.

Broadly speaking, probably the best way to keep costs down, and yet maintain effective investor protection, is for the government to focus its regulatory attention on investment crowdfunding platforms, rather than individual companies or investors. If nothing else, this means requiring that investment crowdfunding take place only on platforms holding an official license from the government. Through the licensing process, a securities regulator like the SEC can monitor and regulate the investment crowdfunding market. There are only a handful of platforms in any given jurisdiction, and often only one or two highly active ones, compared with dozens, hundreds, or thousands of companies participating each year. The regulators should keep an eye on the platforms and count on the platforms to keep an eye on the companies.

It's like regulating a number of pyramids. Rather than check every brick on every face, it is much easier for the regulator to focus just on the apex, and rely on it to regulate the bricks below it. In contrast with the individual companies, platforms are repeat players with extensive experience and long-term interests. They have good incentives to serve as diligent gatekeepers, which legal regulation can sharpen and focus. Competition is vital here, as we want platforms to fear that they could lose business if they fall short in their gatekeeping role.

This focus on platforms, rather than companies, is the essence of the liberal model of investment crowdfunding regulation.

Furthermore, the law should not require any sort of mandatory disclosure by offering companies; rather, disclosure should be a decision for the platform and the company. Crowdfunding investors need information to make investment decisions, obviously. But this does not necessarily mean that the law should mandate the disclosure of certain information.

There are powerful private incentives for crowdfunding entrepreneurs to provide voluntarily disclosure to potential investors, as I discussed in Chapter Four. To recap the point: investors will either refuse to invest, or only accept a very low valuation, unless the entrepreneur shares information about the company. Since the entrepreneur needs the money, she will accommodate (or preempt) the investors' demands by voluntarily disclosing information about the company, regardless of legally mandatory disclosure rules in place. And the usual reasons we might require mandatory disclosure—to inform traders and ameliorate agency costs—are really only relevant to the secondary market, not a primary market like investment crowdfunding.

Moreover, disclosure is useful—but it also costs money to produce. The GAAP-compliant financial statements required by American law clearly provide useful information to investors and the investment crowdfunding market

178 LESSONS LEARNED

as a whole. Yet it is certainly possible that the cost of producing such documents outweighs their value to investors deciding whether to contribute. An efficient system would require companies to produce exactly as much information as is worth producing, and no more. This sort of cost-consciousness is essential for investment crowdfunding, because companies are limited in the amount that they can raise.

Mandatory disclosure rules are unlikely to hit that efficient spot, since they are standardized and apply to every company equally. The proper level and type of disclosure varies from offering to offering, so a mandatory set of rules will not suit any of them perfectly. Yet if disclosure is left to the voluntary choices of companies, guided by platforms, they are more likely to produce and disclose just enough information for investors to make a thoughtful decision.

Beyond theory, the experience in the UK and New Zealand investment crowdfunding markets—where there are no mandatory disclosure rules and no official forms—shows that voluntary disclosure can work just fine. In those jurisdictions, crowdfunding entrepreneurs really do make extensive disclosures, even without a legal obligation to do so, but they don't make wastefully expensive disclosures. In this way, the United Kingdom and New Zealand have been able to keep compliance costs much lower compared to jurisdictions that follow the standard model. Indeed, I believe the lack of mandatory disclosure has been a key factor behind the United Kingdom and New Zealand's status as global leaders for the entire (short) history of investment crowdfunding—and I would recommend that other countries follow in their footsteps.

On the other hand, it is theoretically possible that the mandatory disclosures required by a given jurisdiction are close to, if not precisely the same as, what platforms and companies would have come to voluntarily, if given the chance. In that case, mandatory disclosure is harmless and, in fact, could make it easier to analyze and compare companies. This is particularly true if a jurisdiction has a standard form, like the Form C in the United States, and especially if the data on the form is captured in a digital format, as the SEC does.[1]

Good news: based on my research, I think the disclosures currently required in Australia, Canada, the European Union, and the United States are not too far from what companies would voluntary disclose. Anecdotally, the disclosure in a typical New Zealand offering looks very much like the disclosure in a typical American offering. This would suggest that the mandatory disclosure rules are pretty close to optimal.

---

[1] The SEC website includes data sets, extracted from filed Forms C, in a format that can be transposed to a spreadsheet. These data sets are updated quarterly and are quite useful to researchers in the field.

Still, several key mandatory disclosure rules are pretty clearly different from what private ordering would yield (and has yielded). To take one notable example, Regulation Crowdfunding requires GAAP-compliant financial statements for every offering, no matter how small.[2] If private ordering were allowed to hold sway, it is more likely that platforms and investors would allow companies raising small amounts to provide less formal financial reports, and only demand GAAP-compliant financial statements when relevant, such as for companies seeking to raise over a certain threshold, such as $1 million.

The point is that voluntary disclosure should, in theory, work for investment crowdfunding (since it is a primary market with gatekeepers)—and experience in the liberal jurisdictions of New Zealand and the United Kingdom shows that it does. Mandatory disclosure and standard forms are, I submit, raising compliance costs higher than they ought to be and frustrating the growth and development of investment crowdfunding. The effect is not huge, as the markets in Australia and the United States are growing nicely, but it would be better to reduce mandatory disclosure or, even better, jettison it entirely.

I recognize that a proposal to eliminate mandatory disclosure borders on the heretical, so let me clarify that this argument only applies to a primary offering, not later on. As I explained in Chapters Four and Five, the question of whether mandatory disclosure is necessary does not lend itself to a simple answer. It all depends on the timing.

When a company is itself soliciting funds through an investment crowdfunding platform, that is a "primary" offering. At that moment, the private incentive to voluntarily disclose is most powerful, because the company is trying to convince people to invest. After that moment has passed, however, and the company has the money, the incentive to disclose is greatly reduced. Management suddenly has much less interest in taking the time to inform investors about the company's business and prospects.

This is a species of agency cost, and it is also common sense, as well as consistent with experience. Recall from Chapter Five that a majority of crowdfunded companies in the United States have failed to provide their shareholders with the annual reports required by law. This is not surprising, given the incentives, but it points up a weakness in the standard model of regulation, and indeed the liberal model as well.

Just a moment ago, I suggested that an optimal legal regime for investment crowdfunding would depend on voluntary disclosure, not mandatory disclosure, for purposes of the primary offering on the platform. After the money is raised, however, I would recommend just the opposite: the law should impose

---

[2] 17 C.F.R. § 227.201(t).

180 LESSONS LEARNED

ongoing mandatory disclosure obligations on crowdfunding companies, such as a requirement to provide investors with an annual report.

Many jurisdictions have this exactly backward: they require mandatory disclosures at the primary offering stage, but then leave ongoing disclosures up to the discretion of the company. Regulation Crowdfunding, for instance, effectively requires just one annual report, and then leaves it to the good graces of the management to provide disclosure after that. This should be reversed. It would be better to eliminate mandatory disclosure for crowdfunded offerings, but then impose a long-term duty to keep the investors informed.[3]

Disclosure and licensing aside, there are other useful regulations that are well worth the regulatory burden they impose and thus ought to be adopted, even in a liberal jurisdiction. A boilerplate risk warning costs almost nothing and has at least a little bit of value. A cooling-off period is also a minor inconvenience, as long as the clock starts once the investment is made, which is the case in every jurisdiction except for the United States.

An issuer limit that places a ceiling on how much money a company can raise through investment crowdfunding is a simple and effective way to cabin the harm caused by any given crowdfunding company going bust, honestly or otherwise. It also distinguishes investment crowdfunding from a traditional public offering (IPO), which is not subject to any similar limit.

The issuer limit should be set to the highest level that a typical startup company might realistically seek to raise in an early round of financing. In the United States as of the early 2020s, that level is roughly $5 million (or so I am told). Most companies need much less—in the $100,000s—but many need to raise a couple of million dollars to give them a sufficient "runway" to progress to the next stage of maturity. For this reason, the JOBS Act's original $1 million issuer was overly restrictive. The current, reformed limit of $5 million is appropriate, however, and the same can be said of the limits adopted in Australia (A$5 million), the European Union (€5 million), and the United Kingdom (€8 million).

The issuer limits in New Zealand (NZ$2 million) and Canada (C$1.5 million) are frankly too low, however. This isn't fatal, since platforms can (and do) conduct a parallel accredited-only offering for popular investment opportunities. But this adds cost and complexity, and undermines the unifying, democratizing idea that the whole crowd is investing together. I would recommend that these two countries double their issuer limit.

An investor cap that limits the amount an individual can invest through investment crowdfunding is also a reasonable idea, although not strictly necessary,

---

[3] This line of reasoning does not necessarily suggest that the SEC, or analogous regulator, needs to receive ongoing disclosure. Rather, it is for the investors, and the information may be sensitive, so it probably should not have to be filed with the regulator.

as New Zealand has shown (and the European Union has followed). In a free economy, competent adults are generally free to invest as much as they wish, in whatever they wish, whether gold, government bonds, or their grandma's house. By the same token, they should be allowed to invest as much as they want in startup companies raising money through licensed investment crowdfunding platforms.

On the other hand, the presence of an investor cap acts like a safety net and may embolden a jurisdiction to adopt a more liberal legal regime than it might otherwise.[4] The SEC is much more likely to eliminate mandatory disclosure with an investor cap in place than without one, and for good reason. So it may be, on balance, advisable to adopt an investor cap—as long as it is well designed.

There are several variables to be considered in designing a good investor cap. It can apply either to the cumulative amount invested per year in all crowdfunded companies (as in the United States) or on a per-company basis (as in Australia and Canada). (Theoretically, a jurisdiction could impose both types of caps, but I'm not aware of that actually happening.)

A cumulative cap does a better job protecting investors from loss, as a per-offer cap has no real upper bound. A lot of small investments can add up to a large amount at stake. On the flipside, a per-offer cap does a better job encouraging diversification, since a cumulative cap would allow an investor to put all her money in a single company. Reasonable people can come to different conclusions on which they prefer, as long as they understand the policies behind each type of investor cap.

As for me, I would advocate for a per-offer cap. For one thing, it is simpler, as it doesn't require an investor (or platform) to keep a running ledger of how much she has invested over the prior twelve months. For another, in practice, a per-offer cap does have some loss-prevention effect, as it stops an impulsive investor from putting her entire bank account in a single offering.

Whichever cap is selected, it is better to set it at a specific dollar amount (like Australia and Canada) and avoid a calculation based on the individual investor's financial position. On this point, the JOBS Act blundered, as I recounted in Chapter Five, as it laid down a complex rule that requires investors to state their annual income and net worth, both highly private matters. Investment crowdfunding is supposed to welcome all investors, so it doesn't matter what a person's wealth is—and asking for it discourages people from participating.

Finally, accredited investors should certainly be exempt from the investor cap. Not only do they have the financial resources to absorb a loss, they are the ones

---

[4] *See generally* Abraham J.B. Cable, *Mad Money: Rethinking Private Placements*, 71 WASH. & LEE L. REV. 2253, 2258, 2302 (2014) (recommending broader use of investment caps as a way to contain risk, rather than "trying to engineer each transaction to be safe").

182 LESSONS LEARNED

who serve as lead investors in the syndication process I described in Chapter Four. For them to play that role effectively, they need to be able to invest large sums in a single offering, so they ought not be constrained by an investor cap of any type.

Despite all my grumblings, the status quo is pretty good, on the whole. Putting aside the European Union, whose Regulation (EU) 2020/1503 is not yet in effect at the time of writing, the legal regimes in every jurisdiction I discussed in Chapters Five and Six—the United States, Australia, Canada, New Zealand, and the United Kingdom—are all working reasonably well. The original regulatory schemes in Australia and Canada had fundamental problems, but those have now been corrected. The United States has been reforming and improving its laws, and New Zealand and the United Kingdom have done well with their stripped-down, liberal regimes. There remains, nonetheless, substantial room for improvement, and I have filled this book with my recommendations.

Conclusion

Investment crowdfunding holds tremendous potential and enjoys widespread support from all corners of the globe and across the political spectrum. Startup companies get a new source of capital, helping to grow the economy, create jobs, and develop new products and services. Entrepreneurs of all types, regardless of geography, gender, race, or anything else, are invited to participate. And investment crowdfunding is a democratic market that is open to all investors, not just the wealthy and connected. These investors—being a large, diverse crowd—may appreciate needs and niches that might otherwise have gone unrecognized by traditional VC and angel investing. What's not to like?

Whether investment crowdfunding can realize this great potential depends, however, on the laws and regulations in place to govern it.

As we have seen, investment crowdfunding has flowered in what I have called the "liberal" jurisdictions of the United Kingdom and New Zealand, which adopted a light and inexpensive regulatory regime that relies on private ordering. In jurisdictions like the United States or Australia, which enacted what I've called the "standard model" of investment crowdfunding regulation, the market has been hampered (and sometimes suffocated) by an overly heavy regulatory approach.

Emblematic of the difference between the liberal and standard models is the fact that the United Kingdom and New Zealand were both able to get their investment crowdfunding markets up and running by 2014—years ahead of their standard-model counterparts. By taking a light hand to regulation, the Brits and Kiwis were able to act swiftly and seize the moment, just after the financial crisis, when businesses were in dire need of a new source of capital.

In the United States, the SEC spent years drafting Regulation Crowdfunding and only opened the market in 2016—four years after the JOBS Act was signed into law. In the meantime, the SEC published hundreds and hundreds of pages of proposed and final regulations. Canada, for its part, futzed around for years with multiple sets of conflicting provincial regulations, only adopting a national investment crowdfunding regime in 2021. And the European Union has spent nearly a decade considering, analyzing, and drafting a regulatory regime—and they are not even done yet!

The fact that the standard-model jurisdictions spent literally years crafting regulations for investment crowdfunding indicates that their approach is overkill.

Investment Crowdfunding. Andrew A. Schwartz, Oxford University Press. © Andrew A. Schwartz 2023.
DOI: 10.1093/oso/9780197688526.003.0009

184 CONCLUSION

Moreover, by taking so long to promulgate regulations, these countries deprived their local startup companies of the opportunity to use investment crowdfunding, for years on end. Who knows how many companies needed capital, couldn't get it, and shut down over those years? And even once the markets were up and running, they have been hindered by a restrictive regulatory framework.

It doesn't have to be this way, however, as the liberal jurisdictions have shown. The United Kingdom and New Zealand laid down a spare set of regulations for investment crowdfunding, relying primarily on private ordering to govern the market and protect investors. This keeps the compliance costs very low, which is necessary when a company is raising only a modest amount of capital. These countries' markets have done well, especially in recent years, with investment crowdfunding growing into an important part of the financial markets there.

To their credit, the standard-model jurisdictions have been willing to liberalize their regulations as they have gained experience and comfort with investment crowdfunding, and as they have observed the generally good results coming out of the liberal jurisdictions. In the United States, for example, the SEC liberalized Regulation Crowdfunding after several years' worth of experience by raising the issuer limit to $5 million from $1 million, and excusing accredited investors from the investor cap. In this and other ways, the standard-model jurisdictions are starting to move closer to their liberal brethren.

What about the dangers of investment crowdfunding? Aren't these liberal jurisdictions rife with fraud and business failure since they are so lax? In fact, no. As we have seen, the record in the liberal and standard jurisdictions are quite comparable on these measures, suggesting that the additional regulatory burden imposed by the latter is not worth its cost since you can get the same outcome at a lower price.

Investment crowdfunding poses very little threat to investors, the economy, or anyone else. Thanks to the issuer limit, a standard feature in every jurisdiction, companies can only raise a few million dollars per year, not the unlimited amounts that lead to crazes like the tulip, dot-com, or cryptocurrency bubbles. And thanks to the investor cap adopted by most jurisdictions, investors can only invest a certain amount per company or per year and are protected from unaffordable losses.

Now, will the average crowdfund investor outperform an S&P 500 index fund? Maybe not, as there will be many duds for every gem—just as in all types of investing. But for serious investors, crowdfunding might represent a new type of "non-correlated" asset class—meaning that the value of these investments does not rise and fall in tandem with other types of assets. Non-correlated assets hold special value because they enhance the diversification of a given investment portfolio.

And for amateur investors, crowdfunding gives them a chance to play angel investor on a scale that makes sense for their net worth. Experience shows that there are millions of people interested in doing so, and millions of companies looking for someone to take a chance on them. They might make a decent return from their investments and, in the worst-case scenario, they lose an amount of money they can afford. In doing so, they promote entrepreneurs they believe in, fund research and development into new technology, encourage hiring and job creation, advance diversity and inclusion, and more. Not so bad.

In conclusion, as I have advocated from the beginning of this book until now, I believe all jurisdictions should emulate the liberal model of regulation. Investment crowdfunding has such great potential for good, and so little potential for harm, that we shouldn't tie it down with the red tape of traditional securities regulation. Rather, we should unfetter this promising new capital market so that it may spread its wings and take flight.

Index

For the benefit of digital users, indexed terms that span two pages (e.g., 52–53) may, on occasion, appear on only one of those pages.

Tables are indicated by *t* following the page number

accredited investors
    definition of, 42
    and exemption from registration
        requirement, 2, 20–21, 42, 104–5
    investor cap, not subject to, 32, 125,
        171, 181–82
    investor cap, previously subject to, 100, 125
    as lead investors, 92–93 (*see also*
        syndication)
    and parallel offers (*see* parallel offering)
    and transfer of crowdfunded securities in
        first year, 139
Activated Nutrients, 151
adverse selection, 50–51, 134–35, 168
advertising, 137–38
    in Australia, 150
    in New Zealand, 163
agency costs, 7, 45–46, 53–55
Alberta, 153
all-or-nothing model, 26, 126–29
    and crowdsourced investment analysis,
        89–90, 127
    deadline in, 128–29, 155
    funding target, selection of, 127–28
    gaming of, 127–29
    improvement, proposal for, 129
    Kickstarter, used by, 16
    policy rationale, 126–27
Andrea Moore, 165
angel investors, 1
    geographic focus of, 23, 37–38
    in New Zealand, 160
    and syndication, 92
    in the United Kingdom, 31
annual report. *See* ongoing disclosure
antitrust, 60, 177. *See also* market concentration
    and Crowdcube-Seedrs merger, 9–10, 24,
        67, 172
ASIC, 2, 147, 148
ASX, 151
audited financial statements, 111–12

Australia, 34–35, 146–51, 174*t*, *See also* Crowd-
        Sourced Funding Act
    all-or-nothing model, 129, 148
    cooling off period, 150
    in comparison with New Zealand, 144, 146,
        147, 151
    due diligence, 66
    funding volume, 35*t*, 36*t*
    investor cap, 148–49, 181
    issuer limit, 148, 180, 181
    mandatory disclosure, 148, 178
Australian Securities and Investments
        Commission, 2, 147, 148
Australian Stock Exchange, 151

bad actor exclusion, 136
bicycle sharing, 80. *See also* digital trail
BIPOC entrepreneurs. *See* minority
        entrepreneurs
Birchal, 151
Black entrepreneurs. *See* minority
        entrepreneurs
boilerplate. *See* risk warning
bond, 134. *See also* security
brand ambassadors, 4, 9, 51, 76–79, 151. *See also*
        online reputation
brand assassins, 9, 78
broker, 118. *See also* platform
bulletin board. *See* communication channels

Capital Raising Online While Deterring Fraud
        and Unethical Non-Disclosure Act, 101
Canada, 152–55, 174*t*
    all-or-nothing model, 129
    cooling-off period, 154–55
    due diligence, 65
    history of crowdfunding laws, 152–54
    investor cap, 154, 181
    issuer limit, 154, 180
    mandatory disclosure, 154, 178
Canadian Securities Administrators, 153–54

188 INDEX

cancellation. *See* cooling-off period
Caribu, 40
carried interest. *See* carry
carry, 63, 94
  as employed by angel investors, 92
chat room. *See* communication channels
close corporation, 115, 140–41
Coffee, John, 112–13, 114
Colorado, 102
commission, 63, 114, 118–19, 120, 127–28
communication channels, 130–31
comparative law, 143–74
competition. *See* antitrust
concurrent offering. *See* parallel offering
consumption
  contrasted with investment, 21–22
cooling-off period, 138–39, 180
  all-or-nothing model, relationship with,
    128n.78
  in Australia, 150
  in Canada, 154–55
  compared across jurisdictions, 174*t*
  in New Zealand, absence of, 163–64
  price, impact on, 138
  in United Kingdom, 171
Corporations Amendment (Crowd-Sourced
    Funding) Act. *See* Crowd-Sourced
    Funding Act
COVID-19 pandemic, 103, 172
Crowdcube, 24
  and abandoned merger with Seedrs, 9–10,
    24, 172
  expansion into European Union, 158n.53
  as gatekeeper, 66–67, 170
  origins of, 166–67
CROWDFUND Act, 101
crowdfunding vehicle. *See* SPV
crowdsourced investment analysis, 88–91
  incentive to share information, 89–90
crowd-sourced funding. *See* Australia
Crowd-Sourced Funding Act, 146–50. *See also*
    Australia
crowdsourcing
  and investment analysis (*see* crowdsourced
    investment analysis)
  and remote monitoring, 96
CSA, 153–54
curation. *See* gatekeeping

deadline. *See* all-or-nothing model
debt, 134
definition of investment crowdfunding, 22–24
digital trail, 79–81

disclosure. *See* mandatory disclosure; voluntary
    disclosure
discounted cash flow analysis, 46–47
donation crowdfunding, 16–17
due diligence. *See also* gatekeeping
  disclaimer of, 65
  disclosure of, 169, 170
  by lead investors, 92–93
  mandatory, 119, 150, 158
  market failure, 118–19
  pressure to undertake, 66–67
  as private ordering, 66–67, 170
  touted by platforms, 65–66

entrepreneurship
  job creation due to, 27
  national policy in favor of, 28–29
  social benefit of, 27–29
Equitise, 66, 150–51
equity crowdfunding. *See* New Zealand
European Union, 156–59
  cooling-off period, 158
  funding volume, 156
  gatekeeping, 158
  investor cap, absence of, 158
  issuer limit, 157
  knowledge and experience quiz, 158
  mandatory disclosure, 157, 178
  Regulation (EU) 2020/1503, 156–59
Everydae, 86
exclusivity. *See* gatekeeping
exempt offerings, 20–21, 103, 104–5
exits, 33–34
  in Australia, 151
  few in number, 33, 151
  in United Kingdom, 173

fair dealing. *See* New Zealand; United Kingdom
female entrepreneurs
  difficulty obtaining funding from traditional
    sources, 22, 38
  opportunity provided by investment
    crowdfunding, 22, 38
  success raising money via investment
    crowdfunding, 39–41
Financial Conduct Authority, 165–67, 168–69,
    171–72. *See also* United Kingdom
Financial Markets Authority. *See* FMA
Financial Markets Conduct Act. *See* FMCA
financial statements, 111–12
FINRA, 118
FMA, 74, 106, 161–62. *See also* New Zealand
FMCA, 159–61. *See also* New Zealand

INDEX 189

Form C, 107–8, 112, 113–14, 137–38, 157, 178
  compared with Form S-1, 109–10
Form C-AR, 114–15, 116, 117. *See also* ongoing
  disclosure
Form S-1, 107–8. *See also* IPO
France, 13, 156
fraud
  as criminal violation, 72–73, 107
  in cryptocurrency market, 8, 122
  digital trail as constraint on, 80–81
  enforcement, 72–73
  fear of, 7–8, 52
  gatekeeping as constraint on, 25, 62, 64, 67–
    68, 119 (*see also* gatekeeping)
  information asymmetry, as a type of, 46, 52
  low apparent levels of, 8, 52, 74, 103, 165, 184
  market manipulation, 90–91
  in New Zealand, 74, 165
  online reputation as constraint on, 76
  punishment for, 107
  rescission as remedy for, 72
friends and family. *See* private placement
FrontFundr, 65
funding portal, 118. *See also* platform
funding target. *See* all-or-nothing model
funding volume, 32*t*, 35*t*

GAAP, 73–74, 111, 112, 177–78, 179
gatekeeping, 61–70. *See also* platform
  in Australia, 150
  definition of, 8–9, 25
  economic incentives for, 63
  in the European Union, 158
  inclusivity, tension with, 27, 68–70, 119–21
  JOBS Act, under the, 118–19
  on lower-tier platforms, 67, 68
  in New Zealand, 65, 162–63
  strictness, 64–65
  in the United Kingdom, 66–67, 170
gender. *See* female entrepreneurs
geography. *See* rural entrepreneurs
Germany, 156
Gilson, Ronald, 7, 45–46
GoFundMe, 17
Green Bay Packers, 13–14
Greenfern Industries, 165
grooming, 62

half-truth, 169
von Hayek, Friedrich. *See also* private ordering;
  wisdom of the crowd
  and knowledge of particular circumstances of
    time and place, 84, 88, 89

and spontaneous order, 59, 83, 85–86
herding, 30, 85–87, 121–22, 155, 184. *See also*
  wisdom of the crowd

ICO, 6, 8, 23–24, 81, 122
Igloo Energy, 173
illiquidity, 34, 115, 139–40
inclusive entrepreneurship, 6–7, 18, 37–
  41, 160
  and tension with gatekeeping, 25, 27, 64,
    68–70, 119–21
  and tension with syndication, 94
inclusive investing, 6–7, 23, 41–44, 160. *See also*
  retail investors
Indiegogo, 15. *See also* reward crowdfunding
information asymmetry, 7, 45–46, 49–53
  definition, 49
  fraud as type of (*see* fraud)
  and lemons problem, 50–51
information cascade. *See* herding
information underproduction, 113, 114
initial coin offering. *See* ICO
initial public offering. *See* IPO
intermediary. *See* platform
intrastate crowdfunding, 102–3
investment company exclusion, 136
investor cap, 25–26, 124–26, 180–82
  accredited investors, application to, 100, 125,
    171, 181–82
  all-or-nothing model, relationship with,
    89–90, 127
  in Australia, 148–49
  calculation of, 124–25
  in Canada, 154
  compared across jurisdictions, 174*t*
  complexity of, 124–25
  and diversification, 124, 149, 181
  in European Union, absence of, 158
  in New Zealand, absence of, 161, 162
  as paternalistic, 126, 158
  as price for liberal regime, 126, 181
  as safety net, 126, 181
  in United Kingdom, 170–71
issuer limit, 121–24, 180. *See also* parallel
    offering
  in Canada, 152–53, 154, 180
  compared across jurisdictions, 174*t*
  and herding, 30, 85–86, 184
  imposed by JOBS Act, 123
  in New Zealand, 162, 180
  raised by 2020 amendments to Regulation
    Crowdfunding, 32, 103, 123
  in the United Kingdom, 167

190 INDEX

IPO, 2, 19, 108
  in contrast with investment crowdfunding,
    31, 107–8
  as exit for crowdfunding investors, 151
  high costs of, 121
  and mandatory disclosure, 107–8, 110
  as unlimited fundraising device, 180
Italy, 136, 156

JOBS Act, 99–142. *See also* Regulation
    Crowdfunding; standard model
  companies eligible to participate, 135–37
  as a global model, 143, 146
  legislative history, 4, 101
  as a model for Australian law, 146, 147
  as a model for Canadian law, 152, 156
  as a model for EU law, 156
  as a model for New Zealand law, 159, 160–61
  new exemption to registration requirement,
    104, 105
Jumpstart Our Business Startups Act. *See*
    JOBS Act

key investment information sheet, 157
Kickstarter, 15, 17. *See also* reward
    crowdfunding
KIIS, 157
Kiwis. *See* New Zealand

Latino entrepreneurs. *See* minority
    entrepreneurs
lead investor. *See* syndication
lemons problem, 50–51, 134–35, 168
liberal model
  commendation of, 6, 9–10, 174, 176, 183–85
  definition of, 5, 9–10, 144–46
  New Zealand as exemplar, 159–65
  United Kingdom as exemplar, 165–74
license. *See* platform
liquidity, 34, 115, 139–40
liquidity events. *See* exits

madness of the crowd. *See* herding
mandatory disclosure, 105–14. *See also*
    voluntary disclosure
  in Australia, 148
  in Canada, 154
  compared across jurisdictions, 174*t*
  cost of, 19, 108–10
  criticism of, 100, 141–42, 177–79
  in European Union, 157
  financial statements, 111–12
  Form C (*see* Form C)

  as harmless, 178
  liberal model, abandoned by, 5, 145
  in New Zealand, absence of, 26, 73, 162, 165
  ongoing disclosure (*see* ongoing disclosure)
  in primary market, 112–14, 180
  standard model, retained by, 5, 26, 145
  as touchstone of securities regulation, 106
  in United Kingdom, absence of, 26,
    73, 169–70
March of Dimes, 12
market concentration, 67–68. *See also*
    antitrust
market statistics, 32*t*, 35*t*
Meow Wolf, 33–34, 140–41
messy cap table problem. *See under* SPV
Mindful Chef, 173
minority entrepreneurs
  difficulty obtaining funding from traditional
    sources, 22, 38
  opportunity provided by investment
    crowdfunding, 38
  success raising money via investment
    crowdfunding, 41
  targeted by crowdfunding investors, 22, 41
mom and pop investors. *See* retail investors
Monzo, 77–78, 167, 172
mum and dad investors. *See* retail investors

National Instrument 45-110, 153–55. *See*
    also Canada
New Zealand, 159–65, 174*t*
  advertising, 163
  all-or-nothing model, 128, 163–64
  brand ambassadors, 79
  compliance costs, 164, 178, 184
  contrast with Australia, 144, 146, 147, 162
  crowdsourced investment analysis, 91
  fair dealing requirement, 162–63
  female entrepreneurship, 41
  fraud, 74
  funding volume, 35, 35*t*, 36, 36*t*
  gatekeeping, 65
  investor cap, absence of, 162, 180–81
  issuer limit, 35–36, 180
  mandatory disclosure, absence of, 73,
    162, 165
  secondary market, 163–64
  syndication, 93, 94
  voluntary disclosure, 73–74, 162, 178–79
New Zealand Stock Exchange, 165
NFT, 6, 8, 23–24, 81, 122
non-accredited investors. *See* retail investors
nonfinancial reasons for investing, 21–22

INDEX 191

non-fungible token, 6, 8, 23–24, 81, 122
notice filing, 107, 157
NZX, 165

Obama, Barack, 4–5, 28, 43, 101
Office of the Advocate for Small Business
    Capital Formation, 28–29
ongoing disclosure, 114–17. *See also*
    Form C-AR
  contractual obligation to provide, 116
  failure to provide, consequences of, 136
  mandating, merit in, 114–15
  and market failure, 114–17
online reputation, 75–79. *See also* brand
    ambassadors
  and agency costs, 76
  and information asymmetry, 75–76
  and repeat players, 79
  value of, 75–76, 79
  and voluntary disclosure, 76
Ontario, 152–53
oral solicitation, 137

parallel offering, 35–36, 94, 118, 123–24, 180
  in New Zealand, 94, 164
  and non-integration, 123
platform
  as essential feature, 23–24, 61
  as focus of liberal model regulation, 162,
    169, 177
  as gatekeeper, 61–70 (*see also* gatekeeping)
  independence requirement, 23–24, 81
  license requirement, 24, 118, 174*t*, 177
  mandatory use of, 23–24, 81, 117–18
  as repeat player, 63, 177
PledgeMe, 41, 74, 128
Policy Statement PS14/4, 168–71. *See also*
    United Kingdom
portal. *See* platform
power law, 86–87
primary market, 112–14, 139, 179. *See also*
    secondary market
private ordering, 57–97. *See also* von Hayek,
    Friedrich; liberal model
  babysitting market example, 59–60
private placement
  exclusive nature, 2–3, 42
  exemption from registration, 2, 104, 144
  issuer limit, absence of, 121
  modest means, unavailable to entrepreneurs
    of, 18, 37
  rationale for exemption, 20, 61, 104
promotion. *See* advertising

prospectus, 167. *See also* mandatory
    disclosure
Prosper Marketplace, 19
public company exclusion, 135–36

question-and-answer (Q&A). *See*
    communication channels; crowdsourced
    investment analysis

Rebus, 66–67
reflection period. *See* cooling-off period
Regulation Crowdfunding. *See also* JOBS Act;
    standard model
  liberalized over time, 32, 103, 184
  rulemaking process, 101–2, 119–21
  2020 amendments, 32, 103, 125, 133,
    135, 137–38
Regulation D, 94, 105, 118, 123–24
Regulation (EU) 2020/1503, 156–59. *See also*
    European Union
remote monitoring, 96
Renaissance Brewery, 165
Republic, 63, 65, 66, 67, 127–28
reputation. *See* online reputation
resale restrictions, 139–42
retail investors
  ability to self-certify as a sophisticated
    investors in the UK, 171
  inability to absorb large losses, 21
  primary intended beneficiaries of securities
    regulation, 104, 105
  protected by investor cap, 124, 148–49
returns. *See* exits
reward crowdfunding, 14–16
risk factors, 108, 110
risk warning, 107, 148, 158, 161
rugby in Oceania, 146
Rule 506(b), 105
Rule 506(c), 105
rural entrepreneurship, 37–38

SAFE, 132–34
Saskatchewan, 152
SEC. *See* Regulation Crowdfunding
secondary market, 112–13, 139, 179. *See also*
    illiquidity; resale restrictions
  lack of, 34, 115, 139–40
  and mandatory disclosure theory, 112–
    14, 177
  in New Zealand, 163–64
Securities Act of 1933, 18–19, 20, 80, 99, 104–5
Securities and Exchange Commission. *See*
    Regulation Crowdfunding

192   INDEX

security
    definition of, 1–2, 18, 131
    eligible types compared across jurisdictions, 174
    registration requirement, 2, 19 (*see also*
        exempt offerings)
    variety of, 131–32
Seedinvest, 33, 62, 64–65, 116, 127–28
Seedrs, 172–74
    and abandoned merger with Crowdcube,
        9–10, 24, 172
    and carry, 63
    as gatekeeper, 66, 170
    and grooming, 62
    origins of, 166–67
sex. *See* female entrepreneurship
side-by-side offering. *See* parallel offering
Silicon Valley, 1, 37–38, 39–40
simple agreement for future equity, 132–34
small businesses, 3n.2, 28–29
SMEs, 3n.2
snowball effect. *See* herding
Snowball Effect, 36n.10, 41, 62, 65, 128
social media. *See* advertising; online
    reputation
sophisticated investors. *See* accredited investors
special purpose vehicle. *See* SPV
SPV, 134–35
    messy cap table problem, as solution
        to, 134–35
standard model
    Australia as exemplar, 146–51
    Canada as exemplar, 152–55
    criticism of, 9–10, 176, 178, 183–84
    definition, 5, 9–10, 144–45
    European Union as exemplar, 156–59
    United States as exemplar, 5, 99–142
Startengine, 39–40, 41, 118, 134
    and all-or-nothing model, 127–28
    and crowdsourced investment analysis, 91
    as gatekeeper, 65
    market share of, 67
    SAFE prohibited, 133–34
    secondary market, 139–40
startup company. *See also* entrepreneurship
    defined, 3n.2
Statue of Liberty, 13
Sugru, 48
syndication, 92–95, 100
    abuse, opportunity for, 95
    in angel investing, 92
    inclusive entrepreneurship, tension with, 94
    in New Zealand, 93
    in United Kingdom, 93

target. *See* all-or-nothing model
technology, 48, 50, 60–61, 80, 185
telecommunications, 14, 18, 23, 38, 54
testing the waters, 137–38
transaction fee. *See* commission
transfer. *See* resale restrictions
Tuchman, Maxeme, 40
tulip mania, 85

uncertainty, 7, 45–49
underrepresented groups. *See* minority
    entrepreneurs
United Kingdom, 165–74, 174*t*
    appropriateness test, 169
    cooling off period, 171
    dedicated legal regime, absence of, 165–
        66, 168
    embrace of private ordering, 168–
        69, 171–72
    exits, 173
    fair, clear, and not misleading rule, 169–70,
        174 (*see also* fraud)
    female entrepreneurship, 40
    funding volume, 35*t*, 36*t*, 37
    gatekeeping, 170
    investor cap, 170–71
    mandatory disclosure, absence of,
        73, 169–70
    origins of investment crowdfunding
        in, 166–68
    voluntary disclosure, 73–74, 169–70

valuation, 46–47, 49, 62
    and the SAFE, 112–13
VC. *See* venture capitalists
venture capitalists, 1
    as accredited investors, 2, 25
    and female entrepreneurs, 38, 40
    fleece vests, penchant for, 1
    geographic focus of, 23, 37–38, 60–61
    as lead investors, 93, 94, 151 (*see also*
        syndication)
    and lemons problem, 45, 50–51, 168
    and messy cap table problem, 134
    and minority entrepreneurs, 38, 40, 41
    in New Zealand, 160, 164–65
verbal solicitation, 137
volume of funding, 32*t*, 35*t*
voluntary disclosure, 70–75. *See also* mandatory
    disclosure
    commendation of, 177–78, 179
    economic incentive to provide, 70–72, 108–9
    and information underproduction, 112, 113

and market failure, 112, 114
in New Zealand, 73–74, 178
in primary market, 112–14
and rescission for fraud, 72–73, 74
in secondary market, 113–14
in United Kingdom, 73–74

Wefunder, 33, 39–40, 41, 91
and all-or-nothing model, 127–28
and due diligence, 65
lead investor requirement, 93–94, 141
market share, 67
sample risk factors, 110
wholesale investors. *See* accredited investors
wisdom of the crowd
and communication channels, 91

and crowdsourced investment
analysis, 88–91
herding, potential for, 85–87
heterogeneity, importance of, 83
homogeneity, problem of, 83
and knowledge of particular circumstances of
time and place, 84–85, 88, 89
and lay expertise, 87–88
and power law, 86–87
and progress bar, 83–84
as spontaneous order, 83
theory of, 82–83
weight-judging example, 82
women. *See* female entrepreneurs

Zero Co., 151